## Praise for Prior Books by Randall Hicks

### THE BABY GAME

"Light, easy-to-read prose, self-deprecating humor and constant action place this first novel high on the must-have list."
—*Library Journal*

- Winner Gumshoe Award (Best Debut Mystery, 2005)
- Finalist for the Anthony, Barry and Macavity Awards
- "Book of the Month" selection by Independent Mystery Booksellers Assn. ·

### BABY CRIMES

"Breezy and Beguiling." —*San Diego Union Tribune*

"Randall Hicks has the three vital ingredients for mega success: great narrative, humor and style. It's smart, sassy and with a streak of compassion. Best of all, Hicks has that rarest of all qualities, he's even better on your second reading."
—Ken Bruen (Shamus Award winning author)

### ADOPTING IN AMERICA

"Educational and empowering. No-nonsense, matter-of-fact advice while using a compassionate approach." —*Publishers Weekly*

"Showers the anxious parent with information." —*Booklist*

Featured on *The Today Show, CBS This Morning, PBS, Sally Jessy Raphael, Mike & Maty, The Home and Family Show* and *John & Leeza from Hollywood*

### STEPPARENTING: 50 One-Minute DOs & DON'Ts

"A brilliantly lean book . . . enthusiastically recommended." [Starred Review] —*Library Journal*

# THE GIRL
# WITHOUT A FACE

Randall Hicks
& Hailey Hicks

WORDSLINGER PRESS
San Diego, California

Trade paper ISBN: 978-0-9839425-7-3; Ebook ISBN: 978-0-9839425-8-0; hard-back ISBN: 878-0-9839425-9-7

Cover design: Michaela Apfler

WordSlinger Press / WordSlingerPress.com

Library of Congress Cataloging-in-Publication Data:

Names: Hicks, Randall, 1956- author. | Hicks, Hailey, 1994- author.
Title: The girl without a face / Randall Hicks & Hailey Hicks.
Description: San Diego, California : Wordslinger Press, [2020] | Summary:
   "At age fifteen, Katie Wilder might be one of the greatest figure
   skaters in the world . . . but no one even knows she exists. When a
   childhood accident leaves her face so severely scarred that she wears a
   mask, Katie never leaves the Ice Castle, the rink owned by her father, a
   once-famous coach. Skating since she could walk, and without friends and
   distractions, every moment is dedicated to her passion, skating, under
   her father's guidance. However, when her father returns to coaching and
   Olympic hopefuls come to train, her safe and private world is gone.
   Katie searches for the courage to not only show the world what she can
   do on the ice, but more importantly, make her first friend, and start to
   live a life that extends outside the rink"-- Provided by publisher.
Identifiers: LCCN 2020018414 (print) | LCCN 2020018415 (ebook) | ISBN
   9780983942573 (trade paperback) | ISBN 9780983942580 (ebook)
Subjects: LCSH: Figure skating stories. | Life change events--Fiction.
Classification: LCC PS3608.I285 G57 2020  (print) | LCC PS3608.I285
   (ebook) | DDC 813/.6--dc23
LC record available at https://lccn.loc.gov/2020018414
LC ebook record available at https://lccn.loc.gov/2020018415.

# Acknowledgments

We can't begin to adequately thank the kind and generous people of the figure skating world who have contributed their time, expertise and enthusiasm to this book. They are all people we have admired for many years, and watched on television during countless U.S. national championships, Grand Prix and Olympics. To have them personally sharing their valuable time with us to help make this book as authentic as possible is greatly appreciated. If their name appears in this book, lending it realism, it is a sign of our great respect for their talents.

First and foremost, thanks to one of the world's top coaches, Tom Zakrajsek (Coach Z), coach of countless U.S. national champion and Olympic skaters. He dedicated so much time in answering our questions, and his knowledge and patience were limitless.

Thanks to: Tom Dickson (five-time USFS Choreographer of the Year), for his expertise in music and choreography; Todd Sand (two-time Olympian, world champion medalist and four-time U.S. national champion), for his insight on pairs skating; Jeremy Abbott (two-time Olympian, four-time U.S. national champion, and Grand Prix Final winner), for his singles expertise; Tatjana Flade, leading figure skating journalist, for her insight and expertise; Leslie Deason (Master-Rated coach in Carlsbad, California) for her personal demonstration of some of the technical aspects of figure skating; those who wrote pre-pub reviews: Joanne Vassallo Jamrosz (*Skating*), Susan D. Russell (*IFS*) & Paula Slater (Golden Skate). Also to Ryan Hicks for his suggestions. Thanks to skating icons, Rafael Arutyunyan and the Shib Sibs, Alex & Maia Shibutani, for their kind letters of encouragement after receiving our first draft. We loved the early support!

Special thanks to Brian DeFiore of DeFiore and Company, as well as our many advance readers, especially Barry Meadow, Lisa Albright Ratnavira and Bonnie Hiler.

Any mistakes are those of the authors, not the experts who have advised us. There are a few areas where we have taken literary license and not strictly followed the USFS and ISU rulebooks.

# THE GIRL
# WITHOUT A FACE

# 1

K, here's the bio.

Katie Wilder. Fifteen. Blonde and blue. What my dad calls willowy, which is polite for "no boobs."

Skater. As in ice.

And

    I

    don't

    have

    a

    face.

Legit. No exaggeration.

Not my favorite story, so details later, but third and fourth-degree burns to my face and neck when I was three—think marshmallows in a fire. And yeah, skin really does turn black when it burns. At least the dark skin contrasts nicely with my blonde hair. It gives me more color options when selecting from my many party dresses for the constant invitations I receive for tea parties and social galas.

Don't believe me? Google Image it. You'll even see my face there. Last I checked it was on page four, second row, third from the left, but it moves around the page. So go ahead, do it. You'll see. Not my whole face due to confidentiality, but enough for me to know it's me. In the name of science, shared with the world.

Actually, don't. Because you'll hate me if you do. And yourself.

Trust me, you will. Never having had a single friend in my life (a dad and a dog don't count), I'd given it some thought. Like can't-sleep-all-night thought, and here's the circle of hate . . .

If you see my face, or a face like mine, you will feel

revulsion,

followed by

pity.

Then the revulsion again, wishing you'd never seen it. Like a bloody car wreck you don't want in your memory bank. Now comes the guilt for what you feel, then hating yourself for your shallowness, for wishing people like me didn't exist. So then you'd hate me, for making you hate yourself.

See?

Lose, lose, all the way around.

But in a weird way, figuring it out actually made me feel better, the hatred/fear/pity/revulsion thing in others, and the friendless/face-less thing that is me. Life's like a roll of the dice in the cosmos, and mine came up with a number that is not supposed to exist. Whatever. Still, it gave me some peace in my aloneness. My *me*ness. An acceptance for what is, and what will never be.

And I can live with that.

I have to.

So since no googling (we agreed right?), here's the selfie. Believe me, your imagination will be kinder than reality.

Instructions:

1. Imagine a face made of wax.
2. Put face in oven.
3. Leave face in oven until severely melted.
4. Remove from oven.
5. Vomit.

I've been told I'm actually "lucky." Ha! I guess God really hooked it up for me. At least my body is unaffected. In fact, it's actually perfect. (Well, except for those mosquito bites I have for breasts.) But athletically a perfect body anyway.

Enough about my face though, or lack thereof. I don't dwell on it. What I do instead is skate. Night and day. How good am I? The truth? I mean, I didn't exactly sugarcoat the whole no face thing. So my skating?

Damn good. Olympic good. In the practice rink anyway. Of course, the real test is competition, but that's not possible for me. I know only one rink. My rink. The Ice Castle in Lake Arrowhead, in the San Bernardino mountains of southern California. Yes, SoCal has mountains. Snow even.

Skating is the family business. I may have got a slap in the face from God—wait, that's kind of funny—get it—slap in the face? LOL. Anyway, maybe I got shortchanged in that department, but I got a double dose of skating genes from my parents. Both were figure skaters and almost Olympians. Dad became a coach. Gloria (I refuse to call her Mom) became . . . absent.

I think somehow I'd have found my way on skates even if my dad hadn't laced me up at 18 months. Walking and skating were one and the same, skating just easier. A fish in the ocean could not feel more at home than I do on the ice. I love that I can jump higher than any other woman on blades in the world—at least according to my dad. That I can do a triple Axel as easily as skipping over a crack in the sidewalk—that is if I'd ever walked on a sidewalk. But mostly, I love it for one big reason.

When I'm on the ice, it's the only time I forget that

I

don't

have

a

face.

That's why I live on the ice.

3

# 2

I hate calendars. Calendars are for people with things to do. And people to do them with. Friends. In other words, a life. What could be a crueler invention for someone like me? I've never gone to a movie theater. Never eaten in a restaurant. Been in a store. Gone on a bicycle ride. No grade school sleepovers or Chuck E. Cheese birthday parties. No school. And I'll certainly never get married. Or have a baby.

And
I'll
never
be
kissed.

But I was alright with all that. Really. My world was peaceful. Safe. Predictable. Just the way I wanted it, and just the way things should be for someone like me. Besides, movies taught me all I needed to know about the outside world—and thanks—but I'll take a pass. *Mean Girls, High School Musical* and *The Fault in Our Stars* showed me the teenage life cycle: *dis, dance* and *die*. Hollywood wouldn't lie. So I was content in my perfect solitary world.

And then it all changed.

Forever.

I got up before dawn to get in two hours of ice time before breakfast. I was just getting off the ice when I heard the phone, so it was me getting Uncle Robbie, my dad's brother. Just after 8:00 a.m., early for him to call.

"Katie, Katie!" So excited he said my name twice. "Get your dad! *Please*. Right away!" It was positive excitement, so I wasn't alarmed. Just curious.

"Uncle Robbie, what—"

"Just get him, honey! Please. Right now. *No!* No! Never mind! I'm coming over. Tell him I'll be there in ten minutes."

With that he was gone. Unlike him to interrupt me, not to mention hang up on me. And excitement wasn't a word you'd associate with Uncle Robbie. His idea of excitement was a new sweater vest. On sale.

His cabin was just a mile and a half away, but on the curvy mountain roads of Arrowhead that meant at least ten minutes. That gave me time for my usual after-workout shower, a five-minute blast of steaming water followed by 60 seconds at max cold. I was drying my hair when I heard Uncle Robbie let himself into the kitchen via the back door. I could hear the sound of my dad putting his pot of morning tea on the stove.

The rink has the public entrance in front, with our apartment attached in the back. There is also a string of six cabins behind the rink for resident skaters in training. But that was back in the glory days of the Ice Castle. The glory days of *my father* actually. Before his cover-of-*People*-esque fall from grace. Now the cabins are vacation rentals to bring in some extra money.

I moved closer to the oversized heating vent in my room. It was directly across from the one in the kitchen, so any conversation was as clear as if I was in the room with them. I'd grown up falling asleep listening to the sound of conversations in the kitchen, although usually the "conversations" were just my dad watching TV. He barely had more visitors than I did. Sad considering I had none.

ROBBIE: "Davey! Davey!"

Still with the double naming, although no one called Dad "Davey" but Uncle Robbie. Dad's status as a coach, even now, got him full use of his fancy triple play: David Cole Wilder. Just one of those semi-show biz things of the skating world that he had once been such a part of.

DAD: "Robbie, what's up with you? You look like you're ten years old and it's Christmas morning."

I could hear the amusement in his voice at Uncle Robbie's uncharacteristic excitement.

ROBBIE: "It's Juliette! She's recanting! She's *recanting!*"

I didn't realize my legs had given away until I found myself sitting on the floor.

Juliette?

*Recanting?*

Juliette Francine's name was not a welcome one in our home. Dad had been her coach sixteen years ago, back when my mom was pregnant with me. Juliette was seventeen, a French phenom who'd just won the European Championships and was a favorite to medal in the Olympics. She'd lived here at the Ice Castle, back when it was called *the campus*. The pictures of those glory days were still on the walls.

Thirteen Olympic medals represented by those photographs: five gold, three silver and five bronze. Three of those golds my father's. As a coach anyway. The rink must have been so cool back then, like a tiny college for elite skaters from all over the world. My parents owned the rink, and Dad was the most famous of the resident coaches. The rink was not even open to the public. It was dedicated solely to training high-level skaters.

But it had all ended sixteen years ago, the Winter Olympics in Torino, Italy. Dad and Juliette, both front and center media stars in different ways. Dad, only thirty-eight years old, crazy young for a top coach, and with rock star good looks and an ego to match. And Juliette, his newest star, a *Guess* model on skates.

It took only thirty seconds for both their worlds to end.

# 3

Anticipation had been high. Ladies figure skating is the signature event of every Winter Olympics, and Juliette had been its poster child. She had it all.

Youth,

sex,

innocence,

beauty.

Juliette was one of the favorites to win the gold, with anticipated tens of millions in endorsement dollars awaiting her on the other side. Smile and sell the world soap, face lotion and tampons.

The beginning of the end was just ten seconds into her long program. She was already in first place by the narrowest of margins after the short. Skate a clean program and the gold was hers.

She fell on her first jump, a simple triple toe loop. A jump she— any elite skater—could do in their sleep. Then she caught an edge and fell again on a flying sit spin. When she got up the panic was in her eyes. A deer in headlights. Any chance at the gold was gone. Epic fail. She and everyone knew it. But still an outside chance at a medal.

Silver or bronze.

And then she fell a third time, going down hard and hitting the back of her head, the ice like cement. A sick sound like a stick breaking, echoing through the arena. And she didn't get up. She laid there, lifeless.

At least that's the way it looked. I've seen the video hundreds of times. I torture myself with it. Hating her for not dying. There'd been screams from the crowd followed by absolute silence. They carried her off the ice on a stretcher, my dad at her side, distraught, touchingly pressing his forehead to hers as if transferring life. His lips an inch from hers, speaking silent words. That was the photo that found its way onto every front page and news story around the world.

Juliette, even more famous.

My dad, as it turned out, infamous.

Her press conference was given from her hospital bed two days later—yeah, that's on YouTube too. Concussion, neck brace, the whole dog-and-pony show. But it wasn't the sympathetic puff piece from an adoring press she'd been anticipating. The sympathy was still there, but some questions were being asked by the media. Forcefully. Rumors were swirling of her sneaking out for some late-night partying the night before the long program. Not dedicating herself to her sport and her country. She'd been France's best chance at a gold and they wanted answers.

But the hard questions ended when she burst into tears and haltingly, gasping for air, begged for them to leave her alone. She said she could not hide the truth any longer.

Her truth anyway.

She claimed she'd been in a sexual relationship with my father for months leading up to the Olympics, and she'd felt powerless to say no. Worse, she feared she might be pregnant. It was a wonder she could skate at all, but she had to try for her country. So she said anyway. Poor, poor Juliette.

It turned out there was no pregnancy, but proving there had been no affair was impossible.

He said.

She said.

Skating may look beautiful on the ice, but behind the scenes it can be a brutal, take-no-prisoners world. My dad had told me he'd met the best people of his life in skating, but there was another side too—filled with jealous coaches, maniac parents and prima donna skaters. Dad's fast success—the first ever to coach both the ladies' singles and pairs to gold in the same Olympics—made him a target. Others could only rise with his fall, so the skating world's silence in his support was deafening.

So maybe no surprise that no one heard any words but those from Juliette. She was an adorable and can't-hide-it-even-if-she-tried sexy girl with tears in her eyes, and Dad was a man whose bedroom had been one wall from hers for years of training. No cabin for Juliette. She shared the rink apartment with Dad and Gloria. She had what's now my room in fact.

Maybe making it worse was the world's knowledge that Gloria was pregnant (me), and she was virtually a slightly older clone of Juliette. Both skaters, beautiful and young. So it was easy for the world to imagine Dad's taste ran to the type, and what a sexy story for the normally staid Olympics. Sex triangle on ice!

So Dad was finished. The cover story photograph, initially seen as incredibly touching and sweet, was then seen as evidence of his lechery. No real evidence, so no trial, but abandoned by the skating world. His once famous Ice Castle became a public rink, and his coaching became just local kids with big aspirations and little talent. The locals of Lake Arrowhead knew Dad, so knew the story had to be bogus, so at least we still had a community to support the rink, but little else. The only winner was me, coming along just months later:

The world's best skating coach since I was a toddler.
Focused
only
on
me.

My mind snapped back to the conversation in the next room as I heard the sound of a coffee cup hit the counter. Hard. Like the arm holding it could no longer support it. My dad's I'm sure.

DAD: "What are you saying, Robbie?"

His voice had become quiet and I had to put my ear right to the vent. There was hope in his words.

DAD: "Did . . . did *she* call you? Juliette?"

Uncle Robbie was a lawyer and handled business for Dad, not that there was much of it anymore.

ROBBIE: "That little coward? No. Someone from a book publisher called me. From New York City. An editor named . . . oh, never mind . . . someone called me. She's written a book—"

DAD: "Juliette?"

ROBBIE: "Yes, yes! Juliette! Just listen! There's a book coming out. About her life. Skating and . . . up to now . . . her life. *She's admitting she made the whole thing up!* The truth is finally coming out, Davey. That you did nothing wrong!"

There was silence as my dad absorbed what he was hearing. I could hear the bewilderment in his voice when he finally spoke.

DAD: "Why? Why did she do it?"

A snort from Uncle Robbie.

ROBBIE: "Who cares? Maybe she found Jesus. Or maybe she just wants to sell books. You've got to have something juicy if you want to get on some talk shows, get a bestseller, be famous again."

DAD: "No, I meant, why did she do it back *then*? Why did she lie?"

ROBBIE: "Who knows? The lady who called me promised to FedEx an advance copy for you today. And it's going out to the media too. I guess to get a little buzz going. Then the book is released next week. The short version I got on the phone was Juliette's life was a mess, and she just fell apart. You were her scapegoat."

After her failure at the Olympics, Juliette never skated again, not with any success anyway. Her story was a sad one. She remained a celebrity of sorts, like all the other damaged ones who never seemed to go away. There had been drugs. Alcohol. Arrests for abusing both. But she was still beautiful and sexy and a figure of sympathy. Particularly in Europe, she was a guaranteed headline, usually spotted with a race car driver or somebody super rich. She'd become a dating accessory, a taste of the month, then discarded.

And then Uncle Robbie said out loud what had just occurred to me.

No.

*No!*

*Don't say the words.* Saying them out loud would make them reality. But he said them anyway.

ROBBIE: "You know what this means don't you, Davey? *You're back!* You are going to be back in business!"

Yeah.

They'd be calling.

All of them.

The skaters. The parents. The coaches. The sponsors. The media.

All those people in Dad's old life would be back. Or at least the new crop of them sixteen years later. Their excuse to hate him was gone. The prince was back. And I knew my private world was over.

# 4

I wore my mask to practice that afternoon. I'd found it when I was six and exploring one of the rink's many storage rooms. Discarded skating costumes, old equipment, and the mask. It was nothing but a smooth hard shell with holes for eyes, nostrils and mouth. White with black accents, it looked nothing like a real face. More like Japanese art, a kabuki mask.

Before the mask, I'd just stay in my room when the rink had its public hours, but I wanted every minute on the ice. So one day without even telling my dad, I was out there, the mask a little too big for my face but the pretty pink ribbons from each side tied securely behind my head, weaving between the Saturday night skaters whose only goal was to keep their ankles straight and not fall down, a couple of brave souls skating backwards.

I don't know what they made of me, the little girl skating like a demon, kamikaze maneuvers around the skaters, tossing in singles and doubles when I'd find a clear patch of ice. I had been so focused that I hadn't even noticed when the ice had emptied, all the skaters having moved to the sides to watch me. But when I finished center ice with a scratch spin, I heard them. Their applause. Loud and long. I even bowed. One of the coolest moments of my life. Actually, the *best* moment of my life.

Until the mask fell off.

Maybe I didn't want the applause to end, or I just wanted to show off, but on my way off the ice I tossed in a double Lutz. But not enough speed, caught an edge and went down hard. The mask skidded away, leaving me
   naked.

Every eye fixed on me. Mouths opened in horror, Edvard Munch's *The Scream* times fifty. At least, that's how I remember the faces in the crowd.

And silence.

The mask ten miles away and hours to get to it.

My hair tied back, not hiding my face, even though my little hands tried.

One child crying in fright and confusion at the sight of me. Then two. A collective intake of breath that practically took the air out of the rink. No ears. No nose. Just holes in distorted flesh. An arena so filled with pity that even at age six I knew revulsion was preferable. So what did I learn that day?

*How to tie a freaking knot, that's what!*


So Dad understood the mask. But I'd never worn it when it was just us. Not ever. There was no public to hide from. But on that day it wouldn't be my face I was hiding. It was the emotions it would show.

I'd never lied to my father.

But today was going to be the day.

I loved him too much *not* to lie.

It had been only a minute after Uncle Robbie left that Dad was knocking on my door. Even his knocks radiated his joy. I knew he'd be bursting to share the news with me.

Daughter.

Best friend.

Maybe nerdy shrinks would label it as unhealthy codependence, easy to happen when you are both outcasts, and skating is a shared addiction. But I couldn't be his daughter or his friend at that moment, and I let his knocks go unanswered. I made it to my bed just in time to look like I'd gone back to bed as he opened the door. Then felt shame as he whispered my name, so clearly hoping I was awake. But I kept up the sleep act.

With a whispered, "Love you, sleep well," he closed the door, leaving me with my shame.

And my thoughts.

Because it hadn't taken me long to realize that I'd been wrong earlier that morning. Yeah, my dad's life was going to change. There were less than a dozen elite skating coaches in the world and my dad would take his place there again. Even after an absence of sixteen years and three Olympics, that kind of talent was never forgotten, especially after what they'd now see as his unfair ouster. And I knew one thing no one else did—that he'd never stopped coaching. He'd just been coaching only me.

So the skating world would be waiting with its arms open, and an apology for his wrongful banishment.

But only if he let them.

And he wouldn't.

I knew his mind, and his heart, better than he did. He'd celebrate the news for a while, then tell Uncle Robbie to turn the inquiries away. He'd imagine leaving for weeks at a time for major competitions with me left alone, or only Uncle Robbie to watch me. He'd imagine skaters living at the campus again, and worry about me learning to interact with them 24/7. No privacy to take off my mask. He'd imagine me locking myself in my room each day, becoming the lost girl he'd worked so hard to never let me become.

So Juliette may have freed him, but he still had a jailer.

Me.

# 5

My face might be hideously scarred, but that didn't mean it didn't show emotion, and no one could read me like my dad. So when I went out for my eleven o'clock session, I had the mask on before I even left my room. Dad already had his skates on and had been warming up on the ice. As he skated up to me I could literally see the question forming on his lips: *Why are you wearing the mask?*

But then Parenting101 kicked in and the wisdom of silence took over. Clearly he thought it better to say nothing than the wrong thing. The poor guy. Tucked away somewhere in his room was probably a *Guide to Single-Parenting a Teenage Daughter.* What he needed was *Parenting a Teenage Daughter Without a Face,* but I don't think Amazon or Barnes & Noble stocked that.

So instead he started with, "Uncle Robbie came by this morning." And then he excitedly told me what I already knew.

There was no need to fake a look of surprise with the mask, so I put it into my voice. "Dad!" I ran the few steps between us and gave him a hug. "I'm so happy for you."

His infectious grin flashed. "It's amazing, isn't it? I . . . I don't even know what to think yet."

"Dad, what's to think about? They're going to be begging you to coach again. It's going to be fantastic!" Lie #1 (about the fantastic part anyway).

I sat down to lace up my skates and gave him my profile so he couldn't see the lie in my eyes. I said, "It's going to be so exciting to have some of the best skaters in the world here again, like in the old days." Lie #2. Then sealing it excitedly with, "Dad, don't you know how many times I've looked at the pictures on the walls and wished I'd been alive back when all the top skaters were here? To be a part of that?" Lie #3 (actually some truth in that one).

He stepped off the ice, pausing just to put the guards on his skates, and sat down next to me to get at eye level. His face was doubting, wordlessly asking, *really?*

The fact was that I'd quashed his every effort for me to interact with people since I could remember, so this sudden turnaround wasn't ringing true to him. But he didn't go there. Instead he said, "Well, honey, I don't even know if I *want* to coach again, or if they'll want me. That's way down the road. I'm just so glad to have . . . you know, all the other stuff gone."

I felt a rush of shame. The biggest news for him had nothing to do with coaching again, which was all I was thinking about. I could only imagine what it had been like to live with the accusation hanging over his head that he'd slept with Juliette, and worse, someone he'd been trusted to care for as her coach. If he'd had one wish to grant him anything in the world, he'd use it on me having a normal life. But right behind that—he'd gotten his wish: his name was cleared. I should be celebrating this with him, not hiding behind a mask.

I finally turned to face him. "Dad, what do you mean *if* they want you? Your skaters have won three gold medals! Stop being so modest." I leaned my shoulder into his and gave him a bump. "Don't you want other skaters here too, Dad? Don't you want to coach someone besides me? Someone the world can see? Someone who can *compete*? And *win*?" In other words, someone besides me who we both knew would never leave the rink.

He just stared at me with that sweet face I knew so well, and then as if in slow motion I saw his eyes moisten, then overflow, as ignored tears ran down his face. He gently cupped his hands around my face.

"Oh, honey, is that what you think? That I've been missing something? Do you have any idea how much I've loved teaching you to skate? You're not just my daughter, you're the best and the hardest working skater I've ever coached. You're my life, Katie. I don't *need* anything else. Any*one* else."

Okay, now time for my tears to come. I locked my arms around him. My God, we were living in a Hallmark Channel movie. We just needed an off-screen orchestra for some sappy music. We were linked not just by skating and family blood, but by the accident that destroyed me—or created me. A life changed at age three.

Dad couldn't have avoided the pick-up that hit us. The drums of gasoline it was carrying sent a spray of fuel across my face—like nectar for the fire that followed. He was knocked unconscious, leaving me a prisoner in my car seat in the back when the car erupted in flames. We'd been sledding just a couple miles from home and were headed back, soaked and shivering but laughing. They say our wet winter clothes saved us—but that was no help for a face wet with gasoline. The burns to my body were minor by comparison, as were Dad's. The only reason I still have eyes is that evidently I covered them up with my wet gloves.

I hugged him so tight I think I might have actually hurt him. Here he was, giving me an out, despite the Oscar-caliber lies I'd just delivered. All I had to do was say, "Okay," and keep things just like they were. Just one word from me, and our lives would continue as they were. Just him and me. And skating. Just one little word. But that's not the word I said.

I stood up and pulled the guards off my skates. "No."

He stood up alongside me and I could see the surprise on his face. I didn't even know if I was lying anymore. "Dad, you've got to coach again." And I didn't plan to say it, but the words tumbling after were, "And I need to grow up."

*God, where did that come from?*

But before I could change my mind, or let him change it for me, I said, "Protopopovs, 1965 Worlds."

Dad had converted old TV and film footage to digital so we could study all the great skaters, and we had memorized more than twenty programs, some of them going back even before my dad was born. Oleg Protopopov and his wife, Ludmila Belousova, were one of Russia's greatest pairs skaters, winning gold in two Olympics and four straight World Championships. Unique for their grace and interpretation to their music, they were one of my favorites.

Every day my dad and I would take a break from training and choose a famous pairs program to skate—old school stuff, before fancy overhead lifts and twists. It was my favorite part of every day. Dad was still an excellent skater and incredibly strong, still able to throw me high enough to turn a triple. And as much as I loved skating alone, there was something special about pairs, especially with my dad. Most girls just get their wedding dance with their father. I'd never have that, but what I had was better.

And so after I did my warm-up, we skated. But for the first time ever, my thoughts were elsewhere. What had allowed me to lie so convincingly, first to him then to myself, was that I knew nothing would change immediately. The National Championships were just four months away, with the Olympics another month after that, quickly followed by the Worlds. Top skaters rarely change coaches, and if they do it's usually right after the season ends, so that meant nothing would change for at least four or five months. That's when Olympic expectations for so many would be unfulfilled, coaches blamed, and changes made.

So for now, I could convince myself

the
future
would
never
come.

But I was wrong.

I didn't know it then, but Dad's new skaters would arrive only six days later.

18

# 6

That night I had my dream. The same dream I had every night. The dream that feels like reality when I wake up, and I briefly struggle to leave the dream world and enter the real one.

It starts with me walking alone in a busy shopping mall. I'm holding several shopping bags in each hand. They are all empty and I carry them only so I can try to blend in. But it doesn't work. Everyone is staring at me. At my face. I have no mask. Most people quickly turn away. Some fall to their knees and retch. Some shout not just cruel words but hateful obscenities. The children mimic their parents and do the same. When I pass a sporting goods store, men rush out with baseball bats and golf clubs and start to attack me as the people around us begin to cheer. The attack is well planned. Their first blows are to my legs and I fall to the ground, but my only thought is that I will never skate again. Several of the men are shouting, "Kill it! Kill it!" as they now aim their blows at my face and head. I realize I am not a *her* to them.

I
am
an
*it*.

I can see the joy in their eyes as they try to obliterate me from the earth. They are so excited that spit flies from their mouths. *"Kill it, kill it,"* becomes a chant taken up by the gathering crowd.

Then the ceiling of the mall melts away and a spaceship blocks the sun. A beam of light shoots down and envelops me, and my attackers fall away. Slowly I rise into the air until finally I'm inside the ship. The aliens are about my size, but I can't see their faces, hidden by their space suits. No one says anything to me, but they are kind. One of them approaches me and puts a gentle hand to my heart, and my injuries from the attack melt away. I'm not aware of how long the journey takes, but finally through the window of the spaceship I can see our destination planet ahead. When we land a ladder descends and we all exit the ship. People from the planet gather around me and the crew of the spaceship takes off their spacesuits.

Everyone looks exactly like me.

Wherever I look, I see my own face, or one almost exactly like it, smiling back at me. I realize that I'd simply been born on the wrong planet, and it was here I was meant to be. It took fifteen years, but God found a way to fix His mistake. I can see in the faces around me that they think I'm the prettiest girl on the planet and everyone wants to be my friend.

But I always wake up.


Dad woke me up with breakfast in bed. Parents—they can be so transparent—bless their little hearts. First off, maybe I'm missing something, but what's the big deal? It's breakfast, but you have to eat it in bed, which let's face it, is pretty awkward. Hard to sit up straight. Your legs are uncomfortable trying to balance the tray. Crumbs are falling everywhere that you know will find their way against your skin at night and wake you up. The only good thing about it is that someone made breakfast for you. Dad making me *breakfast at table* sounded better.

But the worst thing about breakfast in bed was that I knew it meant I was getting a Talk. I wasn't sure what the topic would be, but a Talk was clearly on the agenda, and they were

never

ever

good.

Prior Talk subjects, in order, had been:

1. There really is no Santa (which I sort of already knew, but *damn* was I pissed off when I realized that also meant there was no Easter bunny).
2. Mom's not coming back.
3. Mr. Beavers, our rescue from the pound who'd become my best friend, had died in his sleep.
4. I would soon be having my first period.

And worse than discussing your upcoming first menstrual cycle with your dad is when that topic segues into the birds and the bees. Not that he did a bad job of it, but it was so humiliating to know it was information we both knew I didn't need to have. I probably overthought the whole thing—what else is new—but I could imagine my dad's agony on which would be the lesser insult. Let's face it, he was likely the only dad in California who didn't have to worry about his teenage daughter getting pregnant. So does he give the obligatory parental "where babies come from/abstain/but if you don't abstain use a condom" lecture to someone who will never have sex? Or does he never say anything, basically saying, *you are so butt ugly there's no need to worry about the boy issue.* No win for him. No win for me.

The bottom line was, whatever the topic, Talks sucked. Big time.

But one of the mandatory rules of being a child is to protect your parents' feelings, so I let the B.I.B. gushing begin with, "Oh, goody! Cereal! And a smoothie! Breakfast in bed! Wow, thanks, Dad."

Like I hadn't seen those same things since breakfast yesterday.

He sat down on the edge of the bed. "So," he said. "About that *nap* yesterday morning . . ."

Oh, crap.

Busted.

I knew pretending to have gone back to bed to avoid talking to him yesterday was lame. Now I was going to pay for it.

He said, "So, since when do you take a nap right after your morning skate? At eight-thirty in the morning? Then wear your mask at practice?"

Jeez. He was like a lawyer in one of those TV crime shows, laying down the evidence. Gently, but piling on. I wasn't ready to cop to anything so went with chewing. Chewing *really* well. No fear of choking going on here.

"Yum, Dad. Really good bran flakes."

But he wasn't going to be distracted by my perfect mastication. He said, "I'm guessing you overheard me talking to Uncle Robbie. You knew before I told you. Right?"

Damn, the guy was psychic. And oddly, smiling a little. I was glad he found the whole thing amusing. He grabbed one of my extra pillows and flopped down next to me, putting his head by my feet so he could face me. His way of saying he wasn't going anywhere until we'd talked it out. Unlike yesterday, there was no mask to hide behind, clearly part of his dastardly evil plan with the early morning surprise attack.

Well, when you're busted, you're busted.

"You're right," I finally said. "I heard Uncle Robbie when he came over. But I didn't know what to say, so I pretended to be asleep. Then I acted like I didn't know. It was stupid. I'm sorry . . . I didn't mean to be fake about it."

He smiled. "So that whole 'Dad, get some skaters here,' was what? You said that because you think I want that?"

What I really wanted was to delay this conversation. Like maybe until next year. I suddenly didn't feel as brave as yesterday.

"Dad, can we talk about this later? I really want to enjoy this nice breakfast in bed. I don't want my cereal to get soggy."

He gave a little laugh. "Like you care. I could see the look on your face the minute you saw the breakfast tray. You knew something was up."

Damn! Sometimes parents are smarter than you give them credit for. When I didn't say anything he said, "Honey, just tell me what you feel. Please. You're my life. You know that. I know things changed in the outside world yesterday. But that doesn't mean anything has to change for us. Forget whatever you said yesterday. Let's start all over, okay?"

That's my dad. The best.

But I didn't know how to answer. I wanted to masterfully deliver the best lie ever, convincing him I wanted him to coach again. He deserved that. But part of me wanted to say, *You and me alone forever, Daddy, hiding away in our rink in the mountains.* Complicating it all was trying to figure out who put those words into my mouth yesterday: *And I need to grow up.*

BRAIN TO HEART: Dad's been trapped here with you for fifteen years. This is his chance to escape and have a life.

HEART TO BRAIN: Dad loves you. He spends time with you because he wants to be with you. Skating with you. Nothing needs to change. You've created a world where no one can hurt either one of you ever again.

BRAIN TO HEART: Get real. Change happens. Kids have to grow up. He *will* leave eventually. Or do you want him to stay with you until one of you dies?

I made myself say, "I meant what I said yesterday. I really do want you to coach again. If you want to, I mean. You do want to . . . don't you, Dad?"

There, the burden was on him. Then I gave his own words back at him. "So you just tell me what *you* feel."

23

He took even longer to answer than I had. I watched his eyes as they took in all the posters on my walls, all my favorite skaters from past greats to up-and-comers for the Olympic Games in Beijing. He sounded almost wistful as his eyes stuck on the one of Petra Gorbinova, his first Olympic gold medalist, caught in the air in a Russian split, the line of her legs couldn't be straighter if you used a protractor.

He said, "You don't know how many times I've asked myself that in the last twenty-four hours."

Up to this point I'd been wondering why he seemed kind of subdued, yesterday's joy already faded. But something clicked when he said, *twenty-four hours*. Why were we having this conversation so soon? Why not next week? Next month? The answer hit me like a blow to the stomach.

"Dad? You've already got a skater, don't you."

# 7

Two skaters as it turned out.

He pulled his eyes off the poster. "I don't *have* anyone. But I did get a call last night from U.S. Figure Skating. And I have to . . . *we* have to, make a quick decision. I was going to just say no, but I thought I should talk about it with you first."

U.S. Figure Skating is the governing body that runs the sport with a velvet-covered iron fist, everything from approving judges to selecting who would be on the Olympic team. But I didn't want to talk about the USFS. I wanted to know the skater. I couldn't imagine it would be anyone major with Nationals just months away. But then why would there be a rush if it wasn't somebody big?

"Who, Dad? Who's the skater?"

He pointed at one of my newest posters. "Piece of Cake," he said.

It took me a few seconds to realize he was serious. *Piece of Cake!* It was like casually saying Taylor Swift and Justin Timberlake were dropping by for lunch. For a minute I was a normal fifteen-year-old girl and had to remind myself to breathe.

"You've got to be kidding me! Piezov and Cake? Dad, are you serious? *Are you serious?* They want you?"

He gave me mock insulted. "Hey, I'm not good enough? What happened to, *You're a great coach, Dad.*"

Alexander Piezov and Melissa Cake (*Lissy* to her friends according-ing to *Skating* magazine) were the hottest figures pair in the country. Pairs skaters are always referred to by their last names, and during the TV coverage of last year's Nationals, retired skating greats Johnny Weir and Tara Lipinski playfully tweaked Piezov-Cake into *Piece of Cake*. The name stuck. And it was accurate. They did make every-thing on the ice look easy.

Alex and Lissy (so, yeah, as a fellow skater I'm putting myself in the friend category) quickly made the transition from good to great. Two years ago at the Nationals they finished fourth, but just a year later they took the gold, then followed that up against the best on the planet with a bronze medal in the World Championships in Stock-holm. That made them big names in the skating world, favorites for gold again at the upcoming Nationals and solid medal contenders for the Olympics. Still, that wouldn't normally be enough to put them into the public consciousness, at least not until the Olympics actually began and hundreds of millions of Americans began their every-four-year love affair with it.

That was, until *The Kiss*. They had just completed their long pro-gram at Nationals and had skated the performance of their lives. As Alex held Lissy in their finishing position and the crowd cheered, he slowly lowered his lips to hers and delivered the most gentle kiss ever recorded on film. And after a brief moment, she raised her face to his to deliver a kiss just as gentle and sweet. No gross tongue swapping, just the most perfect first kiss any boy had ever given a girl, and vice versa. Even ESPN's SportsCenter, which doesn't exactly fall over it-self to cover figure skating, made it one of their lead stories. Just months ago, both Pepsi and NBC included Alex and Lissy in their pre-Olympic mashup commercials. The Games were still five months away, but NBC wanted you looking forward to watching it, prefera-bly while drinking Pepsi.

Being great skaters in one of the Olympics' premier glamor sports had something to do with their highlights being included with the best U.S. downhill racers, bobsledders and hockey players, but being gorgeous, charming, kissable teenagers didn't hurt either. So Piece of Cake was already becoming a household name, months before their first Olympics even began.

A lot of pressure on them.

And on my dad, if he took the job.

"Dad, you're serious! What's going on? Why do they need a new coach?"

And I didn't say it, but I admit I *was* thinking, *and why you?* I knew their coach was Nick Prado. He was one of the oldest and most respected coaches around. He was so nice (and old) that his nickname was Old Saint Nick. He'd been with Piezov and Cake for years and had brought them together as a pair eight years ago when they were only ten.

"Nick had a heart attack a couple of days ago. It looks like he's going to be okay, but he's going to be on bed rest for a long time, and they say his coaching days are over. I guess he was struggling even before this."

Not only had Nick been Dad's coach back when he was a skater, but also his mentor as he segued into coaching. And I knew Nick Prado had been one of the few people in skating who'd stayed in touch with Dad over the years of his exile.

Dad went on, "And to answer your *why me* question, Nick recommended I take over. We've always had the same philosophy. And let's face it, all the other established coaches have full rosters and would be trying to squeeze them in. So nobody ends up happy, them or the other skaters."

"But they train in Lake Placid, don't they? Would we ... you ... go there to coach?"

He shook his head. "No. I said I wouldn't even consider it unless they trained here." He held up his hands in a stopping motion. "But Katie, you're getting way ahead of things. For one thing, getting a call about possibly coaching them is a long way from actually being chosen to do it. And that's even if we decide I *should* do it. So can we first talk about if we even *want* to do this? And so soon?"

He said *we*, but what he really meant was if *I* was ready.

The truth was, I wasn't going to be able to put one over on my dad, even for his own good. I decided I had nothing to lose by being completely honest. That's the way it had always been between us anyway.

"Well," I pointed out, "You still haven't told me what *you* feel. But okay, I'll go first."

I took a deep breath. "The truth is I was kind of lying yesterday. I was terrified about the idea of people coming to live with us . . . What it'd do to my life. No more privacy. Not as much skating. But mainly just the scared part. Just," I pointed to my face, "dealing with this."

Dad started to speak. "I understand. I'll just tell them—"

"No, please, Dad. Let me finish. I know you've always tried to get me to be around other people. And . . ."

I had to pause to think about how to say what needed to be said. The reality was that I'd rejected every effort my dad had made to *mainstream* me. First it was trying to get me to go to kindergarten. Epic fail. And again years later for third grade. He'd found a small charter school with a lot of nice "special" kids. My word, not his. But both times something between a panic attack and a tantrum hit me before we got to the car. I remember a band tightening around my chest: gasping for air and literally falling to the ground. Then when I recovered enough to breathe—kicking and screaming, my sobs surely piercing his heart.

Other times he'd tried to get me to help teach his beginner skating classes. I said "no" to his every overture. My only interaction with "the world" was masked, helping with the cabin rentals and flying around the rink during the public skating sessions on Friday and Saturday nights. Maybe that's one reason I skate incredibly fast for a figure skater. If I'm a blur then no one can focus on the sides of my face that the mask doesn't cover. Ropey, corded flesh, a lesser version of the horror that is my face.

When I did the public skates, no one ever spoke to me. I sometimes wondered if they had some weird legend about me around our little mountain town. *She skates so well because she is a mutant. She eats small children. At night she flies over the lake on her broomstick. Don't look her in the eyes or she will steal your soul.* But small towns keep their own secrets, and so far no one has come up the mountain to learn about the mystery girl in the mask who can do triple after triple.

The bottom line was my exile was self-imposed. And maybe the reason my dad didn't push harder to get me into the outside world was that he could see I was genuinely happy. Every minute of my days was filled with skating, exercising, studying other skaters, and exploring the world via the Internet. Oh, and Netflix. So compared to other teenagers, I wasn't all that screwed up. The only interaction with the world that I welcomed was through the safety of the phone, handling calls to the rink and about cabin rentals. I actually enjoyed that.

"It's time, Dad. I've always fought you on it, but I know it's time for both of us. You should be coaching and I should be . . . um, expanding my life a little."

It would sound too pitiful to say out loud to my dad, but what I really hoped for was to make a friend. Just one. Maybe not soon, but someday. To me, a friend seemed like both the most remarkable, and impossible, thing to obtain. I'd see friendships in movies and wonder how it happened in real life. To have someone who wasn't your family like you enough to want to hang out with you. To just talk about nothing. To share fears and secrets and dreams with. I just didn't understand how someone took the first step to making a friend. And if I ever learned that first step, I wondered if anyone would accept that offer of friendship, especially people like Alex and Lissy who were skating celebrities.

Dad was looking prouder than when I landed my first triple Salchow.

I said, "Okay, your turn. Be honest. What do *you* want to do?"

# 8

"Okay," he said. "My truth is I'd like to coach again. Part of me is a little nervous though."

"You? Nervous?"

"Katie, being away sixteen years is a long time. Think about it. I missed fifteen National Championships, sixteen Worlds, and three Olympics. I know I've been coaching you, and some locals, but it's going to feel strange doing it at that level again. And what if Alex and Melissa are thinking the same thing? If they don't have complete confidence in me, it's going to make it hard to get the most out of them."

Wow. It never occurred to me my dad could feel any anxiety about anything. That's my job.

"Don't doubt yourself, Dad. Look what you did for me. I'm *incredible*."

I couldn't keep from laughing, but the fact was he'd single-handedly turned me into a great skater. I took a big slurp of my smoothie I'd been ignoring. "So what's next? How do we get them here?" I was already imagining being able to have a private ringside seat to watch them train, and see my dad coaching them. I'd deal with the fear later.

He said, "It was Barbara Felsdorf who called me. She wants to come out tomorrow and talk about it. I told her I'd need to get back to her."

Barbara Felsdorf was a big name in skating, U.S. Figure Skating's Director of Athlete High Performance, just one of a million facts in my skating-OCD mind. The fact it was her calling Dad seemed to indicate how seriously they were looking at him. More than he was admitting to himself.

"Isn't she based in Colorado? Why is she coming in person?"

"She won't come out and say it, but she's basically the advance man—woman—to check everything out and see if the place still measures up. She'll want to make sure the ice is good, check out the rink facilities, the housing arrangements . . . Is it all still suitable for elite skaters? She hasn't been here for what, sixteen years? And she hasn't seen me in about as long. A lot can change."

I said, "Well, I know one thing. We've got great ice."

He held out his knuckles for me to bump. "Damn right we do."

I'd learned from my father that ice is a living, breathing thing. Most people think you put a couple inches of water in a rink and wait for the pipes in the cement underneath to freeze it, then cut it smooth with the Zamboni. But taking care of a top-level ice rink is like being the groundskeeper of a major league baseball team, constantly tinkering to keep everything perfect.

Great ice starts with using special purified and mineral-free water that has to be trucked in, added one-sixteenth of an inch at a time until it is eventually two inches thick, deep enough for our toe picks to get good penetration. Then there's the temperature, which determines the speed of the ice. Keeping the ice at 19 degrees would be great for hockey. Fast ice. But figure skaters want slower, softer ice for better traction and control, closer to 24 degrees. The humidity and temperature of the air inside the rink plays a huge role too, so built into the ceiling we had humidifiers and vents that could open and close, keeping the rink at sixty degrees with ideal humidity.

You do not want to see our electric bill.

Like I said, it's complicated, and it took a lot of my dad's time. In his glory days he had someone to do a lot of those jobs but now everything was divided up between the two of us. Even though the Lake

Arrowhead locals wouldn't know if the ice was second rate, Dad kept the rink at the same level as when it was a training ground for the world's best skaters. For me.

"Will she want to meet me too?" I asked. In other words, will she think her skaters would get freaked out by some geek in a mask hanging around all the time? Was I going to ruin this chance for my dad?

"I'm sure she'd like to meet you. Don't you want to meet her? You could set her straight on how to run U.S. Figure Skating."

I was always pestering my dad with questions about why certain changes in the scoring system weren't made, like bigger mandatory deductions for falls, and why some technical elements were required in a short program but not others . . . I could go on forever about how to make figure skating an even better sport.

"Funny, Dad. You crack me up. Ha ha."

"Anyway, so Barbara will make a decision and either recommend me to Alex and Melissa . . . or not. And if she does, I'd guess I'd Skype with them first, and if that goes well, have them come out for a couple days and we'd all see how it goes."

"So . . . so they could be here in just a few days?"

He gave me a long look. "We haven't even decided if I tell Barbara she can come tomorrow. But if she came out and things went well, then yeah, it could be just a few days. Are you ready for that?"

I nodded. "Tell her to come. I'm ready, Dad."

Ready as in somewhere between completely terrified, and unspeakably excited. I tried to imagine what it would be like to sit with Alex Piezov and Melissa Cake, discussing Salchows and Axels and footwork technique and edges and a million other things. Would they even want to talk to some fifteen-year-old girl in a mask? Would they let me do some drills with them? And if they did, would I skate like one of the best skaters in the world that I knew I was, or would I crash and burn under the pressure as so many skaters did when it mattered the most?

"Good," he said. "Because I have a job for you. I need to go through their programs for the last two years, and the practice footage of their new programs for this season, so that's a lot of video. I've got my Penguins Level One at two today. How about I introduce you and you take over? There should be five kids. The youngest is five and the oldest I think is seven. We're just starting to work on crossovers. What do you think?"

What I thought was my dad was being pretty smart (well, other than labelling his kids' beginner group *Penguins,* which I'd told him was dorky). I'm sure he did have plenty to do, but what he was really doing was giving me a chance to see if I could do what I said I could: interact face-to-face. Mask-to-face anyway. But he wasn't going to say it like that. If I couldn't handle a few kids, how was I going to handle meeting the woman who oversaw Team U.S.A., and later, skating phenoms like Alex Piezov and Melissa Cake.

"Piece of cake, Dad," I said. I know, totally lame. But I said it anyway. "I'll be there at two."

# 9

I had eight hours before my Penguins teaching debut, one advantage of starting every day before the sun came up. My goal every morning was to be in the rink by six a.m. I only need fifteen minutes of bathroom/get dressed time, so my alarm was always set for 5:45. Dad had arrived with my breakfast in bed even earlier than that, so even after we'd talked, I was still on schedule.

I never got over the joy of walking through the door from our hallway and right into the rink. I'd think of all the dedicated skaters around the world who love skating as much as I do, who have to drive hours a day for their ice time. For me, it's my living room.

The sun wouldn't come up for another half hour, so I threw the bank of switches that lit the rink. Hanging from the rafters high above the ice were banners announcing the Olympic, World and National Championships won by Ice Castle skaters, and on the far wall rising up to the ceiling were flags of all the nations represented by those who'd trained here.

I made a quick stop at the skate-rental counter where the sound system controls were. Today I was feeling my Ariana-Selena-Miley mix. Sometimes I liked to crank the music loud and get lost in it, but for my morning session I always kept it pretty quiet. I grabbed the jump rope and did an easy two minutes as a pre-stretch warm-up.

My dad was big into stretching and flexibility, so the next fifteen minutes were spent on the stretch mat. It was a mix of traditional stretches and yoga. I repeat it after each session on the ice too. I do at least three sessions a day, so that's an hour and a half a day I spend stretching. To say the least, my dad is pretty unconventional. I've never worked with any type of fancy exercise machine, used weights, or done any water workouts—none of the things I read about today's skaters doing. We worked my leg and trunk muscles hard, but it was all with isometrics, resistance bands and a medicine ball. And I've never been seriously injured—not once—despite skating more than even any of the top competitive skaters do. I average five to six hours a day. The norm for elites is three.

On the ice I did another warm-up. Around the rink twice just stroking, then reverse and do the same the other way around the rink. A few minutes of alternating outside and inside rocker power pulls, then a few spins: a couple uprights, sits and camels. And finally a series of jumps, easiest to hardest: Salchow, toe loop, loop, flip, Lutz and Axel. Three times through doing a single of each, then doubles. Triples if I'm feeling them, which I pretty much always do, even that early in the morning. No quad. That was an in-progress thing, only in the harness, and under my dad's supervision.

When the warm-up was done, I had a decent sweat going and was feeling good. A short breather and some water, and I could finally get into my session. My first morning session is always just me. Dad usually just joined me for my eleven a.m. and four p.m. sessions. You can only work so much with a coach, especially when it's your dad. Besides, he likes to sleep in on most days and was usually eating his breakfast around eight-thirty, which was when I roll into the kitchen.

My morning session was ninety minutes, not counting the warm-up. If it were football or basketball practice they'd label what I do as drills. There were fifteen I could choose from, each unique and focusing on different elements, ranging from fairly easy to incredibly demanding. Each was designed to take six minutes. This wasn't an arbitrary length. In competition there are two programs: short and long. The short program was two minutes and forty seconds and was made up of seven specific categories of elements, so in competitions each skater was doing similar moves. The long program was four minutes and included twelve elements. It was often called the *free skate* because skaters had more freedom to perform what they wanted. So Dad's theory was if you trained to do a six-minute performance in practice, you'd be strong all the way through four minutes of the real thing. I'd never be competing, but my dad trained me just as he had his competitive skaters back in the day.

I started with *The Brians*, because all the elements of the drill were from Brian Boitano and Brian Orser routines. Their battle for the gold at the Calgary Olympics was legendary. I skated it at top speed and at full effort for the full six minutes, double Axel and Sal, toe and flip, three spin combinations, seven triples, and two complicated footwork sequences. I had my own reward and penalty system. If I performed it well, I got an eight-minute break before the next drill. If I made one major mistake, or two small ones, I only got five minutes. There was a clock on the wall that kept me honest.

The only break I gave myself was that I started hard, then chose easier routines as the session progressed. Otherwise, it would be impossible to do, I don't care how good of shape you're in. If my skating practice were an informercial, flashing on the screen would be:

WARNING! DON'T TRY THIS AT HOME!

Seriously.

Dad said I worked too hard and skated too much. But it's not like he could say, *go outside and play with your friends*. The ice was my best friend—my only friend. With five drills completed, I'd finished my first hour. I took a longer break, then did a long program I'd been choreographing, alternating between imagining I was Yuzuru Hanyu with his elegance, then Evgenia Medvedeva with her passion and artistry. I skated it without music because sometimes I love to hear nothing but the crunch and hiss of my blades on the ice. Like many skaters, to feel the ice better I wore my boots a size smaller than my shoe size, so my feet were yelling for freedom by the time I stepped off the ice. I repeated my stretches and my reward was a short, steaming shower.

I'd repeat the session before lunch and in the afternoon, but different activities for each one. Dad squeezed in some group and private lessons in between two days a week, and we had public skating hours Friday and Saturday nights. Between that, coaching me, some cabin rental stuff and keeping the ice and rink pristine, he stayed pretty busy.

After my shower, I found Dad in the kitchen, eating his breakfast. Actually his breakfast sat next to him, forgotten. Spread out over the table were Piezov-Cake protocols, their score sheets from each competition. I looked over his shoulder and saw he was looking at last season's Skate Canada.

Each page had almost two hundred figures filling countless columns. Every element was listed in shorthand:

$$3T+3T+2Lo \quad (10.1)$$

Translation: triple toe loop - triple toe loop - double loop jump combo. Next to it is its base value—the most difficult moves getting the most possible points. Each triple toe is worth 4.2 and the double loop 1.7, so the element comes to 10.1. Added or subtracted from that was each judge's GOEs—the Grade of Execution—which added or subtracted up to five points for how well each element was performed. The total gave you the *technical* score. But only half the program score came from technical points. The rest was *component* scores, which everyone calls "presentation," judging the skater's choreography, interpretation and skills like transitions and footwork.

You practically need a college degree in skating to decipher a protocol sheet, but it's the key to a skater getting better. It doesn't matter if the skater and the coach thought a routine was amazing if the judges didn't agree. The difference between gold, silver and bronze was often tenths, or even hundredths, of a point.

I said Dad was in the kitchen, but that's not giving the room justice. Other than our two bedrooms and bathrooms, the only other room was what we called our kitchen, but it was a lot more. It was oddly dimensioned, only fifteen feet wide, but absurdly long, almost a hundred feet, running parallel to the side of the rink. Sharing the wall with my bedroom was the actual kitchen area. Next to that was our dining table. In the old days they'd had several picnic tables set up there to accommodate all the resident skaters, so our little table for two looked shrunken and out of place. Then came two sofas and some mismatched soft chairs and a TV, then in the furthest part of the room was a ping pong table, an old pinball machine and a dart board. The room hadn't changed since the days the rink was an international training center. Despite its size, almost every inch of the walls was filled with framed pictures of past skaters, podium shots, and more country flags that couldn't fit into the rink. It was like our personal museum.

I checked the answering machine for cabin rental calls that had come in late yesterday, but there were none. There was a drop box to deposit keys through the wall when guests checked out, and waiting in the tray was the key for cabin 2. That meant there was work waiting for me, and between skating sessions was the ideal time to do it, so no reason to not do it right away. I took a long look out the window to make sure the coast was clear, tied on my mask and stepped outside.

# 10

Behind the rink was a parking lot for the cabin rentals, and from there meandering trails to the six cabins, each far enough apart to give a genuine "in the woods" feel. I always thought of cabin 2 as "The Michelle Kwan." While training here she won the first four of her five World Championship titles, and the first five of her nine National Championships. She was only eleven when she and her older sister and their dad moved here to train full-time, and the banners for all her titles up to 2001 hung in our rafters. Her coach had been Frank Carroll, who was on that same top tier of coaches with my dad and had made the Ice Castle his home rink. My dad told me stories how Michelle had pet hamsters who constantly escaped and there would be a panicked search for them. She was amazingly elegant and according to my dad, just as nice. Her 1996 World Championship gold medal performance of *Salome* when she was only fifteen was one of my favorites.

I didn't like leaving the rink. It's not that I was afraid outside. Not at all. I loved the woods. The blue jays. The woodpeckers. The squirrels. I'd even catch sight of an occasional deer. But I could do without the humans.

I knew they meant well, but I'd pass on
the looks,
the questions,

the awkwardness,

the pity.

And worse, sometimes the fear. Theirs, not mine.

Maybe it was the remote mountain setting, but I'd had guests see me coming and do a frenzied turnaround to their cabins and lock their door. The only question was if they'd call my dad or 911. I guess I couldn't blame them. I did look like a female version of Jason in *Friday the 13th*. His hockey mask not too different from my kabuki. Who was to say I didn't have a hatchet behind my back, ready to Jasonize them?

So I much preferred people on the phone. In fact, I liked that a lot. It was my job to take reservations and process credit cards online. The people renting the cabins were always nice and wanted to chat about the weather, local restaurants, shopping, the ski lifts in nearby Big Bear, or whatever. So I had to know all those things even though I never actually experienced them. Over time I'd actually become a pretty good conversationalist.

My lips only come together with effort, and there had been some damage to my throat, so I have a very minor speech problem. Considering it had been a *major* speech problem before years of work—and multiple surgeries—I was proud of the way I spoke. The funny thing was that on the phone, people were constantly mistaking it for a foreign accent. I was often asked what country I was from. I always asked them to guess. Usually I got eastern European countries like Russia or Romania, but I think people guessed those just because they'd never actually spoken to anyone from there.

I liked to imagine them thinking they'd been chatting with a dazzling foreign beauty.

The cabins pretty much stayed full in the winter when people came up for the skiing or just to enjoy the snow, and in the summer to beat the heat of the valley below. They used to sit empty in the fall and spring, but now we managed to hit at least half occupancy even then. We'd gotten lucky a couple years ago when a small budget movie for the Lifetime Channel used the cabins for some location shooting. It was a film about a gay couple, both dying of cancer, but neither had told the other, and had come to Lake Arrowhead to do so. Sad and romantic, yes. But man did they make Lake Arrowhead and our cabins look good. They were all built in the 1920s and had the original hardwood floors and pine siding, with a potbelly stove and a little kitchenette. Anyway, the movie became quite the hit in the LGBT world, and in no time word spread that the "cute little cabins" in the movie actually existed. The people who mentioned they learned of the cabins from the movie were always our nicest guests.

We made our lives simple by renting them for one week minimums, so we'd basically put fresh sheets on the beds and clean each cabin once a week between rentals, and that was it. We didn't get rich on the cabins, but considering the rink was a money pit and operated at a loss, it leveled out and kept us going.

In the days of training elite skaters and a full staff of coaches, the facility had a second outdoor rink, and a total of twenty-four cabins, a dormitory, swimming pool and a dining hall. But when Dad's coaching days ended, he sold off everything but the rink and six cabins to pay off the mortgage on what we kept.

I opened cabin 2 and did a quick scan. It would be an easy clean. I balled up the bedding and headed back. I divided the sheets and blankets up between our two oversized washing machines and gathered up my cleaning supplies and a fresh set of bedding to head back. My goal was always to get the cabin cleaned before the forty-minute wash cycle ended.

On the pathway I ran into the couple leaving cabin 3 ("The Lu Chen," one World championship and two Olympic bronzes). Sometimes I just couldn't avoid people. They did the usual physical start when they caught sight of me but quickly recovered. They didn't turn around and run, maybe because I looked harmless with both my arms full with a broom, mop and cleaning caddy. The odds of my having a hidden hatchet were evidently perceived as low.

People rarely asked me why I wore a mask. The scars and misshapen flesh around the sides of it and on my throat made the reason clear. So with new people this turned into the world's most awkward conversation where they tried to pretend the scars and the mask didn't exist. I almost preferred being mistaken for an estrogen-filled Jason.

I found the whole thing exhausting, and the worst part was it served no purpose. They were just as anxious as me for the conversation to end, if for no other reason so they could privately talk about "that poor girl." And for some reason it always made me sad they would now know the person they thought of as the clever girl with the cute accent on the phone was actually a deformed, masked girl with a slight speech defect.

So although there were times I yearned to go to a store, a movie, whatever, it just wasn't worth it. But the ice did not

judge me,

fear me,

pity me.

Just the opposite, I felt like it was the domain over which I ruled. And who would ever want to walk when you could skate? Not me anyway.

I cleaned the cabin, got the bed put together and stacked some fresh firewood by the potbelly. I knew Dad was reviewing video on Alex and Lissy so I decided to do the same. We were several months into the new skating season, time skaters used to design and choreograph new short and long program. Soon it'd be time to debut them for the competitive season starting in October, just weeks away—like exhaustive rehearsals before opening a new play on Broadway and hoping for good reviews. Some skaters like to showcase their programs a little early, so Alex and Lissy had competed last month at a small event, the Indy Challenge. I went to every skater's best friend—nbcsportsgold.com—for the video. I'd seen it before, but this time I played the long program a few times and committed it to memory.

When I got on the ice later that morning, I skated through their routine over and over. I couldn't do the throws and lifts, of course, but I moved through those elements in my mind and did the spins and jumps and footwork that I could as a single. I wouldn't expect Piece of Cake to care about the opinion of a nobody like me, but I actually thought their long program had been better last year. I had some ideas I wanted to tell my dad.

With my session over, my mind drifted toward my big teaching debut at two o'clock, an hour away. I gave myself an internal pep talk, remembering past success both with and without the mask. I made a mental list:

1. At the end of each semester I'd go to the school district office to take the home-school final exams. I'd done fine being in a room with a couple dozen other kids as we spent a half-day on tests. That was until some kids blamed their bad grades on me because they couldn't concentrate with me there. Thereafter I had to do mine privately. So never mind that one. Not a confidence booster. Erase, erase.

2. There was Alexa, the college girl who worked our skate rental counter on Friday and Saturday nights. She and I talked sometimes and she was nice.

3. The cabin rental stuff, on the phone and in person.

4. And there were even the people who had to see me without my mask, like when I went to the dentist or the doctor. Most of all there was kindly old Mrs. Gorman. From when I was three until I was seven, she came three times a week. Me, maskless. She, patient and kind. Her gentle hands, without judgment, manipulating my jaw and reconstructed lips. Teaching me to find new ways to use muscles and tendons damaged or destroyed by the fire. Touching me and not cringing at all. Liking me. My Helen Keller to her Anne Sullivan.

So I convinced myself. I could do this. I *would* do this. Besides, how tough could some kindergarteners be?

# 11

Pretty tough, as it turned out.

Dad had asked me to meet him fifteen minutes before the Penguin class was to start. He recommended I be skating when the kids arrived. I figured he thought that would save me awkward questions while waiting for them all to get there, but mainly to give me some cred if they saw me skate.

I was just keeping loose on the ice as the kids came in. Some of the parents would come inside to say hi to my dad, then take off to return an hour later. One of the moms stayed and took a seat. When there were five kids gathered and the clock said two o'clock, I put on a little show, building up my speed, doing two combos, first a triple Lutz - double toe, then a triple flip - double toe, ending in a scratch spin. It was nice to hear the "oohs" and "aahs" from the kids, and they'd all moved to the edge of the ice to get as close as possible.

Dad skated them out. "This is my daughter, Katie. She is going to be your coach today. Why don't you all introduce yourselves."

There were three girls, maybe five or six years old, and two boys a year or two older. The girls all had skating outfits and the boys were in L.A. Kings hockey jerseys. Dad had told me it was important when you coach to remember the kids' names and use them often—it helps them pay attention and shows you care. And the more I said them the faster I'd remember. Made sense. The only problem was that I was now standing in front of the largest group of people I'd ever faced in my life. Thank goodness they were all under four feet tall. But I was wondering how I was going to remember their names.

A blonde girl in orange said, "I'm Brianna. I've seen you on Friday skating nights. You skate so pretty!"

"Thank you, Brianna." I was thinking, orange like honey, honey from bees, "B" for Brianna.

The two remaining girls were both wearing baby blue outfits, so my color coding system was already screwed. One of them said, "I'm Emily, and this is my friend Skyler." Okay, the sky is light blue, like Sky. Emily, well . . . Emily was on her own.

Boy One said, "I'm Brad and this is my brother Bobby." Easy. Both "B"s as in brats. They were already hitting each other with their elbows for no apparent reason.

Loudly from the mom in the seating area, "Bobby! Stop hitting your brother!"

Dad clapped his hands together. "Okay, then. Have a good skate everybody."

And with that, he was heading off the ice and into our apartment. Maybe he thought I'd be nervous with him watching me coach for the first time, and he'd be right. I could handle the humiliation if I failed, but having my father see it happen would make it oh so much worse. I kinda wished the mom would leave too.

Bobby said, "Why are you wearing that mask? Is it a costume?"

Didn't take long to get the obvious question out there. At least I knew it would come and I'd thought about it. I'd decided to just be as honest as I could.

"I wear a mask because my face is disfigured. I—"

"What's dis-fig-erd?" Brad interrupted, stumbling over the word.

The mom again, shouting, "Brad! Don't be rude!"

"Tell you what," I said. "Let's start with some skating. How about if you all show me you can skate to the other side of the rink, then I'll answer your questions. Okay?"

45

Actually, I wanted to move far enough away from Skating Mom to keep her from listening and commenting, and maybe a bonus would be the kids would forget their questions about me and be ready to focus on skating.

I said, "But first, who can tell me how to fall?"

"I don't want to fall!" Brad said. "I want to skate!"

"I want you to skate too. But we all fall down, even the best skaters, and it's important to do it in a way that you don't get hurt, especially if there are a lot of other skaters around. So who can tell me how to fall?"

Brianna raised her hand. "We try to land on our side and slide. And make fists and keep them close to our body."

"So someone won't skate over our fingers and cut them off," said Brad gleefully.

Gross, but accurate. Skates were incredibly sharp.

"Excellent." I had the kids spread out safely apart and as a group we skated to the other side of the rink. No falls. No lost fingers.

Before I could say anything, Brad again: "So what's dis-fig-erd?"

So much for my distraction strategy.

"*Disfigured* means that my face doesn't look right. My face got burned when I was little. I wear a mask because most people would not want to look at me. I guess you'd say I'm ugly." No need to hide behind polite adult words. Ugly is what ugly is.

Brad turned to his brother. "I guess that means you should wear a mask too."

Bobby smacked Brad on the side of the head and then the two brothers were wrestling on the ground. I could hear their mother shouting across the ice, "Stop that! Stop that right now!"

I guess there were some benefits to the fact I'd never be having children. I just ignored them and turned to the girls, who didn't seem surprised by the grade school WWE demonstration at their feet. Maybe it was a feature of every Penguins class.

"Does your face hurt?" Emily asked.

"No, it doesn't hurt."

"Do you look like E.T.?" asked Skylar with innocent wonder.

I could see why she'd ask that. The reality was the skin visible on the sides was kind of like E.T.'s, vaguely reptilian. And although I let my hair loop down into a loose pony tail to cover the fact I didn't have any ears, it still left a sliver of visible skin. At least she compared me to a sweet, lovable alien rather than a lizard or alligator. Honesty with them was one thing, but no need to make them feel bad. Or scared. No need to say the visible parts of my skin did not even come close to the abomination that was my face.

"Yes," I said. "Kind of like that."

Her face was so sweet, and so sad. "I'm sorry," she said. Then hesitantly, "Can I touch it?"

Either because no one was paying attention to them, or they heard the chance to touch something gross, Brad and Bobby got to their feet remarkably fast.

"I want to touch it too!" from both of them.

I didn't know if I should be thrilled or horrified that they wanted to touch me. I kneeled down and turned my head to the side giving them the thin slice of my face between my mask and my hair. With good manners they lined up one by one. It would only be a freak show if I let it.

Brianna and Skylar were first and said nothing, meekly coming forward then stepping back. Emily said, "It's so soft." Bobby said, "Cool!" and Brad said, "Gross!" but somehow not in a mean way. Each was surprisingly gentle.

I stood up. "Okay, can we skate now? Because I love to skate and I want to teach you to be great skaters too."

That got me an enthusiastic chorus of yeahs. "Great," I said. "Here's what I want you to work on today."

I took off and within three strides I was at almost top speed. I circled the rink once, turned backwards and launched into a double Axel-double toe combo, then a spin, first a layback, down into a cannonball, then up into a scratch spin. I knew to them I was a spinning blur until I suddenly stopped. Then I skated straight at them so fast they shrank back and I did a sharp hockey stop, shooting a shower of ice onto their legs.

"Okay, Brad," I said. "You first."

His mouth dropped open.

I laughed. "I'm only kidding. All that's a lot of lessons away. But if you keep trying, maybe you can get there. Today we're going to learn what are called crossovers. The reason I could skate so fast going in a circle was that I moved one skate over and across the other with each step I took. That's what we're going to start learning today."

I took them one by one around the rink, holding both their hands, as I guided them through their first crossovers. The class went so well that when I glanced at the clock to see how much time we had left, I saw it was already a few minutes past three. I'd thought we were less than halfway through. I told them what a great job they had done and that my dad would be back with them for their next class.

They all gave me some version of "bye," and I even got a high five from "B for brat" Brad, who was not such a brat after all, just an eight-year-old boy in a hockey jersey. Emily had stayed behind and took my hand.

"Can you teach our class next time too?" she asked. "Please?"

# 12

I couldn't wait to tell my dad how well the class went. The world wasn't such a scary place, at least not today, although I reminded my-self that my expanded universe had a maximum age of eight, and I hadn't left the security of the rink. Still, I felt like I floated into the kitchen where Dad was on his computer. Alex and Lissy's long pro-gram from the Indy Challenge was playing, the same one I'd been watching earlier. He was intently scribbling notes, but when he heard me come in he paused the screen and gave me all his attention.

I'd taken off my mask the second I was through the door and I'm sure my joy radiated not just from my face but every pore of my body.

"It went that badly, huh?" he said.

"Dad! I should have listened to you before! I really enjoyed teach-ing. It was fun. And they were fine with the mask. I even let them touch my skin. Here." I pointed where they'd gently stroked me like a kitten.

That got me a surprised look. "Wow. So is this your way of saying you'll take over all my classes so I can become a man of leisure? Maybe just drive the Zamboni twice a day to cut your ice?"

"Haha. But seriously, yes! I'll teach your classes. But only so you can teach *them*." I nodded to the screen, where Melissa Cake was fro-zen mid-throw, flying impossibly high above the ice. I pulled up a chair next to him to share the monitor. "Unpause it. I'll watch it with you."

"What are you seeing?" I asked toward the end of the program.

"What are *you* seeing?" he countered, his eyes not leaving the screen.

Whenever we watched skaters—and we watched every competition that made it to TV or the internet—we'd analyze the skater's strengths and weaknesses, and give them scores as if we were judges. He'd spent countless hours teaching me every aspect of a good program. What I learned about choreography was that you should never *notice* it. It should be invisible. All you should be aware of is how beautiful the skating was. If you think about the choreography, it's like seeing the strings on a puppet. Dad compared it to a movie. You don't watch it and think, *oh, that actor just said his line really well.* When you notice the acting, the actors have failed, but great acting makes you forget it's a movie.

I *noticed* Alex and Lissy's choreography. "They aren't using Tom Dickson this year?"

"No," Dad said, his tone giving away his displeasure. "He did their short program, but they switched to Anna Strevoski for the free skate." She was a big name, but was getting older, and it showed—at least to me.

I said, "I think they took a step backwards. Their short program is great, but the free skate is . . . I don't know, but I'm not feeling it."

"The problem," Dad said, "is not that it's a bad program. It's just not a program for two teenage skaters. It's like taking a rock band and making them sing Frank Sinatra."

"Who?"

"That's my point."

I hadn't been able to put my finger on why I didn't like it, but he'd nailed it. The program just didn't let them show the kind of fun and joy that got them gold at Nationals last year. It was the kind of program one of the older Russian pairs would skate.

"And," he added, "the choreography is only half the problem."

Alex and Lissy were a lift and jump-fest—technically brilliant skaters—but they failed to tell a story. They wowed and entertained, but never really touched your heart like the more established pairs. Except for that kiss, that is.

There were three dominant pairs. Everyone in skating called them The Big Three. Russia had not just one but two elite pairs, Romanov-Ludnova and Vrenko-Vlatoya. The third was Peligrino-Maples from Canada. Vrenko-Vlataya had missed last year's World Championships due to an injury, which had opened the door for Alex and Lissy to grab bronze. The bottom line was that if all four pairs performed at their best, Alex and Lissy would usually end up fourth.

Dad said, "I've got a trivia question for you, Miss Skating Encyclopedia. Name the male or female pairs skaters who were eighteen or under when they won a gold medal at the Olympics."

I prided myself on knowing about every aspect of skating history known to mankind, but I was struggling to come up with any names. I knew there had been six girls under eighteen who'd won gold, three of them at only fifteen, but that was for singles.

Dad said, "Actually, it's a trick question, so you can stop thinking. There has never been a *single* male skater younger than twenty-one to win pairs. And there has been only one fe—"

"Ekaterina Gordeeva, Russia," I said. "The 1988 games, sixteen years old." The trivia champ was back.

"Right. Good. But you know the point I'm making. The average top pairs teams are usually well into their twenties."

His point was Alex and Lissy were only eighteen, well below the maturity curve it seemed to take for pairs skaters to emotionally connect to their music, and each other.

"You'll teach them, Dad."

"True dat," he said, ready to give me some knuckles.

But I left him hanging. "Oh, please don't, Dad. *Please*. And I'm begging you, not with Alex and Lissy."

He dropped his fist. "But that was mock! C'mon! Satirical self-parody! Therefore humorous!"

Sometimes he tried too hard. I kept a straight face as I got up to leave.

*"C'mon!"* from behind me as I left the room.

Dad joined me for my afternoon session. We worked on my triple Axel - triple toe combo. The Axel is the only jump where you take off facing forward. The other five jumps all launch while skating backward. So since every jump is landed skating backward, that means a triple Axel is actually three and a half rotations. That made it the hardest jump by far. Putting any two triples back to back is incredibly tough because of the loss of speed after the first jump, but especially when it's an Axel.

We'd measured my distance in the air and it was as far as some of the top men—the combination of strong legs, light body and perfect technique. I loved the feeling of soaring so high and so far, elbows tucked in tight as I rotated, the cold air in my face, and the *crunch* then *hiss* as my blade found the ice. Few women—or men—in the world can land a triple Axel consistently and most don't even try it, usually making the Axel only a double. But the triple Axel was mine. As my dad liked to say, *I owned it.*

We used the harness to work on my quad. Ropes attached above each shoulder, rising above me to what looked almost like a fishing pole. My dad could skate next to me and with just a little tension, keep me upright if needed, like pulling a fish out of water. One of the worst parts of learning new jumps is all the falls, even wearing hip pads, so the harness helped a lot.

It wasn't that long ago that everyone thought a quad was impossible. But athletes love to challenge the impossible, and sure enough, quads have become a staple of the world's best male skaters.

But only one woman had ever landed a quad in senior competition: Miki Ando's quad Salchow back in 2002. That is until 2019, when Russia's Anna Shcherbakova—at only 15 years old—hit not just one, but two quads at Skate America. Then weeks later along came another

15-year-old Russian, Sasha Trusova, who proved she could consistently land them as well. And so began the start of a new revolution in ladies skating.

So, yeah, us 15-year olds got it going on.

Quads are still super rare for the girl skaters though, with most of even the world's top skaters unable to do them. Only one American girl had ever landed one in senior competition; kinda funny considering that the male quad king, Nathan Chen, was an American.

I was working on a quad Lutz. The Lutz was second only to the Axel in difficulty, but it had always been my favorite. I love outside edge takeoffs. I'd gotten up to landing five or six out of ten. The harness would come off when I was at seventy percent.

Before we finished we played around with Alex and Melissa's new program and talked about ways to make it *younger* and showcase what Piece of Cake did best.

I said, "Are you going to mention any of these ideas to them when you guys talk on the phone?"

"Oh, I'm not going to recommend any changes. Not specific ones anyway."

"But . . . why? And then why are we doing this?

"Katie, the desire to make any changes needs to come from them. That's the only way they'll really want to do them—and believe in them. So my job is to make the two of them decide they need some changes, and then lead them to what we just talked about. Or get them to go back to Tom to fix it."

"Geez, Dad. You are so Machiavellian." Yes, even we, the homeschooled, have read about the darkly cunning Machiavelli. "I never knew you were so sneaky."

"Coaching one-oh-one," he said.

"Wait," I said, as something suddenly dawned on me. "So what psychological foo-foo stuff have you been using on *me* all these years?"

"On you?" He gave me an innocent face. "*Never.* You'd see right through me."

I wasn't so sure about that, but whatever he used to get me to be the skater I was, it was okay with me, sneaky or not. I thought I knew a lot about the coaching side of skating but evidently not.

When I went to bed I was so happy. It had been a great day. Taking over Dad's class. Landing the quad six out of ten tries—in a harness, but still. And working with him on Alex and Lissy's program. I knew it wasn't a sure thing they would come, but we were getting ready just in case. One thing I did know was my dad could make them better if they gave him the chance. Although he was trying to play it cool, I could see him getting excited about the possibility as well. Their weaknesses were his strengths, so a perfect pairing. And sometime tomorrow Barbara Felsdorf was coming. We'd know a lot more then.

# 13

*Dear Mommy,*

*Today is my birthday. I am eight. We have a dog now his name is Mister Beavers and we gave him a bath so he can sleep in bed with me!! I am sorry my face is not fixed yet so you can come home. I had five surgerys on my mouth so I can talk very good now! But I had a heart attack when they did the last one and now they wont do any more surgerys. I am sorry. I can do all my doubles. My salchow lutz, loop, flip, and toe loop are really good now, and even my double axel is almost as good!*
*I love you.*

*Katie*

I kept my old letters in my desk drawer, covered with notebooks and out of sight, but never out of mind. I could remember sitting with a dictionary to try to make my letters perfect. I never had an address to mail them, so I kept them for when she came home. I had imagined putting them in a pretty basket with flowers, and she'd cry when I gave them to her because she'd know I'd never forgotten her. That fantasy ended a long time ago, but I kept the letters. I don't know why.

I didn't technically have a heart attack like I'd thought of it then. It had been a cardiac arrest. That's when it's not your heart that has the defect, it's another part of your body shutting down your heart. For me it happened during my fifth surgery, something to do with my body's reaction to anesthesia and a lot of five-syllable words. But the bottom line was even though I'd made it through the first four surgeries with no problems, almost losing me during the fifth didn't make doctors excited about me as a future patient. And my dad wasn't willing to give them another chance anyway. No matter how many surgeries I would have had, I'd still never look normal. I could see and speak and hear, and I was grateful for that.

One good thing about reading the letters was they fired me up for practice: *Rage v. Mom = fire on ice.* By seven-thirty that morning I had more than my usual sweat going. I was on the last drill of the morning. Usually I go hardest to easiest, but I was feeling so strong I repeated the hardest drill last. Today Justin Timberlake was accompanying me with how he *Can't Stop the Feeling*, and I timed my last two moves, the triple Axel - triple toe combo, then right into a very tricky change of foot combination spin, to end right on his last note.

And I freaking nailed them!

The entire six minutes had been close to perfect, and the two final elements ridiculously good. I held my final position long enough to let the audience, had there been one, finish their standing ovation. I waved to the imaginary crowd as I moved off the ice.

And stopped.

There was someone in the lobby.

My mind clicked like a very slow computer. Black lady, regal-looking, like her profile belonged on British money. In her 50s. I'd seen her picture countless times in *Skating* magazine. Due here today but not this morning. Barbara Felsdorf.

Thankfully I was wearing my mask. I'd realized last night that if Alex and Lissy were coming, I'd have to wear it all the time when I was out of my room. Although I did wear it for public skates, I preferred to skate without it since it made seeing a little harder, cutting down my peripheral vision. So I needed the practice skating with it.

"Oh," I said. "Um, hello."

She stepped away from the wall toward the ice. "Hello. You must be David's daughter."

"Um . . . ah . . . um, yes."

*Um, ah, um.* Seriously? Such an idiot.

"I'm Barbara Felsdorf. I got in late last night and your father put me up in one of the cabins. I saw the lights on in here and decided to check it out. It's been a long time since I was here. The place looks good."

"Our ice is great."

*Seriously?* That was smooth. Oh, my God. Next, drool will run down my chin.

She smiled. "Yes, great ice. Of that I had no doubt."

I had nothing. I just stood there. Finally, I said, "I'm Katie. It's nice to meet you ma'am."

"The skating world is pretty informal, Katie. You don't need to call me ma'am. Call me Mrs. Felsdorf."

"Oh, okay. Well, nice to meet you Mrs. Felsdorf."

"Katie, that was a joke. Call me Barbara."

She must have been thinking she was talking to a moron. A masked moron.

"Oh, okay. Ah, Barbara."

I could see something click in her mind. "Ah. So that was *you* . . . I saw your video."

What? My video? Oh.

That day I'd worn my mask for the first time at the public skate. Someone had started videoing about halfway into it and posted it on YouTube. No information, just the title, *Little Skater Girl*. Thankfully they didn't include the part with me falling and the mask skidding away. Along with the countless cute cat videos that found their few minutes of internet fame, I'd had mine—thankfully anonymously.

It had something like four million views in a few days. I had no idea how those things happened. I hadn't thought of it in a long time.

"How old were you in that?" she asked. "Eight?"

"Six."

She shook her head thoughtfully. "Hmm, perfect double Lutz - double toe combos at six. I don't think I've ever seen that. You know, I called your father when I saw it. I recognized the rink. But he never called me back."

Dad had never told me.

"Oh."

I wasn't exactly holding up my end of the conversation so I didn't blame her when she'd evidently had enough. After a long pause she said, "Well, it was very nice to meet you, Katie. I'm headed out to breakfast. Is that place, Vilmer's, still there?"

"The Villager. Yes. It was nice to meet you too . . . Barbara."

She got as far as the door and turned around. "Would you like to join me?"

*Yes! Yes! Say yes!* This was the skating equivalent of the President of the United States asking me to breakfast. But I said, "No, I'm sorry . . . I don't leave. The property I mean."

She gave me a long look, her face expressionless. Finally, she nodded. "I understand."

Her hand was on the doorknob when I pulled up some courage. "Um, Mrs. . . . Barbara?"

She turned back. "Yes?"

"How much of my skating did you see?"

That got me another long look. Her answer was so soft it was as if she were speaking to herself. "Enough," she said. And with that she was out the door.

# 14

The emotional high from my great session was gone. I was too busy punishing myself for looking like such an idiot with Barbara Felsdorf. *Um, ah, um . . . Our ice is great! Um, ah, I'm a freak who never leaves the rink, um ah, um.* But it could have gone worse. She must have at least seen my triple Axel - triple toe combo. There wasn't another woman in the world who could do it. I wanted her to know my dad still had it as a coach. I mean, she had to be thinking if he could do that with some dork in a mask, think what he could do with Alex Piezov and Melissa Cake. At least that's what I hoped she was thinking. Not necessarily the dork part, but the rest of it.

I found my dad in the kitchen. "Dad, I just met Barbara in the rink."

He raised his eyebrows. *"Barbara?"* I met few outsiders, but I'd been taught it was always "mister" or "missus."

"She told me to call me that." I actually felt kind of proud of that. "So, Dad, did you guys talk yet?"

Head shake. "No, she ended up getting here after you went to bed. We're going to talk at ten."

Two hours away.

"Can I . . . should I, be there?"

I could tell he hadn't thought about it. "Well, if you don't mind, at the start, probably no. Sometimes there are some personal things about the skaters I need to know. Everyone has their private stuff."

The heating grate to my room had no privacy filter . . . an ethical quandary maybe. . . but it's not like I had anyone to tell. So . . .

He added, "But I'll make sure you get a chance to say 'hi.' Well, 'goodbye' I guess, before she goes if you want."

I did want. I wanted her to see I could carry on a conversation better than I had in the rink. I'm sure her review of everything to Alex and Lissy would include that the coach's daughter was disfigured and wore a mask. You don't leave a thing like that unsaid. So that would be bad enough, but I didn't want it to include: *Speak to her slowly, in short and simple sentences.*

"That'd be great, Dad. Thanks."


Later that morning I put together my usual smoothie. One orange, a full bunch of spinach, a third of a cuc, big slice of lime with peel, a couple celery tops, a handful of fruit, which today was pineapple and mango, five ice cubes, and a little water to pull down everything into the blades. Yeah, green, but tasted red. I poured it into my Nathan Chen mug, custom ordered for me by my dad, showing him holding up his gold medal at the 2019 Worlds.

I really wanted to hear how Dad would break down Alex and Lissy's skating to Barbara—to hear if he was more, or less, blunt about their strengths and weaknesses with her than with me. I'd only had one hour as a coach, but I wanted to learn more. Maybe that was where I was meant to fit in. I could almost imagine teaching classes like yesterday, and being good at it.

Dad broke into my daydreaming.

"Honey, number five checked out. Can you get it cleaned up? I put Barbara in number two by the way.

"Okay, Dad." So much for maybe listening in. When they met, I'd be working.

60

The cabin ended up needing more than usual, so by the time I was done it was past eleven, an hour into their meeting. I literally ran to my room and sank to the grate. They seemed to be just catching up on old times. Did I miss the good stuff? Barbara was laughing about a Fourth of July when she'd been visiting and they'd rented a party boat and all the skaters and coaches had gone out on the lake to watch the fireworks. The American skaters had sung God Bless America, which then prompted all the skaters from other countries to sing their national anthems too.

Dad brought the conversation back to Alex and Lissy.

DAD: "So, what do you really think, Barbara? Are they going to be more receptive to me than they were to Nick?"

So maybe things weren't exactly nirvana with Nick before he had his heart attack. The skate bloggers were usually pretty up-to-date on all the inside skating gossip, but I'd heard of no dissension.

BARBARA: "Ah, David. They are so damn *young*. In a way getting the bronze at Worlds was the worst thing that could have happened. It made them think they're even better than they are. And getting famous so early is not helping. I know your approach is pretty soft, but I think you'll need to be pretty blunt with them. Like *rude* blunt. The truth is that just getting the bronze at their age would be *huge* for us."

She was referring to the Olympics, and "us" was U.S. figure skating, where for some reason pairs had been a weakness at the international level, compared to ice dancing where we'd medaled in the last four Olympics.

DAD: "Well, we'll see how the call goes. If they're game, I am too."

I heard the sounds of them getting up, and then the noises people make when they're hugging. So I'd missed the whole discussion. She was clearly leaving.

BARBARA: "Don't let Melissa know that I told you. Okay? Let her bring it up."

Damn! I'd missed something juicy. Melissa had a secret?

BARBARA: "And think about what I said about your daughter."
Wait. *What?!?*

DAD: "Will do, Barbara. Oh, let me get Katie. I know she wants to say goodbye."

I quickly got up off the floor and sat at my desk, posed over homework, when my dad knocked.

"Come in."

"Honey, Barbara is leaving. Do you want to see her before she takes off?"

I nodded my "yes," masked up, and followed him into the kitchen.

Dad said, "So, I know you met each other this morning. Barbara, do you know Katie is quite the student of all-things-skating? When you have the time she can tell you how U.S. Figure Skating should be run."

*"Daaaad!"*

She laughed, "Don't worry, you're not the only one. Go ahead, give me your one best recommendation."

Should I? Why not. Just one. "Okay . . . the system gives too many points for flawed jumps. And shouldn't a toe loop be worth more than a flip? They've got it backwards."

I'd snuck in two.

She seemed to study me, then said, "Very astute. That, Katie, is something I've been advocating for years."

She took a long time shaking my hand then walked outside with my dad. At least this time I'd spoken intelligently. And she'd even agreed with me! Very cool. But as much as I'd wanted her here, now I wanted her gone so my dad could tell me how their meeting had gone. From what I could tell, as far as Barbara was concerned, he was in.

# 15

"Tell me everything, Dad," I said, as soon as he walked back in.

"Is there any of your smoothie left?" He opened the fridge door with incredible fake interest.

"C'mon, Dad. Stop goofing around. Tell me."

"Okay, okay." He grabbed an apple before shutting the fridge. "It went well. Really well. I told Barbara exactly what I thought, and most of it was the same stuff she'd been thinking. She told me she's going to call Alex and Melissa to recommend they start training here full time as soon as possible. So we'll see. She's going to see if they can Skype today at four."

*Yes!* Four o'clock couldn't come soon enough. I said, "She walked into the rink when I was doing my last drill. I'm not sure how much she saw, but I think she saw at least my triple Axel combo. Did she say anything?" She was the Numero Uno talent-rater in U.S Figure Skating. What serious skater wouldn't want her opinion?

"As a matter of fact, she did bring you up, even before I did. And she saw more than that. She said she watched you for several minutes."

I couldn't believe he just stopped there. *"Well?"*

"And she thought you were exceptional. Are you surprised? I've been telling you that forever."

I couldn't keep the grin off my face. Hearing it from him was one thing, but from someone like Barbara Felsdorf, that was something else.

"I wanted to do well so she'd know you're still the world's best coach, Dad." I paused. "And maybe, maybe that means I can still skate when Alex and Lissy are here, maybe even skate with them a little in drills?"

The smile slowly dropped from his face. "Oh, honey. You've been thinking you weren't going to skate anymore? Or that I wasn't going to keep coaching you? Why didn't you tell me that?

"Well . . ."

"Katie, there's no way I'd stop working with you. Yeah, you can't be quite the ice queen you are right now with no one else here, but there will be plenty of time for you, and yes, of course you guys would share some ice time."

I guess I knew he wouldn't shut me out completely. Still, it felt good to hear him say it. "Thanks, Dad. I know they need to come first though. They're the ones going for a medal."

"It will work out, Katie. That is, if they come, and we don't even know that yet."

But by four o'clock, we might know.

I remembered something. "Hey Dad, Barbara said she saw that video a long time ago. The one of me skating. She said she called you but you never called back."

Silence.

"Yeeeessssss," he finally said, looking a bit uncomfortable. "That was what, ten years ago? You're right. She *did* leave a message. And I . . . didn't call her back. Are you saying you would have wanted me to?"

"Well, what would she have been calling about?"

"You know what. And actually, just so you know, she didn't call just once. She left five or six messages. You were what, six then? How many kids that age do you think can do double Lutz - loop combos, or spins and footwork sequences like you did? I don't mean just do them, but do them extremely well."

When I didn't say anything, he said, "I'm seriously asking you. How many six-year-old girls do you think could do that?"

"Ah, none?" And no boys either, btw.

"None would be right. But *you* could. Most kids don't even start until that age, but you had a couple thousand hours in by then. From the time you were walking I couldn't *get* you off the ice. It was like your version of playing on the lawn. Your first words were practically, *'Daddy, teach me!'* . . . So that's Barbara's job. Find great skaters and have them represent the U.S.A. She wanted to know who you were."

"But why didn't you tell me she called?"

He looked crushed. "I didn't want you to get hurt. Honey . . . are you saying you'd have wanted to go through testing, and start competing?"

"No . . . I just . . . I don't know." I paused to think. "I'm sorry, Dad. I can tell I'm making you sad and I don't want that. Especially today."

Dad's eyes looked shiny and I felt so bad. He said, "Skating is so beautiful, Katie. I want you to love it your entire life—for it to be part of you, like it is for me. But the competitive side of skating . . . I've told you about it. How brutal it can be. Not *can* be. *Is.* For some people, it becomes a job and not a joy. So many kids start out loving it, and end up giving up on it. I didn't want that for you. I mean, maybe if things had been different . . ."

He didn't have to say it.

"You're right, Dad. I remember what it was like. What I was like."

He couldn't help it. He laughed. "You were impossible. You don't remember, but every time I tried to get you to go someplace, or if you'd see someone new coming over, you'd scream like you were being murdered. I'm surprised the police didn't show up."

Actually I did remember. And I remembered the moment that things changed for me. It was actually one of the oldest memories I had. Her name was Cheryl and she wore a pretty lime green dress with a pink bow around the waist. She was a "friend" brought over to play with me. Another of my dad's attempts to get me into the world. She was a couple years older than me, about six to my four. When we were in my room she told me her mom made her come to play with me, and she'd get a vanilla ice cream cone from McDonalds afterward if she was nice to me.

I'm sure I've forgotten a million things from that long ago but I still remember Cheryl and her vanilla ice cream. She told me my face looked like some kind of animal, like a pig or a dog, but uglier. Not in a mean way, just facts, like she'd say my room was yellow. I remember feeling the duty to keep playing with her, because that was expected of me. It took all my strength, but I can still remember not wanting her to see me cry.

And she didn't.

But when she left, the dam broke. Suddenly all the stares I'd known took on a different meaning. So that was the last day of my semi-public life. Years later, when I found the mask, I had my chance to go out in public again, but only at the Ice Castle. That's why that first skate had been with such a vengeance. Like saying "I'm back!" but on my very limited terms, where I could be in control.

Home ice.

Dad said, "Well listen, it's not too late. Barbara would love to see you test and start competing. That's what she told me. She kept talking about how you skated." He looked at me searchingly. "Do you want to do that?"

In other words, see if I was the skater Dad and I thought I was, or if I was only great in practice. It would mean competitions in faraway places . . . airplanes, hotels, surrounded by uncountable strangers. Audiences of thousands of people. TV cameras at the big tournaments and Nationals. A weird girl skating in a mask. A freak on ice.

Easy decision. No thanks.

# 16

Barbara called. The Skype call was on for four. The funny thing was that I don't even Skype—for obvious reasons—but every time my dad did I had to set it up for him. I'd shown him at least five or six times. He just didn't get it. So I was in the kitchen with him for the call, but only he was in front of the monitor. I stayed to the side, out of camera range.

Baby steps.

And there they were! *Piece of Cake was in my kitchen.* On video anyway. They were sitting close, side-by-side, smiling and looking totally perfect and adorable. God, I was such a stalker. They both said "hi" at the same time, but Alex said "Hi, coach," and Lissy said, "Hi, David." It was a little thing but I liked the sign of respect from Alex.

The three of them talked for quite a while. Dad asked about their training routine, on ice and off, and their goals for the rest of the season.

They were both bright and they didn't get to where they were in skating by not knowing what to ask. You don't rise to the top of any sport without having tremendous focus and desire. Their questions about how Dad ran his practices and his ideas about training were good ones. I'm sure they had already got all that information from Barbara and also talked to some of his past skaters. The skating community was a small one. Regardless, they wanted to hear it directly from him. There was a lot of back and forth, general skater talk. Alex asked if we had Dartfish, which was a computer video analysis program that allowed skaters to compare their moves on either a split screen or superimposition. We didn't, just old-school video, but they seemed okay with that.

As things were winding down, in what felt like kind of a, *This has been great, let's wrap it up* moment, Melissa said, "So what do you think, David? You think we can win the gold?" She was clearly expecting a rah-rah "Let's go win a gold medal" moment.

But Dad's bluntness surprised even me.

"Listen, you're incredible skaters," he said. "So yes, you've got a shot at gold. Someday. But not this year. Not unless you make some big changes."

*Not this year?* Great, Dad. Go ahead. Chase them away before they ever get here. Basically, *you can't win.* Barbara must have convinced him he didn't have time to be blunt.

His words just hung there and nobody said anything. Alex was stoic but Melissa looked like she had a bitter taste in her mouth. But the lemon-face faded as my dad started talking again. He broke down their long program, especially the transitions between their lifts and throws and jumps, the little things that come together to give a program life, then he talked about the music.

"Tell me, really . . . do you guys get on the ice every day and get pumped about the idea of skating to Bette Midler singing *Wind Beneath My Wings*?"

Alex looked at Lissy and laughed. "He's right. Our music really isn't any fun."

Melissa addressed both Alex and Dad, "But Anna Strevoski put our program together. She did Romanov and Ludova's program last year that won Worlds."

"Right," Dad said. "And they're thirty-two and twenty-eight. Your program would be great for them, but last I checked you guys were eighteen."

"It's too late to scrap our program," Lissy said flatly.

My dad shook his head. "It doesn't need to be scrapped. But I think you need new music. Music that matches your spirit . . . and that is actually fun to skate to. And you need some changes with your transitions . . . Sorry, but that's what I think. I'd suggest you get Tom Dickson back for five, six days. That's all it would take. He did a brilliant job on your short."

He didn't stop there, giving both compliments and critiques, everything from the depth of their knees to their edge work. He said he thought they were among the best in the world technically, but their presentation still didn't match the artistic interpretation of The Big Three, and that's where the real work would be. Looking at their faces, I could tell he was telling them what they already knew, but that no one had told them so bluntly.

Alex turned to Lissy. "Admit it, we haven't been feeling it with the new program at all. He's completely right."

It looked like she was going to say something then changed her mind. "Okay . . . Can Alex and I talk about it and call you with our decision tomorrow?"

Before my dad could answer, Alex said, "Lissy, why wait? We pretty much made up our minds before we even called. Have we heard anything to make us change our minds? If anything, I'm even more excited to start than before." He gave her a playful nudge. "C'mon."

I think my dad felt uncomfortable with Lissy being put on the spot. Before she could reply he said, "How about you two talk privately and get back to me. Tomorrow is fine."

Not ten minutes after their goodbyes, Alex called back. Discussion over. They were in. An hour later their manager called, dealing with money and contracts and things I didn't care about. But what did matter to me was they'd be here on Saturday, the day after tomorrow.


Saturday came fast and hard. And for all my brave talk, I ended up hiding in my room. I got in my six a.m. skate, and by ten I heard the first of four caravanning cars driving into the lot. For some reason I guess I just expected just Alex and Lissy to pull up and unload a couple suitcases. I guess that was naive of me. They'd have their little entourage, and since they were still teenagers, I'm sure their parents would be with them.

I angled my window blinds so I could see out but they couldn't see in. At least I hoped not, or they'd have one more thing to laugh at me about. Alex was driving the lead car, a bright-blue Mustang. Right behind him was Lissy in a red Mercedes SUV. Alex got out and walked over to Lissy, giving her a quick hug just as two more cars pulled in, the end of their mini-convoy. One car was driven by a lady I was guessing was Alex's mom, with a couple middle-school-aged boys in the back seat. They looked like little Alexes so had to be his brothers. I'd seen Lissy's famous dad on TV many times, so I'd recognize him, but he wasn't there. In the last car was the woman who I was guessing was the physio and dance instructor that Dad had told me travelled with them.

Imagining them here was already different than actually *having* them here. I literally started trembling. What had I been thinking? Suddenly I felt totally inadequate. Dad tapped on my door, giving me just enough time to move away from the window before he stuck his head in.

"They're here," he said. "Do you want to come out with me?"

No way. My only goal at that moment was to keep Dad from seeing my tremors and hyperventilating. "Not yet, Dad. I'll say hi to them later. I heard a lot of cars pull up. I'll wait until things calm down a bit."

He walked over and gave me a hug. Maybe I didn't fake my bravery as well as I thought. "It's going to be fine," he said. "Better than fine. You'll see. Just come out whenever you're ready."

As he went outside to greet everyone I returned to my horizontal-slatted peep. I could see introductions being made, smiles all around, and necks being craned at the mammoth pines overhead and I imagined the usual, "It's so beautiful here!" comments.

The more I watched, the madder I got—at myself. All those brave thoughts of a new me, taking a chance. Taking charge. Gone. Instead, hiding in my room. Pitiful. I laid down a quite rare, but exquisitely delivered, f bomb and headed for the door. On my way out I did maybe the dumbest thing in the universe. After I tied on my mask, I paused in front of the mirror to check out my hair.

*Seriously?*

I mean, I did have to make sure my hair curved down to cover my ears—or lack of them—but that was about it. At least I was laughing at myself as I was headed outside. As I came out the back door everyone turned to look at me:

1. Surprise on my dad's face that I'd changed my mind.
2. Double takes from Alex and Lissy.
3. Something between confusion and discomfort from Alex's mom.
4. Outright laughter from Alex's little brothers.
5. A split second of revulsion from the physio before she covered it up.

Nothing new for me—the same mixture of reactions I got every time I crossed paths with someone for the first time. I could read every reaction instantly and knew the thoughts behind them. I was sure Alex and Lissy had been told at least about my existence from Barbara, but the double takes were still an understandable reaction. Clearly though, they hadn't mentioned the face-thing to the others in their group. Actually it was nice that they hadn't. *Oh, and by the way, there's some deformed girl who lives there and hides behind a mask, so be nice to her.*

Alex's brothers' laughter faded as I got close. That's when they saw the scarring around the mask and realized the mask wasn't some joke. So there was nothing mean in the laughter. Still, I felt bad for my dad hearing it. I always tried my best to protect him. I got the reaction from guests a lot on the paths to the cabins as I got close.

When I wasn't getting the *Here comes Jasonette with a hatchet* look, it was the short-term laughter. People would think it was just a teen-ager goofing with a mask. Then they'd see the scars and the laughter died.

I was saved by, of all people, Alex Piezov. He took a few steps toward me just as I was reaching them. He was very formal and held out his hand to shake.

"Hi, I'm Alex."

And coming right next to him was Melissa Cake. "And I'm Lissy. You must be Katie."

Okay, I'll admit it. Even with my discomfort, *"And I'm Lissy"* practically stopped my heart. Not Melissa. *Lissy.* I couldn't imagine calling her that though, at least not out loud.

I had two thoughts. One was that they were being incredibly nice. The other was that they were gorgeous. Like perfect golden people. As far as I was on one side of the scale of human perfection, they were on the other. I remember a female reporter had teasingly called Alex "farm fresh." And he was, like he was posing on a tractor in a cornfield in a Calvin Klein ad—straw-colored hair, an infectious smile and a V-shaped chest like a swimmer. His contrast with Lissy was striking. Her Polynesian mother gave her gorgeous dark hair and golden brown skin; the green eyes must have come from her father. Even though they were American skating royalty, I'd told myself I was just as good a skater, actually better, but that thought seemed laughable at the moment.

Alex introduced me to their group. The young woman was their physio, Bridget. She was buff and so pretty she almost made Lissy look average, with her blonde hair braided intricately and perfect translucent skin. A slight accent I guessed was Swedish. Or Danish. Or Finnish. Definitely a Scandinavian *ish* of some type. She gave me a curt nod without moving from her spot.

As I'd guessed, the middle-aged woman was Alex's mom. I knew his parents were divorced. His dad had been a professional hockey player and was now an assistant coach with the New York Rangers, so no surprise he wasn't here. The two kids were indeed Alex's younger brothers. Their mom told us they lived in San Diego, just a few hours away, and they'd be coming up to visit every week or so.

"My dad had an emergency and couldn't fly out," Lissy said. "He'll try to come by in a couple days."

Everyone in skating knew about Lissy's dad—make that *Super Dad*. Her mom had died many years ago, but her dad was a self-made celebrity. He was the founder of Zip It, the express shipping company. He did funny commercials featuring himself in some foreign locale with something to deliver and he'd say, "Don't ship it, *Zip It*." He was a magnet for the TV cameras at all of Lissy's competitions. Usually after her program was done, they'd replay the footage of his anguished parental gyrations as he lived and died through each of his daughter's jumps and throws. Sometimes the camera shot included whichever Victoria's Secret model he was dating at the moment. His over-the-top generosity toward his daughter was legendary, not only constantly sending her flowers and gifts, but to her friends as well. Despite all that wealth, other skaters on the blogs described Lissy as pretty normal. At least as normal as one of the world's top skaters could be.

Dad said, "I was just about to take them to the cabins. Do you want to show them?"

"Sure, Dad." Doing that would be much easier than to keep standing there talking. "The cabins are this way. Follow me."

As we went down the path I heard my dad's voice behind me. "We have six cabins and three are rented right now. So we have three you can choose from."

"I got dibs!" Alex said quickly, then laughed. "Kidding. You can choose first, Lissy."

"Well, I would expect so," she said with fake haughtiness.

I couldn't believe how normal they seemed. Even though they oozed confidence, they didn't have any of the big ego that my dad had described with some of his big-name skaters. Maybe their fame was too new to have made a dent yet. I stopped where the path divided into six gravel walkways.

"The ones we have open are those two." I pointed to my right through the trees. "Four and five. And we have number two down that way." To the left.

Lissy said, "This is going to be so cool. I've never had my own cabin." She turned to Alex. "Let's be next to each other."

Dad forked left with Bridget to cabin number two. I didn't hold the flash of revulsion I'd caught on her face against her. Some people just couldn't help it at first. She was probably in her late twenties. If she were a little older I'd try to get her interested in my dad. He hadn't had a date since Gloria walked out.

The rest of the group trailed after me down the path. I said, "I'll show you both of them but they're exactly the same, just decorated a little differently."

Alex's mom said, "Alex told me this was once a big training center. So all the skaters lived here?"

"Yes. Another coach owned it and my dad bought it from him a long time ago. Back then there were twenty-four cabins and a dormitory, a dining hall, a gym, even a pool. But my dad sold it all off after I was born. So now we just have the six."

I opened up cabin 4 and stepped aside. Lissy, Alex and his mom followed me in while his brothers explored outside.

"Oh, it's so cute!" Lissy said. "Even a little kitchenette!"

I was relieved. I thought Billionaire Daughter Syndrome might raise its snooty head. But no. She'd been living at training centers off and on for years, so a hotel-style lifestyle must have been the norm for her. So maybe by comparison a cabin was cool.

She opened the closet door, which was just big enough to stand in. She laughed. "Okaaaay . . . so I'll need about ten of these."

Well, maybe a little bit of Billionaire Daughter. I said, "Yeah, sorry. The closets are really small. People usually just come up for a week. I pointed out the dresser and said, "The dressers are pretty big, though, and we have empty closet space in our place to keep your extra stuff if you want."

"Okay," she said. "Thanks."

She and Alex made their way to the cabin's little wall of fame, pictures I'd framed of the famous skaters who had stayed in each cabin. There was Robin Cousins winning his Olympic gold in 1980, Lu Chen who won two Olympic bronzes and one World Championship, and Peggy Fleming. Her glory years were before my dad's time, but she'd often come to stay for a few days to visit other skaters. She won the Olympic gold in 1968 and three World Championships and was the most famous American skater of her generation. I hoped they appreciated skating history like I did.

"So is it okay if I take these down and put up some posters?" Alex asked.

"Um, sure." I hid my disappointment. "They are kind of old."

Lissy turned to me. "Can I have the key and check out the other cabin?"

I gave it to her and she headed out the door with Alex right behind her. I knew they were boyfriend and girlfriend and wondered if they'd be sneaking to each other's cabins at night, and if that was something the parents worried about, even though living away from home was nothing new for them.

Alex's mom asked me some practical questions about doing laundry and cooking arrangements. I let her know we'd take care of everything because I didn't know what else to say. The only guest laundry we did was sheets and bedding. I washed my own clothes, but did people like Alex and Lissy? For some reason I couldn't imagine them schlepping their laundry bags over to our laundry room a couple times a week.

Alex and Lissy came back and Lissy said, "I'll take this one." She plopped on the bed and gave a theatrical relaxed sigh.

Alex said, "Hey, can we see the rink?"

# 17

"Oh yeah. Let me show you."

I led our little line, Alex's brothers joining us again, back toward the rink. As we were walking I gave myself a pat on the back. I thought I'd done really well with them. In fact, I couldn't believe how normal our conversations had been. And they'd been really good about the mask. I did catch them staring at me when they didn't think I was looking, but I was used to that. It's just natural to stare at things both beautiful and repulsive. I was sneaking looks at them too.

Dad and Bridget were already at the back door waiting for us and I let Dad take over as tour guide. Our first stop was the kitchen, which was a hit. The flags and pictures, not to mention the ping pong table and pinball machine, made it a fun room. Dad said, "So any meals you guys want to join us for, you're welcome. Or you can just come in and cook what you want in here, or in your own kitchens. And we've got some great restaurants within walking distance."

Then we were in the rink. I knew their last training center in Lake Placid had three rinks and more than twenty coaches on staff. I'd been a bit worried that even with its history, that the Ice Castle wouldn't measure up.

"It's so retro," Alex said. "Very cool. We checked out some pictures online but it's even bigger than I thought."

The rink was beyond regulation size since it was designed to accommodate a lot of skaters at the same time. It was built just for figure skating so it wasn't surrounded by hockey boards like other rinks. It was like an indoor frozen pond that you could step on from anywhere.

Lissy looked up. "Look at all those banners, Alex. I want ours up there."

"Oh that reminds me," Alex said to my dad. "We talked to Larissa Collins. She said to say hi. She also said you're going to be an amazing coach for us."

Larissa had been his first skater to win an Olympic medal. Before connecting with my dad she'd been infamous for choking and finishing way off the podium despite great talent. She publicly credited my dad for her silver medal. But my dad never had any interest in getting compliments so he turned the conversation to their schedule on the ice tomorrow.

Alex and Lissy's first session would be at eight, just as I was finishing mine. They knew we didn't have a traditional gym so they were going to unpack then head into town with Bridget to check out the one in town, and they were all going to stay in town for dinner.

On the way back through our apartment Lissy asked me about the extra closet space I'd mentioned. If my dad was thinking *what extra closet space,* he kept it to himself. I said, "Well, it's in my room. But you can share it and just take stuff when you need it."

I assumed only she would follow me, but the entire group tagged behind. My room had two big sliding doors to a closet that was about ten feet wide, but I only used a foot of it to hang clothes. Most of my clothes fit in my dresser—so she had nine feet to herself.

"Oh," she said, surprised. "But where are your clothes?"

How to answer that? "Well, I don't really have many clothes. I mean, I don't exactly go anywhere." Somewhat defensively I added, "My dresser is pretty full." Which it really wasn't. Three of the six drawers had only books and old DVDs.

The truth was I had a lot of skating pants and tops, but the rest of my clothes you could fit in a couple drawers—kind of embarrassing now that I thought about it. I had no need for dresses or fancy shoes. My dad let me buy what I wanted online, but my needs were pretty simple.

Hopefully no one would look in my bathroom, which was equally bare. I certainly didn't need the makeup and beauty products that filled most teenage girls' bathroom counters. I had a toothbrush, toothpaste, floss and a hair brush. That was it. And no lotions or creams. It wasn't like I was going to scrutinize my face in the mirror and think, *hmm, better keep this baby soft.*

Thank goodness my walls were filled with posters so it looked like someone actually lived in my room. Nathan Chen (aka The Gorgeous One, at least to me), Evgenia Medvedeva, Michelle Kwan, Anna Shcherbakova, every inch of the wall was covered. And Jason Brown, who skated so beautifully he'd once actually made me cry. Alex nodded at the Piece of Cake poster. "Alright," he grinned.

Well, *that* was embarrassing. At least they couldn't see the picture of them I kept under my pillow. Kidding.

As everyone's eyes took in the posters I quickly turned the framed selfie on my bureau face down. Me, three years old, on a sled with my dad. My last picture with a face, minutes before the accident.


The next morning, I set my alarm for an hour earlier than usual so I could skate from five to seven. My dad didn't ask me to, but I wanted time to drive the Zamboni so there was fresh ice for Alex and Lissy. With them due at eight, I finished with about ten minutes to spare, but as I waited for them to come in, I suddenly forgot how to stand. Or sit. Whatever position I took as I waited for them felt strangely unnatural, like some weirdly twisted mannequin. Totally fake.

After a few minutes of posing every which way, I gave up. Easier to just come back when they were busy on the ice. So I took a shower, made my breakfast, even did a little homework—yeah, 'cause I'm soooo cool—no need to rush just because Piece of Cake was skating a hundred feet from my bedroom. That attempt at self-deception disappeared the second I opened the door to the rink. Even before the door was open all the way, I could hear the sound of their blades on the ice. You could *hear* the speed.

And there they were, on my home ice.

But it almost didn't feel like mine. The star power of Alex and Lissy made me feel like I'd just walked onto a movie set. They were just stroking backwards around the ice, but they were *flying,* in perfect unison. Legs churning, arm positions perfectly matched, heads steady. The only other high-level skater I'd ever seen skate in person was my dad, and his best days were thirty-plus years ago. I'd seen myself on video but had no idea how I looked live. I could only hope I looked that good.

The music playing was the soon-to-be-replaced *Wind Beneath My Wings* by Bette Midler. I could tell they were at the end of their long program as they moved into their final lift, a lasso lift with an axel entry where Alex lifted Lissy above his head, his arms locked with hers, supporting her spread-eagled above him as he rotated three and a half times, then flipped her over once before her blades touched the ice, and transitioned seamlessly into a side by side flying combination change of foot spin as the music ended. So amazing for me to watch in person—but from their reaction, another ho-hum day in the practice rink for them.

I was so excited I didn't know where to go. Stay by the door? Take a seat? Stand by the ice? The whole thing was captivating. Not just Alex and Lissy, but watching my dad as a coach. This was all really happening, and I was here to watch it. Not just today but for who knew how long. Incredible beyond words.

Dad must have said to take a break because they skated over to their water bottles. They saw me and gave a little wave but I stayed by the door. Just a few minutes later, they were working on their side-by-side combination jump, a triple Lutz - double toe loop, this time without music, which let me hear the sweetest music of all—the sound of their blades. Dad was having them do what he did with me, do the entire program once, then work on one or two particular elements. They were circling the ice and doing their combos on each long side of the rink, giving them plenty of space for a lot of speed, but evidently not enough for my dad.

"Push it! Push it!" Skater talk for *faster*. "C'mon, grab speed from every stroke."

Seriously? To me it looked like they were flying. Around and around they went, Dad calling out comments.

"Beautiful, but hold that landing. *Savor it!* Extend the line . . ." Then, "Both of you . . . beautiful position on the landing but you're still rushing out of it. You're a seagull riding the wind over a calm, flat ocean. Let's see it, here we go, seagulls over a glassy sea. Let me see you savor it." My dad the poet, talking like Hemingway. But the funny thing was it came out legit. His whole demeanor was different, more intense than with me.

I realized I had a big grin on my face, not that anyone could see it. So I let it stay, silly and sappy on my face as I walked closer.

To end their session, Dad put them into what he called Presentation Cardio, stroking laps at top speed—but while still emoting to the audience. Dad was center ice, skating in tiny circles to watch them as they raced around the rink. "Almost done. Just four more. I know you're tired, but you're still *happy*. Happy that you're so young, and so graceful, and so fast on the ice. Everyone in the audience should be feeling that from you, that joy, even just stroking. C'mon, all I'm seeing is that you're tired. Make me not want to take my eyes off you."

They did, in fact, look tired. And the joy and confidence he wanted to see in their faces looked pretty fake at the moment, but they were trying and it was a start. They finished their laps and bent over, hands on knees, gasping for air, letting their momentum carry them around the rink.

As Alex and Lissy glided slowly past me, Alex got out a few words in between sucking lungfuls of air each time he'd pass me, "We'd say hi . . . but then we . . . couldn't breathe."

He was a pretty funny guy. Dad hadn't moved from the center of the rink and gave a head nod to have them join him. I walked out on the ice to hear his wrap-up.

He said, "Really nice work guys. Really nice. So . . . tell me, why did we end with ten full-speed laps? And why are you so tired?" A beat of silence, then he added, "Hint. The answer is in the second question."

Lissy said, "You're saying we aren't . . . in good enough shape?" I hoped my dad wasn't going to point to me and let them know I did twice as many laps at the end of all my sessions.

"You tell me. We worked for forty-five minutes. A pretty easy forty-five minutes you'd have to agree since it was our first time together and we did so much talking. But you don't look tired. Tired is okay. You look completely exhausted."

"It wasn't the skating," Alex said. "It was all that smiling."

That got a laugh from my dad. "Yeah, right. Listen, no one can perform at their best when they're tired. Both the mind and the body start shutting down. Maybe just five or six percent, but it's enough. I want the *other* skaters to lose that percentage, not you. I want you to be in better shape than any other skater out there. And to go out there with the confidence knowing that you're going to be as strong in the fourth minute as the first."

"I have the feeling I know where this is headed," Alex said, looking sideways at Lissy. "I think we have a lot of laps in our future."

"I think we're in great shape," Lissy said, a tad defensively.

Dad nodded agreeably, "Says the girl so winded she still has her hands on her knees because she's too tired to stand up." Ouch. Slaying with a smile, Dad.

She gave kind of an, *Okay you got me* nod.

"Here's the thing," Dad said. "I looked at your scores for your last two years and from Indy." He paused until both of them met his eyes. "Do you know that in both your short and frees, that your *first* two element scores averaged eleven percent lower GOEs than the rest of your program? And in your free skates in the *last* thirty seconds they averaged eight percent lower?"

From the look Alex and Lissy gave each other they didn't know that. And they took it seriously.

"So what do you think that means?" asked Lissy, although I was sure she knew the answer.

"How about you guys tell me. Can you join us for lunch today? At one?" He got yesses back and said, "Great. Tell me then. Do a cooldown and I'll see you at lunch."

When they'd finished and left the rink I said, "Dad, did you see they didn't stretch before they left?" No way he'd ever let me do that.

But he didn't seem perturbed about it. "One thing at a time. Most people think a cooldown skate is enough. You only know my way of doing things. Not everyone agrees with it."

I didn't see how they couldn't. Maybe my dad had just hammered it into me, but a full stretch after a workout was the best way to really enhance your flexibility and help your muscles recover faster. And they even had Bridget, their own physio to advise them.

"So," I said, "what do you hope they're going to say at lunch?"

"Well, I hope the answer is pretty obvious. To them and to you. I guess we'll find out at lunch." Then he changed gears and asked me what we had in the fridge. Maybe he was just realizing he was going to have to start shopping for four—five if you counted Bridget. He said, "But the main reason I want them to come to lunch is to get them comfortable hanging out in the kitchen, whether it's making their own food or eating with us. The sooner this feels like home to them the better."

And I bet he wanted more opportunities to talk skating with them, without it being a "learning moment" on the ice. I think I learned more about skating from him over the kitchen table than I did in the rink, just talking and hearing his stories.

I was feeling pretty lucky. One minute I had Alex and Lissy in my rink. Now they were going to be in my kitchen, sharing a meal. And not just one—it sounded like there would be a lot of them. There was only one negative to them eating with us. I'd have to wear my mask, so how was I going to eat?

# 18

Dad had another Penguins class. I found it hilarious he went from coaching U.S. National champions to the Penguins, but he didn't want to cancel lessons already scheduled, which I thought was pretty classy of him. This week he'd be letting the groups know I'd be taking over for him.

I was in the kitchen making sandwiches with my favorite organic Dave's Killer Bread when Alex and Lissy came in. They kind of awkwardly knocked on the open kitchen door as they walked in, as if asking permission to enter. Next to the cutting board I had a little cheat sheet to remind me of things to say. Hopefully, the words would come out naturally. At least I had a poker face.

"Hi, Katie," from them both. Then Alex observed, "New table."

Well, a new, old table. Earlier this morning Dad had me help him carry in one of the old picnic tables from the storage room. It was one of the original three that had been in the kitchen during the old days of the Ice Castle. What made it so neat was that skaters had carved silly things into it; names in hearts and goofy stuff like that, so it was completely scarred up. One more piece of skating history in the room.

"Yeah, from the old days," I said.

They sat down facing me and checked out the table, getting into it as they realized whose names they were seeing scratched into it. Hopefully they appreciated it like I did. I turned my back to them and went back to the cutting board. "My dad will be here in a few minutes. Is sliced barbecued chicken on wheat bread okay? And I'll make a smoothie?"

They said that was great and I went back to my cutting, cheating a look at my reminder list. Next up was "fruit" to ask them what they liked in their smoothie. But before I could, they both started laughing. Actually, more like trying to hide their laughter. Somehow I knew I was the butt of the joke.

And I'd thought they were nice. Maybe that was only when my dad was around. But do I turn around? Or ignore it? It was like being four years-old again and Ice Cream Cheryl telling me I looked like an ugly animal.

Alex said, "Oh, man. I'm sorry." More laughter from them both. "But you were humping the counter." And off they went again, laughing even louder.

*Oh, my God.* I realized what they'd been laughing about. I tend to work my body all the time, and there was never anyone around to worry about. But I'd been doing my butt clenches while I'd been cutting. I'd squeeze my butt cheeks together and do a little pelvic thrust. Works the glutes and the lower back. I tend to do them when I'm doing something boring like making meals or brushing my teeth.

Lissy tried to stop laughing. "Katie, we didn't mean to laugh. But it was pretty funny."

And then I remembered thinking I was the butt of their joke, and that made me laugh too. I turned to face them. I felt so bad because even though they were still giggling a bit, I could see they felt guilty. Laugh at the deformed girl. But that wasn't what they were laughing about. And it *was* funny.

I said, "Oh, sorry. I, ah, I'm always exercising. I'm just not used to having anyone around." Then I added, "I'll stop humping."

Which got them going again.

I moved the cutting board to the island counter facing them (and no, not because I was going to continue doing my butt clenches). "What do you guys like in your sandwiches?"

84

Alex got up and moved toward the kitchen. "Hey, we can help."

Lissy got up as well, saying, "Watch out. She's a humper."

They were so nice! And funny. And normal. They seemed to make themselves comfortable really fast. Maybe that came from having so many "homes" in all the training centers they'd lived at. I felt really good about holding my own with them so far and realized they deserved a lot of the credit. They weren't treating me at one of the usual extremes: either grossed out or acting all syrupy sweet because I'm "special." They just acted like I was a girl sharing the kitchen.

"Tomato for both of us," Alex said, pulling things toward him. "Onion and spinach . . . and do you have any mustard?"

"Fridge," I said. "In the door."

Lissy pushed herself up and sat on the counter, legs dangling, as he came back and pulled a knife from the block and started cutting. *Alex and Lissy in my kitchen! Making sandwiches!* Oh how I wished I had a friend so I could casually mention, *"So, yeah, I was in the kitchen yesterday, making sandwiches with Piece of Cake . . ."*

Since he was taking over on the sandwiches, I said, "I can make a smoothie. Is there anything you don't like?"

"No," Lissy said. "We're good with anything. Make us whatever you think will be good." She reached over and grabbed the piece of paper next to the cutting board. "Are these your ingredients?"

*My conversation reminders!* Potential embarrassment beyond words.

I risked being rude and kind of snatched it. "Um, sorry," I said. "Yeah, I need that."

I usually go for mainly veggie smoothies, but I didn't want to scare them away by being too healthy, so went fruit-heavy: mango, orange, pineapple, cucumber and a slice of lime. I was putting it in the Vitamix when Alex pronounced the sandwiches done. And he said, "Hey, do you mind if we add some vegetables in there too? How about this extra spinach, and maybe you have some carrots? You've got a lot of sugars in there."

Unbelievable. As in unbelievably good. I said, "Actually, I usually make just green ones, but I didn't know if you were into that."

Alex gave me stern and pointed to himself then Lissy. "Hey, perfect bodies like these don't just happen."

I had to admit, part of me kept thinking of them more as celebrities than top athletes, which is what they were. Well, I guess they were both. So with their blessing, in went a big handful of spinach, two carrots, some kale and ginger. The three of us were so healthy it was disgusting. No one could talk over the blender so I handed Alex two plates for the sandwiches.

"Where is yours?" he shouted.

When the blender stopped I said, "I already ate. But I'll have some of the smoothie."

As we were sitting at the table I wondered what happened to my dad. But in a way I was enjoying just being alone with Alex and Lissy. They asked me questions about Lake Arrowhead and our little town of Blue Jay, while I hungrily used a straw between questions for my smoothie.

After a while Alex asked, "So, did you really already eat, or do you not want to take your mask off?" Then, "I mean, we've already seen you have sex in the kitchen. I think we know you well enough to ask, right?"

They must have talked about bringing it up because Lissy quickly added, "We're going to be here, in your house, like . . . for a long time. We just want you to be . . . you know . . . comfortable. It's your house."

It was actually a relief to get the subject out of the way. I just wished I had a conversation cheat sheet for it to be better prepared. "Well, I don't . . . I don't wear it around my dad. But I just feel more comfortable with it on . . . the rest of the time."

"Really?" Alex said. "We've seen some really freaky things. Show her your feet, Lissy."

"Shut up!" She gave him a pretty hard elbow.

Figure skaters have the ugliest feet in the universe, the result of being crammed into tight skates for half the day, and putting such demands on them. I guess that literally made me ugly from head to toe. Nicely balanced, one could say.

"Seriously," he said. "Barbara said you're a skater. How do you even skate with that on? That's got to be hard."

"Yeah," I conceded. "It is."

"So, c'mon," he said. "Just get it over with. Just flash that baby up, then back down. Quick little flash. Like when Lissy flashes her boobs out the car window."

She just patiently shook her head from side to side and gave me a *He's hopeless look.*

He went on, "Then again tomorrow, little bit longer. It's like when I had roommates when we trained in Lake Placid. At first we were all shy around each other. And after a while we're like walking around naked after a shower and no one cares."

Lissy said, "She's fifteen, Alex. Stop trying to get her naked."

"Haha. You both know what I mean. I'm just . . . We just don't want you to have to wear it just because we're here."

For a brief second, I wanted to do just what he'd said. To pull the mask off. To be myself, like with my dad. But no matter what they said, and no matter how sincere, reality was a different thing. The truth was I couldn't risk losing them so soon. My face was that horrible.

So I said, "Thanks. You guys are being really nice. But you can see how my face is around my mask? Well it's not like that under it. It's . . . a lot worse. It honestly is." Then I added, "Maybe even worse than Lissy's feet."

I loved that I was making them laugh. I was actually pretty good at this conversation stuff. Good training, all those years on the phone. And I'd just used *Lissy* out loud. It still felt strange saying it, like if I called my dad by his first name. But I was going to keep at it.

I was thinking how great things were going when Bridget came in. I could see a look of surprise flash across her face when she found us all laughing. But just as quickly it was gone. She stayed just long enough to tell Alex and Lissy that they needed to be in the rink in ten minutes. No hello to me. Still, I raised my hand to offer a wave but she was gone. When I brought my hand down it caught the lip of my glass and I ended up with green smoothie all over me. Such a dork. I was so embarrassed that I just sat there, like if I didn't acknowledge the green slime dripping down my clothes then it wouldn't exist. Kind of like closing my eyes to become invisible—which last I checked didn't work.

Finally I said, "Um, I'm going to go change. I'll be right back."

To look even stupider, I first picked up everyone's dishes and put them in the sink, dripping green to the kitchen then into my room. I got out of my clothes and was pulling on some new ones when I heard Alex and Lissy through the vent. I could hear the sounds of glasses being put on the counter. That was nice—they'd finished cleaning the table for me. My head was only a few feet from theirs so I could hear Alex even though he was practically whispering.

ALEX: "Man, this is *so hard*."

LISSY: "Stop it. She is so sweet. And she's trying so hard. Just be nice."

ALEX: "I *am* being nice. But c'mon, you've got to admit . . . that mask is freaky. It's like talking to a wall. You can't see her expression or anything. And everything she says comes out so awkward, like she's memorized it or something."

There was a pause and I could almost visualize Lissy turning toward Alex and taking his hands in hers.

LISSY: "Alex, can you imagine how hard this is for her? She's never had any friends or anything. But she's trying her best. And you think it's hard for *you*?"

A long sigh from Alex.

ALEX: "Yeah, yeah. I know. But c'mon, you know what I mean. I get used to her mask . . . then I turn away for a second and look back and . . . *pow!* It's like it hits me in the face all over again. It's exhausting."

Either they stopped talking or they moved too far away to hear. I realized I was as still as a statue and the only thing moving were the tears streaming down my face. I'd been such an idiot. I had thought I'd been doing so well the last couple of days, but I'd really only been making a fool of myself. And they were like everybody else, looking at me with pity. A freak. They were just better actors.

But as quickly as my anger toward Alex and Lissy appeared, it circled back to me. Why was I mad at them? Did they say anything that wasn't true? I was the oddity. The monstrosity behind a mask. Even my mom had bailed. But here were two kids my age, making an effort. They'd come here to skate. To be coached. Not to get stuck with a freak show. But despite that, they were trying. And Lissy had even called me *sweet*.

My emotions were swinging so rapidly I'd have to google *bipolar* when I had time. I went from thinking I'd just avoid them forever, to wanting to hug them, not that I would or could.

When I got back to the kitchen, only Lissy was there. She said, "You were taking awhile so Alex went to get started with Bridget. I just didn't want to leave without saying bye."

"Oh, thanks. I'm sorry. I didn't mean to keep you. I know you have your session."

She looked like she wanted to say something but just nodded and headed for the door. But when she got there she turned around and said, almost shyly, "Can I ask you something? . . . Barbara told me you were Little Skater Girl. Is that true?"

Wow, she said it like I was famous. Or had been. I didn't know the video was a thing in the skating world. Cool if it was.

"Ah, yeah, that was me."

She literally beamed at me. "Do you know I'm probably skating because of you? I was eight years old. I watched that video like fifty times in a week. I'd never even skated before. A month later I was taking lessons. I can't believe it . . . Little Skater Girl."

# 19

"What happened, Dad?" I asked when he joined me midway through my session. "I thought you were going to talk to Alex and Lissy at lunch." I'd wanted to hear what he was going to say about their dip in scores at the start and end of their programs.

He smiled. "Well, I got as far as the hallway . . . and I heard a lot of laughter. It sounded like you were having fun."

His smile turned into a sappy grin. All my dad wanted was to see me happy. He had likely been doing shadow high-fives and a happy dance there in the hallway, listening to his daughter having a good time with someone her own age. Maybe I was a walking social experiment but I didn't care.

"So, did you just stand out there listening?"

Guilty. "Ah . . . no?"

I gave him a hug. "Liar."

Hopefully his eavesdropping missed the part about me humping the kitchen counter, but he'd laugh at that too. I told him what Lissy had told me about her starting to skate after seeing that old YouTube video of me. I think at first he thought I was kidding. He'd only seen the video a few times and didn't quite get YouTube's reach.

He said, "She actually said she started skating because of you? Wow. So then, who is the fan of who?"

Huh. What a freaky thought.

My session started with edge drills. Judges were nuts about edges. The blade on a skate has two sharp edges, with a channel running down the middle—so there is an inside and an outside edge on each skate—matching the inside and outside of your foot. Each jump requires that the takeoff and landing be on a particular edge. The only difference between a Lutz and a flip is the Lutz requires a takeoff from the outside edge, and a flip from the inside. When skaters launched with both edges, it was bastardized into a *flutz*, and judges would make you pay. To the casual fan, the jumps all looked the same, and didn't know skaters were being rewarded or penalized by judges for the quality of their edges.

Next we worked on my footwork. Most skaters hated footwork and neglected it, considering it grunt work compared to the glory of jumps and spins—but I loved it, maybe because I was so good at it. My dad's off-ice ladder drills were all about developing quick feet and I'd been doing them since I was three. We finished, as usual, working on my quad. Again, I landed six out of ten, but the difference this time was I missed on the first four, then closed with six in a row. And they were solid, even landing a couple of them as softly as if I'd just turned a single. *Like a marshmallow*, my dad liked to say.

"Dad? Let me go without the harness. Okay?"

The harness saved me countless falls but I still couldn't wait to jump without it. He'd been telling me I had to get to seven out of ten, but he must have seen something in the last six that changed his mind. He didn't say anything, just reached over and disconnected the harness. He gave me a nod and off I went.

I circled the rink once, got my speed and launched. As soon as I lifted off the ice I knew it would be perfect. And it was. I landed it so clean I could have gone right into a combo if I wanted. I raised my hands above my head as I circled around the rink. "Wheeeeew. Yeah!"

In a perfect world Alex and Lissy would have walked in just then to catch it. No such luck, but I didn't need them for my moment. I skated up to my dad and gave him a hug. "Thanks, Dad. We nailed it. That felt soooooo good."

"*You* nailed it."

"No more harness?"

"No more harness. But how about quads only when I'm here. For now."

"Deal."

There is nothing like mastering a new move. I practically floated off the ice. The move was mine now after almost a year's work. Something had clicked. I was taking ownership. It was like training a wild stallion that now moved at my command. Now and forever, I had the quad. *I had the quad!*

I had wanted to watch all of Alex and Lissy's final session of the day but my online homework, and catching up on the record-keeping for the cabins, were both overdue. So their session was more than half-way through when I finally made it in. As soon as I opened the door I could hear their long program music. I paused at the door just as Alex lifted Lissy into their modified lasso star lift. It was their signature lift that no other pairs skaters could match. Every pair had a best move and this was theirs. Alex lifts Lissy above his head, then holds her aloft with only one hand on her right hip. Her arms and legs are extended like a four pointed star, her body facing sideways out to the audience, as Alex rotates three and a half times before she cartwheels down into his arms. Other pairs did the move, but none one-handed. With every other pair, the woman needed to keep one arm secured on the man's shoulder to balance the lift. Making it even more beautiful was how fast they were skating as they did it. It actually took my breath away to see it done right in front of me.

"Where's the joy of flying?" Dad shouted over the music. "Lissy, you are *flying!* Love it. And Alex, you . . ."

Dad cut the music and signaled them over. "That move . . . it's exceptional . . ." He was speaking softly and slowly, as he always did with me when he really wanted me to listen. He told me once that was a coach's trick: if you want to be heard, speak softly. He went on, "But just performing it isn't enough. It's still looking like, *And here is our amazing trick!* You aren't letting us feel how wonderful the experience is for you. You both have these gorgeous smiles, but I don't want you putting on a show. You need to welcome people *inside* you. To be so transparent that they can feel exactly what you're feeling. So, Lissy, imagine you are *literally* flying."

She looked at him expectantly and he said, "Seriously, can you imagine how much joy that would bring you? To fly?" He didn't wait for an answer. "Close your eyes . . . please . . . yes, now . . ." He waited until she actually closed them, then continued. "I'm not asking you to do something silly and flap your arms and skate around the rink, but I want you to hold your arms out like wings, and imagine yourself floating up into the air. You're flying over the lake, then between the trees, up into the clouds, effortlessly riding the air currents. And you, Alex, close your eyes . . . Hold your right arm up in the air because it's you who is giving her that gift of flight. Think about that incredible gift you're giving her . . . So both of you, imagine the absolute wonder of what that feels like. To give it. To receive it."

Lissy, eyes closed, started to speak, but Dad gave her a "Shhh. Really. Imagine."

And they did. Or at least, it looked like they did.

"Okay, again," Dad said. "Pick it up at your choreo sequence, and when you get there, *live* that moment. Don't *show* it. *Live* it."

No music this time. I was right on the edge of the ice but I don't think Alex and Lissy even noticed me. They were so focused on my dad. His intensity today basically demanded it. As they stroked into position, Dad shouted, "Now live the moment. You are flying. Don't try to show me anything. Just love that you are flying!"

And, yes! I could actually see a little change. Not one-hundred percent pulling me in, but the show smiles were gone.

"Excellent," Dad said. "Very nice job. Keep that thought in your mind all day. Of flying. Of giving flight. Let that feeling naturally find its way not just to your faces but your whole body. Now ten laps. Go."

Without a word they were off into their Presentation Cardio. Dad skated over to me.

"Nice job, Dad."

"It's not me. They listen really well. And you know what, they're even better skaters than I thought they'd be." It was like his body was buzzing. He was jazzed.

When he left, I saw him pausing to talk to Bridget when she came in. I could tell she didn't like what she was hearing. When they were done, even though I was in a straight line to the ice, she detoured away from me and stood waiting for Alex and Lissy about twenty feet away. She hadn't said a single word to me since they'd arrived, but I was sure no one noticed that but me.

The brief look in her eyes the first time we met had been no stranger to me. I'd seen it too many times. She saw a beast, best kept out of sight so as not to offend. Still, I thought maybe I could change that in her—help her see the person within the beast.

I walked over and her eyes darted to me then quickly back to Alex and Lissy. I said, "That's a pretty sweater."

She ignored the compliment. With her eyes still on Alex and Lissy, she said, "So, your father tell me he already discuss with Alex and Lissy that they are to do a full stretch after each session, here and at the gym. This we will do." Her pretty accent and stilted English didn't hide the tone, civil but cold.

"Oh, well that's good, right?" I said. "Isn't that pretty normal?"

"Not full stretch, no. But I do as I am told."

Was she annoyed because my dad was changing her training program? I knew she technically didn't work for him, she worked for Alex and Lissy, but he still oversaw everything. I had the feeling in the outside world that extreme beauty like hers got a lot of privileges and deference. There'd be none of that from my dad though.

She moved a little away from me and laid out two mats, then put oversized towels on top. My first thought was I'd never seen towels so nice, so thick and soft-looking. My second was how much room they'd take up in the dryer when I did the laundry.

Alex and Lissy took off their skates and walked over in their socks, heading to me rather than to where Bridget stood waiting. They were both still breathing hard. "Man," Alex said. "Your dad works us *hard*. And now we gotta do our full stretch again." But it was good-natured complaining.

I said, "I saw you working on your lift. That is such an amazing move. I really can't believe how beautifully you do it."

"Hey, thanks," Lissy said. "Compliments accepted."

From Alex: "And needed."

Bridget cleared her throat. "Alex? Lissy?" A hint of, *I'm waiting.*

As they were getting settled on their mats I followed them over. "Hey, do you mind if I watch and see your stretches? I've never seen what other skaters do."

Bridget shot me a look and I suddenly realized why. She was thinking I was there to make sure she did as my dad had told her. Great, another reason for her to hate me. I thought about telling her I was next up on the ice and was only there to do my own stretching, but over-explaining might make it worse.

Lissy said, "Sure, but we want to see what you do too. Where's your mat?"

The entire floor was hard rubber, but even though we kept it spotless, you wouldn't want to lay on it. I headed over to the skate rental counter where I kept my mat. I still hadn't skated with them, but even stretching together would be awesome.

As we went through our stretches, I saw that our routines weren't all that different. Bridget's job seemed to be to say soft words of encouragement, and for some of the bigger muscle stretches to provide a little extra pressure. They finished before me so they were all staring at me as I went through my last stretches. When I slid down into a full Russian split then easily bent down and touched my forehead to one knee, I got, "Oh, man" from Lissy and a "Wow" from Alex.

I usually finish with a resting pose called Nidrasana. I rolled onto my back and pulled one foot behind my head, then did the same with the other foot, crossing them behind my head like a pillow. It looked physically impossible, like someone folded me backward. From Alex and Lissy's face I could tell they'd never seen the pose before.

Alex said, "Oh, my God. That's, ah . . . incredible." He was looking at me kind of funny, and I noticed his eyes drop down where they shouldn't be, then guiltily back up, which made me feel . . . I don't know actually, but I quickly got out of the pose and stood up.

Lissy seemed genuinely excited. "What do you call that?"

"It's a kind of yoga called Ashtanga. I've been doing it since I was a kid. I was three, maybe? One day I just laid down next to my dad and tried to copy what he was doing. And I've been doing it ever since."

"Bridget," Alex said, "she's even more flexible than you. I thought that was impossible."

I looked her way but her face was like stone, showing nothing.

"Show us what else you can do," Alex said, laughing.

So I did a Biellmann pose. The Biellmann was created in the '80s by Swiss skater Denise Biellmann. She'd spin on one leg while lifting the other leg directly behind her, then reaching over her shoulders to grab the skate blade with both hands and lifting it all the way above her head. It was a beautiful and very sexy move and not every top skater could do it well. Some in skating had initially thought it was too sexual, but it had become a mainstream move regardless.

With no blade to grab I just looped my hand around my ankle, which was much harder than if I had a skate blade. Then I converted it to what some skaters called a Candle. It took even more flexibility and is rarely seen, but I straightened the leg I was holding over my head so both legs were in a straight line, reaching over my shoulders to grab my upper leg at the calf.

Alex looked at Lissy. "Holy crap. Do you see that?" Then to me, "You've got to show us that on the ice."

I didn't know what to say. No one had ever admired me for anything. My dad encouraged and praised me, but he never looked at me like they were. I felt a mix of pride and discomfort. I guess my flexibility was one more way to be freaky, if even in a good way.

"I want to try some of that Ashtanga stuff," Lissy said. "Will you show me?"

Before I could say "yes," Alex said, "Yeah, I want to give it a try too."

They were both getting down on their mats like it was already decided as he looked up at Bridget and said, "We got it from here, Bridge. You can take off if you want." I don't think he meant it dismissively, but it came out that way.

I didn't know how to feel. I was thrilled I was not only getting to talk more to Alex and Lissy, but they even wanted to learn something from me. But I wanted to fix things with Bridget.

I made it super friendly: "Do you want to join us, Bridget?"

Alex and Lissy didn't bother turning around as she said, "No, thanks. I'll catch you guys later."

She'd made her voice light and casual, but she was behind them so only I could see her face, and the hostility in her eyes.

# 20

Later, Dad told me that Alex and Lissy as well as Bridget were joining us for dinner, and we could have the conversation we were to have had at lunch. A lunch, now dinner. I hadn't expected to be having so much contact with them and I couldn't be happier. But once again I'd have to eat before or after and just drink with a straw during dinner. A small price to pay.

By six o'clock we were all at the table. There was a big plate of grilled salmon to serve ourselves from, as well as steamed broccoli and cauliflower, and a salad of mixed dark greens. Salmon by Dad, the rest by me. The room smelled like roses thanks to Lissy. Her father had a huge bouquet delivered, and she'd split off half for the kitchen. It was nice to sit around the table and hear everyone talking about mutual skaters they knew or admired, and some blunt assessments of who was on the rise and the decline.

It was exactly the kind of conversation I'd dreamed of being a part of, even if I was mainly listening. Bridget wasn't a skater and was clearly bored. I had the feeling she was used to being the center of attention, one of the rights of beauty. As soon as we finished eating, she thanked my dad for dinner and got up to leave. Everyone was so engrossed in a "best female skater of all time" discussion that no one acknowledged her departure, so I made sure to give her a friendly, "Bye, Bridget."

I'd hoped to erase the look she'd given me in the rink, but as she turned back I didn't get the smile I'd hoped for. Did she think I was being sarcastic with the friendly "bye," as if I was glad to see her go? First she thought I was spying on her for my dad, then the stretching, now this. I couldn't do anything right with her.

My dad finally got around to the "assignment" he'd given and I pushed Bridget from my mind.

"We've got the answers you requested, professor," Alex said studiously. "Lissy would like to present them to the class."

"I would? Okay, fine." She turned to my dad. "First off, that's pretty cool that you noticed the score drops. We appreciate it. We never caught it and never did anyone who's coached us, so . . . thanks." She got a little nod from my dad and went on, "Anyway, the lower scores at the start must mean that we're a little tight. And the fact that we have a little lower scores at the end of the free skate, but not the short, would indicate we're getting tired."

That's exactly what I figured too. Dad nodded his agreement. "Okay. So what are you going to do about that?"

Alex raised his hand like he was in class. "Me! Me! Me!" Then he got serious. "Well, we're already working on the get-in-better-shape part. That's what the extra laps are about, right?"

"Yup," my dad said. "We're going to keep doing that. Same theory as running with a weight on your back. When you take it off, the run is so much easier. So to skate for *four* minutes, we'll train you for six. When we're done, you'll be strong to the last second. Did you ever do anything like that with Nick?"

Lissy said, "Not that way, no. Our cardio was separate and in the gym. I like your idea though. Makes sense. But what about the tension at the start? Alex is pretty loose, so I have to admit, it's mainly me." She made a face. "No, it *is* me. I still get a little nervous, even after all these years. I asked Larissa Collins what you did to help her but she just said *you'd* tell me." She smiled. "Trade secrets, I guess."

I said a silent prayer my dad wouldn't say, "I could tell you but then I'd have to kill you." That would be almost as bad as "true dat."

"No," he said, "not trade secrets, just different for everybody. I'm guessing Nick still works with Julie Reynolds, the sports psychologist?"

"Yeah," Alex said. "Dr. Julie. She worked with all of us. Lots of positive thought training. Visualization. Ways to eliminate negative imagery."

"Good," my dad said, "All those things are incredibly helpful. I just have a few different . . . no, not different . . . more like *extra* ways of looking at it. My thinking is the first step is being *glad* you have anxiety."

"Oookaaay," Lissy said.

He said, "The thing is, you can learn to make anxiety work for you. So it actually makes you *better*. The last thing you want is to be an emotionless skater. Don't you think the best actors on Broadway have their stomachs churning before they go onstage? You bet they do. Anyway . . . there are like fifty mental keys I can tell you, but the reality is that a lot of them may not help. But eventually, I'll tell you one, and it will be the one that resonates in you. So we just have to keep going until we find that one. It's like learning fractions and suddenly the light goes on. Okay?"

When Lissy nodded, Dad leaned forward. "Here's the bottom line. You *will* learn to defeat anxiety." He locked eyes with her. "I promise you."

She nodded and her face said, *I believe you.*

"Alright. So here's tonight's thought . . . From this day forward, whenever you're getting ready to perform, you are never again going to have any anxiety . . ."

No, he wasn't hypnotizing her, but he was speaking very quietly and intently. It was fascinating to watch my dad work with someone else.

". . . That's because we're going to *re-label* it. If you think about it, the things you feel when you're nervous—the racing heart, that feeling in your stomach, faster breathing—are the same things you feel when you're super excited. Right? But anxiety is a *negative* emotion. Excitement is *positive*. We're going to eliminate the negative interpretation. So from this day forward, whenever you get that feeling, you don't tell yourself you're getting nervous. Instead you think 'I'm feeling so excited about what's about to happen.' Seriously, the words anxiety and nerves just stop existing for you forever, starting right now."

He sat back. "In a couple days we'll talk about how that feeling of excitement is actually a good thing and how to use it, okay?"

I noticed even now it was *excitement* and not *anxiety*.

Lissy said, "Oh, I really liked what you just said! But you can't just stop there." She playfully indicated Alex, "There's two of us. So, c'mon, one for Alex."

Dad laughed. "Okay, but only because the two go together. And just a short version for now. So . . . when your brain perceives something as scary, it triggers our natural 'fight or flight' response—I'm sure Dr. Julie talked about that. It goes back to caveman days where our survival depended on it. So that strange feeling you've chosen to perceive as fear is your body being flooded with adrenaline and dopamine and cortisol . . . all these natural chemicals your body has in reserve to give you extra strength when you need it. So here's the thing . . . *They're literally there to give you power.* Do you understand what I'm saying? To help your body overcome what your mind perceives as a crisis. It's a scientific fact. But if you don't know how to use that power, all those chemicals are just piling up with nowhere to go, so your heart is racing and you're breathing faster and your body is literally shaking. You're wasting all those magical things your body is trying to do for you. So we're going to train you to actually *welcome* that rush. You *want it* . . . and you *invite it in*. You're going to start thinking, *Yes! Here's my secret power boost to make me even better.*"

Lissy had closed her eyes in concentration as he was speaking. Maybe he actually was doing some kind of hypnosis or something. Now she opened them and gave Dad a grin. "Excellent. Dr. Julie did talk about sort of the same thing, but the way you said it . . . I can use that. It makes absolutely perfect sense. Really, David, thank you."

They got up to leave and were saying their goodnights when Dad acted like they weren't halfway out the door.

He said, "Do you guys want to take care of the dishes?" But it wasn't really a question. "The cooks will put away the food." Reminding them he and I had done the cooking.

They weren't able to keep the surprise off their faces, but to their credit they went to work without complaint. We didn't have a dishwasher so they had to be done by hand, and it was clear they'd never done dishes before, so they needed some instruction.

We were just finishing as Lissy's phone rang and Alex turned to me. "Lissy's dad. He always calls at seven on the dot." Lissy got a big smile on her face and moved toward the ping pong table for privacy. "It's her daddy time," he said. "Never even lets me say hi."

When they'd left and it was just Dad and me, I said, "Seriously? Doing the dishes?"

He shrugged. "Hey, we cooked for forty-five minutes. They can wash and dry for ten. Besides . . . nice kids, but a little entitlement going on there."

Earlier today Alex and Lissy had appeared in front of my dad, each with a pillowcase of dirty clothes. Alex's question had evidently been, "Who do we give our dirty laundry to?" Dad called me out of my room, not to do their laundry thankfully, but to teach them how to use a washer and dryer. As I walked them over to our laundry room I told them there was a laundry service in town they could use, but they were both game to do it themselves.

Since the Ice Castle used to have twenty-four cabins and so many skaters did their laundry here, we had two oversized commercial washers and dryers. They were all way older than me but still worked great. I'd washed my own clothes for as long as I could remember, not to mention all the bedding from the cabins, so I used them almost every day. I explained separating whites and colors, water temperature, measuring detergent, fabric softener, what dryer setting to use for cottons versus polyester and what they needed to hang dry. They looked at me like I was a laundry savant. At one point Alex even took out his phone to take notes.

Lissy had asked, "So do we do our sheets and towels and stuff like that here too?"

"Um, no. We have someone who does that for you. Once a week."

That someone was me. I wasn't ashamed of being a maid. Well, at least I hadn't been until that moment. But I wanted them to see me as a skater, not the girl who changed their beds and cleaned their bathrooms. As long as I did it during their ice time they'd never know.

So when my dad called them "entitled" I didn't really agree. It wasn't their fault someone had always done everything for them. True, they hadn't been thrilled with the fact they'd have to do it themselves, but they hadn't openly complained either. I was just glad Dad hadn't handed Bridget a dishcloth. That would not have gone over well.

"So, Dad, that was really cool what you were telling Lissy about anxiety. You should write a book or something."

He laughed. "What I know could fill a napkin, and still have room left over."

"Okay, Mister Modest, but I thought it was cool."

He just gave me a nod.

I had something I needed to bring up but for some reason it was awkward. "Um, Dad, can I use the credit card to buy some clothes?"

He was probably thinking it had something to do with the empty closet embarrassment a few days ago. But it wasn't that. "Sure. What do you need?"

"I'm just ah . . ." I held my hands out in front of my chest. "Growing a bit."

"Ah, gotcha. Well . . . ah . . . congratulations?"

"Dad! You don't say congratulations for needing a new bra."

"Oh, sorry. I didn't know what the appropriate comment was. I just assumed a girl would be happy about that kind of thing."

"Well, maybe yeah, but you don't say anything."

"Okay, this is me saying nothing about your maturing bust line."

It was still a pretty modest "bust line," and likely always would be. I was close to sixteen, and from pictures I'd seen of the svelte Gloria (aka mom), I'd stay that way. But still, I could tell that I had added a bit. So an A to a B. More like a B minus to be honest, but that was fine with me. At least the order form would no longer refer to them as "training bras." I always wondered, did the word *training* refer to the bra, or the breasts?

But big breasts were not on my wish list. Just the opposite. There was not a big demand for top-heavy skaters. In fact, the last thing I wanted was a growth spurt of any type. Many a promising teenage skater dropped from sight never to be seen again because they couldn't adjust to their new bodies.

I'd taken off my mask as soon as Alex and Lissy left. As Dad said goodnight he gave me his usual kiss on the forehead. "Do you want to share some ice time tomorrow?"

He didn't have to say with whom. "Really? Do you think they'd mind?" I didn't think it would happen so soon.

"Actually, they're the ones that brought it up. I think you had them at *cold water rinse*."

# 21

The next morning I had just finished my Scott Hamilton drill, lots of nice footwork and triples, when I saw that Alex, Lissy and Bridget had come in and were into their stretches. When they came out on the ice to warm-up with some stroking, I fell in with them.

Lissy said, "Hey, we caught the end . . . really nice footwork."

It felt amazing just to be circling the ice with them. Part of me felt like an imposter, that any moment someone was going to point at me, shouting, *"Fake! She does not belong here!"* I fell into formation behind them, which was actually in front of them since we were stroking backwards, them the base of the triangle. I had no problem matching their speed and was soon in sync with them, three pairs of legs and arms in perfect unison. So cool. Like three fighter jets flying in formation.

When Dad arrived he sent us off to each grab a section of ice to warm-up with some rocker power pulls, then huddled up with us center ice. He told us we'd be doing Sals, toe loops and Lutzes, which were the jumps in Alex and Lissy's programs. "I want our focus to be on an effortless takeoff, and extending and holding the landings. *Savoring* them. And if you like what you're doing, *which you will*, I expect to see that joy naturally on your face."

Well, not my face, but he wasn't talking to me anyway.

"Let's warm-up with some double toes. One on each long side of the rink, so two each time around. Okay? I'll space you out. Alex, go."

The toe loop, like the flip and the Lutz, were all launched by driving a toe pick into the ice. The Axel, Sal and loop all had a takeoff just from the blade, with no assistance from a pick. I'd noticed that like most skaters, Alex and Lissy's best jumps were with the toe pick boost.

Alex took off, then Dad started Lissy a few seconds later, then me. I couldn't watch them, and they couldn't watch me, since we were all busy with our own jumps. That was fine with me since my heart was beating in overtime. My dad was yelling both instructions and compliments. "Alex, hold that finish longer. At least a three count. Savor the landing . . . like that, yeah. Fantastic." And, "Lissy, beautiful landing. But let me see how much you enjoyed it. Don't *show* me. Just let me in enough to see it."

Then we did a couple laps of triples. "Alex, extend those arms a tad higher on the finish, chest out, arms up, and hold it . . . Lissy, I'm seeing too much shoulder turn. Initiate with your hip . . . yeah, there you go."

And to me, "Katie, tighter in those rotations . . . hands on your heart. I don't want to see any air." His way of telling me to be a tight coil in the air on my jumps, elbows in and legs tight, with no visible space. My nerves were making me sloppy.

We took a break then Dad had us do the same doubles and triples with Salchows and Lutzes. Out of the corner of my eye I saw them each fall on one of their triple Lutzes. Then he changed it up. "Okay, this time we're going to go one at a time. The two with me are judges. I want to hear what's not perfect." He gave Alex a little push. "Alex, go. Double Sals. Twice around."

Alex's jumps were solid. Lissy said to my dad, "He's signaling a little."

I'd noticed it too but wasn't about to say it. Even the best of skaters sometime took a little pause before a big move, mentally preparing themselves. But it was like saying *here comes a trick*. Not a good thing, but not uncommon even at the Olympic level.

My dad gave Lissy a nod of agreement. "Um hum."

It made me think of my first few years skating. He'd have me watch him skate then make me tell him what he needed to improve. It wasn't until years later that I figured out he was intentionally making mistakes on things he wanted me to work on in my own skating. It was his way to make me self-correct. The guy was sly. So maybe this was a version of that. One thing I knew for sure was Lissy would not be signaling her jumps when her turn came.

As Alex skated up, Dad said, "Okay, Lissy, your turn. Extend those landings. And don't *show* me how good you feel, just *be*. Let yourself be so vulnerable that your emotions are transparent. Not just your face. Every part of your body. Okay? And push it. I want speed."

She did as told and both her entry and finishing positions were lovely. Alex's only comment was "hands could be a little higher on the landings." It was a reach but Dad did ask for comments so Alex had to come up with something. I'd like to say I didn't contribute to the critique out of courtesy, but the reality was I was focusing on not throwing up.

It had come out of nowhere, just as my turn was approaching, my chance to be "judged" by the U.S. National champions. Their first chance to see me skate. To show I was their equal. That this was the one place I belonged. It wasn't just my stomach—my heart was beating out of my chest and it was hard to breathe. I hadn't felt like this since Dad was trying to take me to the first day of school. What I wanted to do was make an excuse and skate off the ice.

But when Lissy finished and Dad said, "Go," I did.

At least we were only doing double Sals. I could do them in my sleep. At least, on any other day. I managed to land the first one, barely. Somehow I pulled out the landing. I could imagine Alex and Lissy were saying, "Not enough speed into the takeoff, arms dropped on her rotations, under-rotated the landing . . ." The rest were no better. Not one clean landing and each one out of balance.

When I joined them center ice my dad's eyes were giving me a "What's up?" look he but didn't say anything. I could imagine Lissy thinking, *What happened to Little Skater Girl?* At age six I'd skated better than I just did. But the worst was Alex. He gave me a big grin. "Nice doubles, Katie! Way to go."

He couldn't have been more patronizing than if he'd patted me on the head. I don't know if I was more furious at myself for the way I'd just skated, or at him for thinking that was the best I could do. I understood his whole "trying to be nice" thing, but the one place I didn't need their pity was on the ice.

When it was time for triple Sals, I watched Alex and Lissy but didn't see a thing. I think Alex fell on one but I wasn't even sure. I was just focused on my nerves, and the anger I felt rising up that I was feeling nerves at all. When Dad called my name, out I went.

I could feel myself out of balance before I've even completed one rotation and I went down. Hard. If Alex and Lissy were even bothering to critique jumps this bad I could imagine them saying, "Still not enough speed, her left side got away from her, and all around horrendously pitiful."

"Up, up!" My dad yelled. He always wanted his skaters to hop up and keep skating, just as they would if they fell when they were actually performing, so I did as taught. And fell again. Even harder. I stayed down.

A humiliation.

Dad skated over, Alex and Lissy behind him. "You okay?" he asked. "That last fall was pretty nasty."

No, I wasn't okay. The body, yeah. The rest of me, not so much. Then the worst thing happened. As if I was a little kid, I started to cry. What was with all the crying lately? And not just tears but sobs. I just couldn't help it. My emotions were all over the place. Humiliation. Shame. I reached for my knee like I was in pain to give a reason for my tears.

I was so ashamed of myself as everyone fussed over me. Worst of all was my dad knew the knee injury was a complete sham. In the thousands of falls I'd had learning to skate, I'd never cried. Not once. But he covered for me and helped me get up.

Alex said, "Hey, don't go gouging our ice. We still have to finish our session."

"Yeah," Lissy added. "But at least you didn't leave any blood, so that's good."

Skater humor. I appreciated the effort. But I knew what they were thinking.

Poser.

Coach's kid who thinks she can skate.

I said, "Dad, I'll be fine. I'm going to go stretch the knee and ice it. Okay?" Then to fully disgust myself, I sold the injury with a fake limp as I skated off. How pitiful could I be?

# 22

Dad knocked on my door about an hour later, like I knew he would. I needed one of the world's best coaches right now, and maybe a dad too. "C'mon in, Dad."

I was on the bed, reading a John Green novel. I'd read all his books about five times, and today's reread was *Looking for Alaska*. I just wished he didn't make so many kids smoke in his books. There was probably some literary reason for it that I wasn't smart enough to understand. But still, gross.

"So," Dad said. "I'm here to collect your skates. Surely after that embarrassment you're going to do the decent thing . . . retire from skating and never go on the ice again." When I didn't rise to the bait, he went on, "I mean, I know you're one of the few women in the world who can do a quad, and triple Axels, but still. Better to give it all up now than risk *that* happening again."

"Enough, Dad. I get it." And I did.

"So . . . nerves for the first time in your life, huh?"

On the ice anyway. When I just nodded, he went on. "It happens to everyone, honey. Ev-er-y-one. That's the first time you ever had an audience you wanted to impress. Cut yourself some slack. If Gwen Stefani showed up to watch me skate, I couldn't even lace up my skates." He was rabid over Gwen.

"What about Katarina Witt?" I asked. She was his other fantasy woman, a real hottie in her day, wearing outfits so sexy the International Skating Union made rules to limit excessively sexual and theatrical costumes. She was an amazing skater who dominated in her day. He'd told me when he was a teenager he had her posters all over his walls.

He said, "If Katarina Witt was in the room with me, I wouldn't even be able to walk."

I gave him the smile he expected but didn't say anything. He let the silence go on. Finally, I said, "What do I do, Dad? I never thought I'd be a choker. And here I am. A choker. Just like all those skaters we talk about."

He shook his head. "That wasn't choking."

Yeah, right. "I guess I should have been paying better attention when you were talking about it with Lissy. But my mind just went blank. All I could think of was, *Don't fall in front of them.*"

"Like I said, it wasn't choking. It was bad coaching. I owe you an apology. Asking everyone to comment like that was a mistake. It was your first time skating with them and I know how you look up to them. You're just such a confident skater, it didn't even occur to me that it'd be an issue for you. Personally, I'd fire me and hire a new coach. What do you think?"

"Well, I'm not going to fire you. But I am going to start withholding your pay. From now on you have to coach me for free."

He nodded. "Only fair."

"But Dad, seriously, the reality was I did feel the nerves . . . So I'm going to do what you talked to Lissy about." I ticked them off on my fingers, "I'm going to re-label it. When I get that feeling next time, I'll tell myself it's a good thing—it's excitement . . . and welcome it because it's going to make me skate even better . . . that all that adrenaline is there to help my body be stronger and perform better, not hurt it." I nodded to myself like it was a done deal.

I was glad he wasn't going to over-talk it. He walked to the door. "So do you want to join them for part of their last session today? Or tomorrow?"

"Daaaad. Neither. I'll just do my own. I'll join you guys in a few days."

"Ah, let me think about that," he said, then clearly without doing so said, "No. This afternoon or tomorrow, take your pick. Get right back up on the horse."

"Don't have a horse. Don't want a horse."

"Mmm hmm, right. So, this afternoon or tomorrow?"

"Isn't my knee supposed to be injured?"

"We'll label it a magically quick recovery."

After Dad left I shut my book and closed my eyes. I imagined I was a superhero—I already had the mask—and adrenaline gave me super powers. I reminded myself the ice was my friend, the only playmate of my life. It wanted good things for me. I'd set low expectations about life with Alex and Lissy off the ice, but *on* the ice I'd hoped to be their equal, and be respected as a legitimate skater.

The real me would take the ice next time.


Alex, Lissy and Bridget had plans to go into town for lunch and my dad was doing his weekly Zamboni maintenance, which principally involved praying it would keep running, so I figured I'd be alone for lunch. I was getting stuff out of the fridge to make a sandwich, thinking I could actually take off my mask to eat when I heard Alex's voice behind me. "Hey, your limp is gone. You feeling better?"

"Oh, hi. I thought you were going into town."

He laughed. "Man, your dad is killing us. I laid down for a second and I guess I fell asleep. Bridge and Lissy left without me. So, your knee is okay?"

"Yeah, thanks. All good." I hadn't put the food away so started making an extra sandwich. "I must have looked pretty lame. I'm . . . I'm usually better."

"Like Lissy and I never fall? And we saw your footwork when we came in . . . it was awesome. You just weren't on with your jumps today, that's all. They were actually pretty good."

I'd had enough.

"Alex. Stop it." I could hear the emotion in my voice but I didn't care. "I get it. I'm the scarred up, weird girl in a mask, and you want to be nice to me. Okay? I understand. And yeah, I haven't had any practice talking to people my own age, so I'm not very good at that either. I really appreciate how nice you and Lissy are being. But don't tell me those were good jumps. They were *garbage.*"

I don't know what I expected from Alex, but it wasn't for him to casually lean against the counter and grin. "Okay, truth." He laughed. "They were crap."

My little speech had taken the anger out of me and I laughed too. "Well, okay then . . . Thanks. For saying my jumps are crap."

He seemed to consider for a second then said, "And thank you."

"For what?"

"For what you were just saying. When you were mad? That's the first real thing you've said since I met you. Usually you're . . . um . . ."

"Awkward," I filled in. "Yeah, I know."

He scrunched up his face in thought. "No. How about . . . just trying too hard. Like you're putting everything through a filter before you say it."

Hmm. Pretty dead-on actually and I gave him a nod. He gave me one back and I felt like a small bridge had been crossed.

When I'd finished the sandwiches and added a scoop of cold pasta-veggie salad to our plates, he said, "You know what? Let's eat outside. At that picnic table out there."

I resisted the temptation to turn around to see if he was talking to someone else. "Um, okay."

Did that make it a picnic? If so, I'd never been on one. In fact, now that I thought about it, I'd never eaten outside. And certainly never with a boy. Not that he saw me that way, but still.

I divided up my smoothie into two glasses and he grabbed the plates and we went outside. He put the food and drinks in a tight grouping on the table and then took out his cell phone and snapped a picture. He showed it to me. "Look okay?"

"I guess." If you really wanted a picture of our lunch.

He was quickly typing into his phone and talking out loud as he did. "Great training session this morning and lunch under the pines of Lake Arrowhead. Sandwiches and smoothies by Katie Wilder!" He pushed *send*. "There, Twitter post done for today."

"What? That was a tweet? With my name in it?"

"Yeah, isn't that okay? You *are* following me right? How else am I going to catch up to the Shib Sibs."

Alex and Maia Shibutani were a brother-and-sister ice dancing team, and social media mavens.

"Are you being serious? I can't tell. Did you really just send a tweet?"

"Yeah. Why are you surprised? Just go on your phone. Eighty-five thousand people are asking themselves right now, *Who is Katie Wilder? And why is she making Alex Piezov a smoothie?* Oh, tongues will wag." He seemed to find the whole thing pretty funny and I still didn't know if he was kidding.

I said, "Well, first off, I don't have a Twitter account, and I don't have a Twitter account because I don't have a cell phone." I didn't add that I didn't really get the whole social media thing.

He put down his sandwich. "Are you serious? You don't have a cell phone?"

"Of course I'm serious. I don't go anywhere. Why would I need a cell phone?" I didn't add, *And if I did go anywhere, I didn't have any friends to call.*

He pretended to study me with extreme seriousness. "I've never met a fifteen-year-old girl without a cell phone. You might get your own Wikipedia page for that."

But he had me thinking about Twitter. "So show me on your phone what your tweet looks like."

He did, and it was just as he'd read it. Of course, all I saw was *Katie Wilder.* I have to admit it gave me a thrill, especially considering who had sent it. I said, "So, you have to think of something to write every day? And . . . *why?* I still don't see the purpose."

"I guess it is kind of silly, but yeah . . . I try to write one at least every other day. Instagram too. But what's kind of a pain is with the whole ridiculous Piece of Cake thing taking off, we had to start one with that name too. So we take turns on that one. Seventy thousand followers so far." He tried to not look proud but failed, and even though he was acting like it was all a burden, he was clearly thrilled by the whole thing. I wondered if I was a famous skater if I'd have an ego that big.

I couldn't help but rib him. "And you tell them what you eat? How exciting for them."

"You are such a wise ass. I just do silly ones like that sometimes. We talk about our training and our competitions coming up. Give props to other skaters. Or like last month, we did Scott Hamilton's Skate to Eliminate Cancer." He gave me a sideways look, "Wait, don't tell me you don't have a computer either?"

"No. Of course I have a computer."

"*Of course* says the girl with no cell phone. Anyway, you can see Twitter on your computer. And Instagram too. I actually like it better. I can't believe you aren't following all the skaters you like."

Okay, maybe there was more to social media than I thought. I guess it wasn't that different than all the skater blogs and vlogs and websites I spent so much time on. "Okay," I said. "First thing when I get to my room I'm signing up for Twitter. And Instagram. Really."

"And . . ." he prompted.

"And I'm following Alex Piezov and Lissy Cake . . . and Piece of Cake." And what the heck, all my favorites past and present: Evgenia, Nathan, Shcherbakova, Kostornaia, Chock and Bates. Lots. One thing I did know was *I'd* never have a follower.

We ate our lunch in a nice companionable silence. And yes, I actually ate, but I turned my face to lift my mask for each bite. I'd thought about it and realized I couldn't stop eating every time they were around; they might train with my dad for years. Even lifting my mask with my face averted was a big step for me, having Alex only a few feet away.

I said, "So Lissy and Bridget went to lunch in Blue Jay?"

"Well, they're in town, but not together. Bridget isn't exactly Lissy's favorite person."

That was news to me. "Why?"

He shrugged and looked uncomfortable. "It's not a big deal. Bridget is a good physio and a great dance teacher. That's what counts."

Whatever. I told him I'd be joining them for one of their sessions tomorrow, and he said he'd be checking his social media and if he didn't see me as a new follower I'd be banned from the ice.

Then he got serious, "And hey, just so you know . . . I'd be happy to work with you on your jumps if you ever want. I could probably show you a few things that might help."

I didn't want to tell him that, excluding yesterday anyway, I was actually the better skater. I couldn't do any of the lifts and twists that pairs skaters could do, but jumps and spins were the domain of the singles skater. But once again, he was being so sweet, and I could tell, sincere. And it didn't feel like pity, just one fellow skater offering to help another.

So I said, "Okay . . . wow. Thanks. Maybe we can all just skate for fun after dinner sometime."

As if we'd made a deal, he offered his knuckles to bump. It felt amazing to do it with someone other than my dad. We didn't say anything for awhile and didn't need to. There was no awkwardness to the silence. My mind was busy though, filled with the thought that maybe I was making a friend.

The day felt indescribably beautiful. The sky had never been so blue or the clouds so white, and the trees were alive with sound and movement: squirrels and blue jays and red-chested woodpeckers. I felt a little like Alice in Wonderland, with life exploding all around me. And even a boy at my side.

# 23

I had to cut my late afternoon session short so I could fit in one of the groups I was taking over for my dad. There were ten in the class: eight women and two men. Three of the girls looked like they were just a little older than me. When the class started I gave the same little speech I'd given the kids about my mask to get it out of the way. Thankfully, the only difference was no one asked to touch my face. But unlike the kids, they all seemed familiar with me already. They were anonymous faces to me, but many of them told me they'd been out on the ice when I came out for the public skates.

They had all been taking lessons for a while so were all decent skaters. They had advanced to spins and we worked on the two foot spin. When the class ended, two of the teenage girls stayed behind. They were really friendly and I'd loved how much fun they had learning their spins. They thanked me for the lesson then one of them said the strangest thing. "Wow, this is so funny. It turns out you're really nice. We all thought you were stuck up or something."

Wait, what?

"Why would you think that?" I was the last person in the world to be stuck up about anything.

She said, "Well, we've been out here skating on Friday nights for years, and you come out and do all this amazing stuff. You're like a legend around here . . . we all wait for you to come out. But then it's like you can't leave fast enough, like . . . I don't know. It's just, you never talk to anyone or even look at anyone. It's like we aren't even there and you don't even hear us clapping."

The other girl said, "But it turns out you're so nice and such a fun teacher." She laughed. "So does this mean on Friday night you'll stop and talk to us?"

Wow.

"Um. Yeah, of course."

As they were leaving I could hear one of them say, "Alright! No one is going to believe it when they see that!"

I didn't leave the ice for a while. With the rink again empty I just did some lazy stroking. And thinking. Was that the image I gave to all the skaters on public nights? A conceited girl who didn't think they were worth her time? A cheerleader walking with her nose in the air past the dork table at lunch? The kind of girls I despised when I saw them in movies?

That was me? To them anyway.

And what had she said: A *legend around here*. Not the words about me I'd put in their minds, like *mutant, witch* and worse. The truth was I wanted to move like lightning on the ice, then get off as quickly as possible to avoid close inspection. Yes, I liked the admiration of my skating, *needed* it in a way, but I didn't want the pity that came with a slo-mo close-up. I wanted to skate off the ice with images of beauty and grace, not scars and ugliness.

To have that image in their minds, therefore in mine.

But was I not giving people enough credit? Was I rejecting them before they could reject me? Doing to others exactly what I didn't want done to me? Was I excluding myself more than others were excluding me, like my dad had been saying in his own way for so long?


That night it was just Dad and me at dinner. Alex's family had driven up and they were all going out for an early dinner, then a tour boat cruise around the lake. So it was actually kind of nice for it to be just

118

the two of us. With all his time with Alex and Lissy, I was seeing less of him than I was used to and I missed him. After dinner we dug out some games we hadn't played in weeks, like Sorry and Kerplunk. Since the listed recommended age to play was "five and above," we qualified.

As I was getting ready for bed I remembered that Alex had asked me if he could have an extra pillow, and I'd forgotten all about it. But it was only eight-thirty so not too late to run one over. I was looking forward to at least twenty minutes to read in bed before I'd get sleep around eight-thirty.

My plans for the evening did not include seeing my first live penis, although that's what ended up happening. I say *live* penis because I confess to having seen one on the internet. Well, more than one. In a scientific way anyway.

I am a girl after all, and curious like anyone else. So one day last year I decided to see what all the fuss was about and Google Imaged *penis*. And there they were. Row after row, column after column of them in their Google glory, some drawings and some actual. I can frankly say I'd never seen a body part more ludicrous in my life. I literally laughed out loud. And when you include testicles in the package, it goes off-the-chart ridiculous. If aliens are really coming to earth to kidnap people to do scientific experiments on them like some people think, now I knew why. Other planets must be coming just to check out the whole penis thing. Like, *Let's check out Niagara Falls, the Northern Lights, giraffes and penises.* God must have been drinking a lot of holy wine the day He came up with the design for male genitalia—no offense to God, or those unfortunates He gave penises to. Thank God I was born a woman.

And I don't know what had possessed me, but my next search had been *erect penis*. I mean, why not get the whole subject out of the way and never go back? When those images came up I was on the floor, laughing. At this point I was sure someone had hacked my computer and was playing a joke on me. C'mon. Be serious. No wonder so many boys had anger issues. It must be suppressed anger over possessing such a ridiculous body part and having to carry it every-where they went.

At least there was one advantage to the way I looked. I'd never have to touch one of those things, or have someone that owned one want to touch me with it. Thank you, God.

But back to the live penis. I could see the lights were on in Alex's cabin. I don't know why I didn't just knock on his door as I'd planned, but for some reason I assumed he was at Lissy's, so when I noticed a gap in the curtains of his front window, I looked inside.

And there he was.

Naked.

Naked as in, as the movies say, full frontal nudity.

He must have just gotten out of the shower because he was drying his hair as he walked. And the body movement made certain body parts, ah, jiggle and sway.

And all of a sudden that body part was no longer at all ridiculous. Completely terrifying, yes, but at the same time . . . I couldn't look away. It was dark outside and I knew he couldn't see me even if he glanced up. So I'm ashamed to say I was in no hurry to leave. But in my own defense, I wasn't sure what to do. I couldn't go knock on the door, pillow in hand, knowing he was standing naked on the other side of the door. That would be very improper (says the girl standing in the dark outside staring through the curtains at a naked boy). And when he turned around, his butt was just as interesting, muscles clenching as he walked. I changed my mind about the whole boy-girl thing. It made sense now.

Alex seemed perfectly comfortable to move around his room with-out any clothes on, and I was in no hurry to leave.

"Want to get your camera?" A voice whispered in my ear. Bridget. I cut off my scream.

I'd been so focused on Alex's—well, on Alex—that I didn't even hear her. Now she stood next to me. The tiny ribbon of light from the window barely lit her smirking face. I moved further away from the cabin so Alex wouldn't hear us and she followed me.

"I did not take you for a peeper, Katie." Then in a slightly louder voice, letting me know it could quickly get a lot louder, "Want me to call to him? Let him know you've been peeking for a few minutes?"

She'd been watching me that whole time?

"Oh, no," I whispered. "*Please* . . . I didn't mean . . . it's just . . . I just had his pillow and . . ."

The only thing more humiliating than Bridget catching me there would be if she called out to Alex. I'd never be able to face him—to ever come out of my room. And not just Alex. What about Lissy? How would she react to me peeking in Alex's window and seeing her boyfriend naked. Accidentally at first, yeah, but I'd stayed. And what would my father think?

Bridget just stared at me. Then, "Starting tomorrow, I'd like my sheets changed every day, no more of this once a week crap. And not all wrinkly out of the dryer. I like them . . . how do you say it . . . ironed. We understand each other?"

So much for my secret cabin cleaning. She must have seen me coming out of the cabin next to hers with my cleaning caddy after the guests had checked out. Hopefully she was keeping it to herself.

"Yes," I said. "I understand."

She locked eyes with me for a minute, then finally said, "Fine." She took the pillow from me. "I'll let Alex know you dropped this by."

She wasn't done with me though. With her eyes still locked on mine, she started to *hum*. And smile. Too, too weird. Finally, she turned away, still humming.

It wasn't until I got to my room that I realized what she'd been humming. *The Phantom of the Opera*, that's what. A popular choice by many skaters for their programs, so not a surprise to hear it around a skating rink. But not an innocent choice by Bridget. It was the story of a grossly deformed man who lived hidden in the sewers under the Paris Opera and wore a mask to hide his face.

# 24

My first thought when I woke up the next morning was of the dream I'd just left behind—the people in the mall, their eyes filled with hate as they tried to eliminate me from their sight. I realized it was the same look I'd seen in Bridget's eyes.

My exposure to the outside world was almost nonexistent, but my window to it—movies and the Internet—had quickly taught me the prevalence of hate. Joy in attacking people—even strangers—for their looks, weight, skin color, religion, sexual preference . . . whatever. Hate knew no bounds. My own theory was people wanted to take your happiness away when they didn't have it themselves. And those people particularly raged when they saw joy in someone they deemed not worthy of it, not possessing the very quality they thought should be a prerequisite.

In Bridget's case, beauty.

Or at least, not the polar opposite of it. No matter how nice I was to her, she'd find me repulsive, and resent that I dared to try to have the same full life that she had.

The funny thing was I actually felt guilty about Bridget. I'm sure she imagined my face crumbling behind my mask under her withering stares, or her humming *Phantom*, but once I'd pegged her for a hater, it was easy to dismiss her. And her words. I'd had too much practice dealing with it before she came along. She didn't know she was humiliating herself more and more with each attempt to diminish me.

So Bridget? Sorry. But you've been marginalized.

And you don't even know it. Blackmailing me into being your maid doesn't make you stronger; it shows how weak you are.

Once she was pushed out of my mind I focused on my skate today with Alex and Lissy. My chance at redemption. My dad had been right to force me to skate today. I reminded myself all I had to do was skate like I did every day. Nothing more. And I'd follow his advice about dealing with anxiety. But most of all, I had a secret weapon to call upon.

I didn't join Alex and Lissy until their last session of the day. Dad first ran us through our spins and some footwork exercises. He'd told us earlier in the day we'd each be doing a full program, so when he asked who wanted to go first first, I volunteered. I decided to go with one of my drills. It was kind of like doing a program, but I packed in more than the twelve elements allowed in a free skate. So it was actually an *uber-program.*

I told them, "My dad and I make up a lot of drills and name them after who inspired them. So this one is *The Scotty,* after Scott Hamilton."

He had four national titles, four Worlds and an Olympic gold. I varied the music with my drills and today I was going with Miley Cyrus's *Party in the U.S.A.* I'd let the elements fall wherever they felt right.

As I waited for my dad to queue my music, I listened to my breaths and found my center. (Fancy yoga-talk for focusing on the best part of me.) Any remnants of nerves that were left . . . I welcomed as excitement. Then I did something I'd been doing since I was a little girl, and that I'd forgotten to do yesterday—the thing I felt gave me almost magical powers. I spoke to the ice as if it was my friend, which it was and always had been—the only constant in my life besides my dad.

I silently said, *You are my best friend. Take care of me.*

I opened with a sequence of three fast single toe-loops, which in my mind was like a deer jumping through the forest. I'd never do single jumps if I were competing since they weren't worth many points, but I liked their simple beauty. Then right into a triple Lutz and a triple Sal. My footwork sequence went flawlessly, then a triple toe loop - triple loop combo. Sometimes I throw in something for fun and I did a rarely seen Chinese Attitude, which is a Biellmann, but instead of a spin I made it a spiral, holding the position as I glided straight across the ice. My last jump was my big combo, the triple Axel - triple toe combo, something no woman in the world could do, and maybe three men. I hit it big and flawless. Then I wrapped it up with a nice choreo sequence and a three-variation layback spin into a scratch spin. On the spur of the moment I made it headless, where during the spin I tilted my head all the way back, making it look like I was spinning without a head, a cool effect.

I turned to my audience of two. *Now* they'd seen me skate.

But they were just staring.

Finally, Lissy jumped up with a *"Yes!"* and sprinted out on the ice to give me an enthusiastic high five. "That triple Axel combo! Katie! That was amazing! . . . It was *all* amazing." She kept going on with words too nice to hear.

Alex was standing as still as a statue, his face blank. I looked over at my dad and could see a tiny smile. He said, "You opened up a little on that triple toe."

I nodded. "Yeah, Dad. Sorry."

Dad's words seemed to finally rouse Alex. He looked at my dad. *"Seriously?* She skates like that and . . . *'You opened up on your triple toe?'"*

And then as his eyes went from my dad to me, he seemed to get it. That it was just a standard skate for me. Dad and Lissy's attention may have been on me, but mine was on Alex. But I didn't understand what I was seeing. Emotions chased across his face. First there was a split second of anger, then embarrassment, like someone had played a trick on him. Then resignation. I didn't understand any of them.

Why wasn't he happy for me, as Lissy clearly was? An equal on the ice. A worthy training partner. Instead, I could feel the little bridge we'd built when he'd offered to help me with my jumps, and the first steps toward friendship, get washed away in the empty air between us.

Or was I wrong? Because now there was a smile on his face. He said, "Wow, Katie, that was . . . incredible."

To me the words sounded hollow, but my dad and Lissy didn't give any sign they'd picked up on it. Was I imagining the whole thing?

My dad said, "Okay, short program. Alex, Lissy, let's go."

I welcomed thinking about something else, not to mention the chance to watch them skate again. They had only been working with my dad for a few days, but I'd already noticed some progress in their interpretation of the music.

Their old choreographer, Tom Dickson, was due later today to start revamping their long program. We didn't have an empty cabin so he'd be staying at a local hotel and coming over for one session a day for three or four days, as well as some off-ice time. I was sure his changes would help with their presentation score even more.

But when Alex and Lissy went into their program, it was obvious from their first element that they were off. When Alex tossed Lissy up into her twist she came down hard and their shoulders collided. In their next element, their side by side triple Lutzes, they were badly out of sync and Alex had to put his hand down to save the jump. The rest of the program had no glaring technical errors, but it was clear they were going through the motions and the fake smiles were back.

What surprised me even more was that my dad said nothing. Usually he'd be chattering all the way through. Not a word this time, as if he'd written it off seconds into the program, somehow knowing it wasn't salvageable. And when they were done, he just said to shake it off, that it was one of those days, and to do their Presentation Cardio.

I went out to join them as my dad left, but neither Alex or Lissy cracked a smile as we all circled the ice, no attempt at presentation. I had the feeling that even if my dad was watching, he wouldn't have said anything. So the three of us skated with our matching slack faces, instead of the happy ones I'd anticipated after showing I deserved to be on the ice with them.

Afterwards, I was the first to lay out my mat to stretch, but when Bridget came in a moment later, Alex and Lissy were still talking on the other side of the rink. I had been waiting for them to join me before I started, but I watched as Bridget spread out their mats where they stood. Lissy gave me a little shrug and a smile but stayed where she was.

So I stretched by myself, trying to figure out what I'd done wrong. I felt more alone than if I were the only person in the rink.

# 25

Dad came in as I was getting ready for bed. As if the late visit wasn't enough of a warning, I knew something was up when he told me for the second time that day he was proud of me for my good skate with Alex and Lissy. Finally he got to the point, trying to make it sound casual.

"So . . . I'm going to put the shared workouts on hold for awhile. I think I need to focus just on Alex and Lissy when I'm with them. Probably just for a week or so. That okay with you?"

Clearly it didn't really matter if it was okay with me. I was being told the way it would be.

"What did I do wrong, Dad?"

I knew the words came out pitiful but I didn't know how else to ask. Worse, I didn't have a clue as to the answer. I mean, I wasn't blind. I knew my skate had changed things. Alex's emotions. Their bad skate. Stretching on the other side of the rink. Alex's forced cheerfulness saying bye as they left the rink. Not joining us for dinner afterwards. But why?

Before he could answer I said, "I thought when they saw I could skate like them they'd like me more." Again, pitiful, but it was the truth. That had been my hope. My only route to their acceptance. "But . . . I think Alex was mad. I just don't . . . I just don't understand what I did wrong."

His face softened and he shook his head. "Oh, honey. You didn't do anything wrong. And . . ." His voice turned rueful. "You *didn't* skate like them. That's the problem."

When I just looked at him, he said, "Katie . . . you *schooled* them. You buried them. They'll never do a triple Axel. They'll never have a jump technique like you. They'll never do a spin so fast or with your extension. They'll never have footwork like you. And . . ." He tried to fight down a laugh, "Where the *heck* did that Chinese Attitude come from? That was beautiful . . . Anyway, that's another thing they'll also never be able to do."

I could feel my mouth open to speak, close, then open and close yet again, before the words came.

"*What?* . . . you're saying I was too *good?* But I can't do *any* of the things they can do. I can't do lifts. I can't do twists. That can't . . . Dad, that can't be it."

But as I looked into his eyes I could see it was true. At least, he thought it was.

He gave a little sigh. "Alex came to me yesterday, after your bad skate. He wanted my permission for him to help you with your jumps. It was kind of sweet actually. He seemed really happy about it." He raised his eyebrows. "Was that something you two talked about?"

When I nodded he went on. "So . . . I couldn't exactly say you could give *him* lessons. So I said you'd just had an off day, but that I was sure you'd love to get out on the ice with him." He grimaced. "I guess I needed to be more blunt. Anyway—"

"So, what did Alex say today, Dad? That he didn't want to skate with me anymore?"

He didn't answer and I could see a battle going on in his head. He was Dad to me, but coach to Alex and Lissy, with loyalties to each.

"No," he finally said. "Alex didn't say anything."

"So *you* decided?" It stung that my own dad thought of me as so toxic that I shouldn't skate with them. With Alex anyway. That we couldn't just all talk about it.

He shook his head. "No actually, I didn't." Then he said what I least expected to hear. "It was Lissy."

*Lissy?* But she'd been so happy for me. And there was no way that was fake.

I was speechless and my dad filled the silence. "And actually, she's right. Listen . . . I'm sure she'd love to have you out there, but she knows what's best for her partner . . . that he needs to get his confidence back. You saw how they skated after you. So she's just being a good partner. I would have come to the same conclusion if she didn't say something first. He just needs a few days."

I hadn't meant to make Alex think I needed help, then throw it in his face by out-skating him. He had to know that. So I told my dad that, adding, "And if it's all about me being better, why was Lissy so happy for me? She wasn't mad at all."

He laughed. "The difference is Alex is a *teenage male.* There is no more insecure animal on the planet. Their egos are more fragile than an egg. Especially a teenage male *figure skater*, with all the baggage that carries. Of all the young skaters I've coached, it's the girls that are the strong ones mentally. Always. Boys like to posture that they're tough, but usually . . . just the opposite."

Jeez. If my dad was right—and I was assuming he was, given he'd *been* a teenage male—how had this whole reality of *Teenage Boy Fragilitis* escaped me through all the books I'd read, and the movies I'd seen?

"So . . . what do I do? . . . Dad, I want them to like me. Do I just never skate with them again?" I felt myself getting angry. "Or do I skate badly on purpose?"

That wiped the smile off his face. "Don't you dare. And let me tell you, you're actually going to make them better skaters. As a coach you always want a skater that your other skaters can aspire to match. But . . . short term . . . just give him a few days. I can almost guarantee that if you just act like nothing happened, in a few days, so will Alex."

Do *nothing?* That was the answer?

"Shouldn't I talk to him about it? About his feelings, I mean?"

He bit back a laugh. "No. Definitely not. Boys don't talk about feelings. The last thing he'll want to admit to you—or even himself— is that he felt that way. At least for now. Just . . . trust me on this."

I was definitely going to have to talk to all those novelists and Hollywood screenwriters. They had done a terrible job preparing me for dealing with real life boys. Or maybe that's what moms were for, and I'd missed all those lessons.

He said, "It's not that boys mind girls being better at something, like in school, or . . . well, about anything but sports actually. And this is the one thing Alex does best in the world. Skating is his whole iden- tity." He gave me a, *Are you getting it?* look. I guess he could tell I wasn't because he went on. "And he got schooled by not just a girl, and not just a younger girl, but a younger girl who has never even competed."

Part of me wanted to argue, but dumb or not, the reality was that I got it. In fact, now I was actually feeling guilty about the whole thing. And stupid. My mind was visualizing Alex asking my dad for per- mission to help me with my jumps. Like my dad had said, that had been sweet. I tortured myself with the memory of how he'd been so nice to compliment my pitiful jumps that first day, trying to cheer me up . . .having lunch with me and telling me he'd work with me on my jumps. Then his unguarded look of embarrassment when I'd done my real skating the next day.

The day before Alex and Lissy had arrived I researched "How to make friends." Humiliating, yeah, I know. But I didn't know how else to prepare for them. The online articles' advice of *"Just be yourself!"* and *"Get yourself out there!"* was of no help at all. But one thing I read did make sense. It was that people want to be around other peo- ple who make them feel good about themselves. I actually wrote that one down.

So, I hadn't meant to, but I'd done just the opposite with Alex. I said, "Okay, Dad. I understand." And I actually did.

The next few days were kind of awkward. I'd pass Alex and Lissy in the hallway or in the rink, and they'd both give me a friendly "hi," but not stop to talk. Lissy would give me a look like we shared a secret, but I didn't quite understand what the message was. Unfortunately, I didn't speak *girl* any better than I spoke *boy*. At least one person was happy: Bridget. She noticed the shift and was practically glowing.

But just as quickly it changed back. First, Alex and Lissy showed up at dinner. The next day, lunch. The day after that, lunch and dinner. A few nights later they even took me up on my offer to play some games. They kind of rolled their eyes at the sight of *Sorry, Trouble* and *Kerplunk*, but they had fun once we started. Note to self: go online to find some games for teenagers and adults.

But better than after-dinner games was when Alex and Lissy asked me if I wanted to join them for their last session everyday, starting tomorrow. I calmly accepted while my heart was doing cartwheels in my chest.

# 26

It was a few weeks later and my dad and I were halfway through my late-morning session when he said, "Oh, by the way, I'm setting up an impromptu show for tonight. A few hundred people."

That seemed to be a pretty significant event to be a "by the way." A few hundred people? And *a show*?

He said, "I'm having Alexa call everyone we give lessons to and telling them they can each invite up to ten people." Alexa was the girl who worked our skate rental counter on Friday and Saturday nights. "It's tonight at six. I didn't want to set it up too much in advance or it'd get out and we'd end up with too many people here. Alexa will come and help with the crowd."

Word had spread that Alex and Lissy were training here, and we'd been getting a lot of calls, from local media asking for interviews, to people just asking if they were allowed to come and watch them practice. But the rink doors had stayed locked so far to both. I could bet my dad had a couple goals with his "show." One was to give Alex and Lissy an audience for their new program, but also to give Lissy some practice with handling her early-program jitters.

They were set to compete at The U.S. International Classic, just a week away in Salt Lake City, followed by two international-level competitions, Skate America in October, and two weeks later in Paris for the Trophee de France. After that, a month to Nationals, and five weeks later—the big prize, the Olympics—then three weeks to the Worlds in Montpellier, France. The skating world usually took a short nap after that, then it was time for a new season all over again with new programs.

"I already told Alex and Lissy," he said.

His former skater, Petra Gorbinova, had written a book, *Skating to Gold*, and she wrote stuff about my dad that even I hadn't known— like to keep skaters fresh and be ready to adapt to new situations, he'd throw surprises at them. One "surprise" was unannounced performances, where the skater thought they had their usual training session later in the day, only to find out they'd be skating their program in front of a few hundred people, or someone famous, like the one-person show she did for Matt Damon, who'd been up here on a ski vacation. Another time he'd invited in the cheerleaders from our local Rim of the World High School and had them stationed around the rink doing cheers while she did her program. That was to help her deal with distractions—all little steps on the way to her gold medal.

He said, "They did have one request though. They want their training partner to skate too."

I was about to ask who that was when I realized the obvious. Me.

"They want *me* to skate?"

"Sure. Why don't you? You do the public skates all the time. And it'd be nice for the audience. One long program is only four minutes. That's kind of a short show. It'd be nice to have at least have two programs. In the old days we'd have seven or eight skaters perform."

So easy to say "no." And so safe. And the Katie Wilder of just weeks ago would have said that. But this was the Katie Wilder who'd been skating with Piezov and Cake, whose name was in a tweet, who'd gone on a picnic, who'd seen a naked boy. "Okay, Dad. I will. Thanks for including me."

"So, what do you want to skate?"

So far, in my shared sessions with Alex and Lissy, I'd always done one of my drills, never a true program. I'm not sure why. But I had many of the greatest skaters' programs memorized, and my dad and I had choreographed several original ones just for me. I said, "Um . . . how about *One Call Away*. That was the newest program we'd done and I loved it, like I loved Charlie Puth singing it. Everything flowed together so naturally and beautifully.

Like all skaters, I was thrilled a few years ago when the rules were changed on music. Previously, only orchestral tracks were permitted, not songs with lyrics. But now we could use pop and rock songs. It made performing more fun for the skater, and the audience.

"Good choice. I'll have the music loaded." He told me we'd all be skipping our afternoon sessions and meeting on the ice at five. Evidently he was trying to make it feel like a real event, where skaters have limited time on the ice before they perform.

"So, Dad . . . do you think I should do the quad?"

His face was saying "no," but trying not to show it. "Where would you put it? In place of the Sal?"

"Yeah, or the triple loop."

He surprised me. "Hmm. Well, I say . . . if you're feeling it, go for it. It's all about having fun out there." Then he laughed. "Just know that no one will know you did it."

What he meant was that unless you were a skater, the rotations were too fast to count. To the casual fan, a double jump looked about the same as a triple, and a triple almost the same as a quad. But it didn't matter. Just like the average person watching figure skating on TV didn't know the difference between an Axel and a Salchow, or a toe loop and a flip, you didn't have to know the name of something to know it was beautiful.

# 27

I was the first one in the rink at five and already stretching when Alex, Lissy and Bridget came in. As soon as I saw them I realized how out of place I looked. Alex and Lissy looked great in their performance costumes. Alex wasn't a glitter or ruffles kind of guy so his outfit was basic but elegant, dark grey pants with a light blue shirt. It really accented his build nicely. Lissy's outfit was a matching light blue with grey ruffled accents. She'd done her hair nicely too. Their boots were polished and gleaming. She saw me and her face fell. "Oh, I thought you were going to skate with us."

How embarrassing. "I am. Sorry, I don't have any fancy outfits. But you guys look amazing."

I'd chosen my favorite workout clothes, my Lululemon skating pants and top, blue over black. I'd never had the need for an actual skating outfit. And my boots were all scuffed. It hadn't even occurred to me to polish them. But did it matter what I wore? I mean, when you're skating with my face and a mask, would anyone even notice the costume?

"You look great," Lissy said. "I'm sorry, I just wasn't thinking. We should have come casual too."

That was nice of her. I said, "No, to be honest, I didn't even think about it. This is the first time I've done anything like this."

"It's all about the skating," Alex said. "When they see what you can do, they won't be thinking about your outfit."

We got on the ice for some warm-up laps. I saw Dad blocking off a small area directly off the ice and set up three folding chairs inside it. It looked like he was creating our own little Kiss and Cry, which was what they called the area where the skaters wait for their scores. There would be no judges tonight, so hopefully no crying. Maybe a happy kiss between Alex and Lissy though. I was actually surprised I had not seen a single kiss between them since they arrived, but maybe they weren't into PDAs.

Dad had them run through their long program, then I had a chance to do mine. I didn't feel the quad so left it out, but that didn't stop me from getting rave reviews from Alex and Lissy. That was the first time they'd ever seen me do an actual program, not that it was that different from my drills, but I did have some cool moves in it.

My dad joined us. "Okay, let me tell you what this is going to be like. Most of the people coming tonight aren't skaters and only watch figure skating during the Olympics. They will be loud and close and enthusiastic. They're going to cheer at inappropriate times and even though I'll tell them not to, someone will end up taking a flash picture right in your eye-line. Some people will yell things out while you're skating, like they're at a Little League game. They don't know any better, but they're going to be doing those things because they're so excited to be watching you." Then just to Alex and Lissy, "This isn't the big arenas you're used to, but it's great practice. We used to do these little exhibitions in the old days and some of the biggest skaters in the world found the environment . . . well, you'll see. It's great prep. That's why we're doing this."

We gave him, *we got it* nods.

He grinned. "You are all going to do great and we're going to have fun." He turned to Alex and Lissy. "And are you going to 'put on a show?' Or are you going to savor your music, and realize how beautiful what you're doing is, and let it fill you with joy?"

Playfully from Alex, "Nothing but joy, coach. Nothing but joy."

The front doors of the rink were all glass and I could see a crowd outside. A few dozen even had their faces to the glass, trying to get a peek at Piece of Cake. It was funny that now that I knew them, I found the name hilarious, as they'd told me they did.

Alexa was looking our way, waiting for the signal to let everyone in.

Dad held up a finger to her as if to say "one minute," and turned to us. "We didn't talk about who's skating first. Anyone care? Or should I flip my imaginary coin?"

Lissy gave an "I don't care" shrug, but Alex said, "It doesn't matter, but shouldn't Lissy and I go last?" His unspoken words were *headliners went last*. He was right. They were the big names so I should be the opening act.

I was slowly learning about the male ego—Alex's anyway—over the last few weeks. He now seemed fine with the fact I was a better skater, but he still flared up once in awhile. Like now.

Dad ignored Alex's comment and poised his invisible coin to flip. "Call it Alex."

"Imaginary tails," Alex said. "Loser goes first."

Dad mimed the flip. "Tails. Piezov and Cake go first. Katie Wilder second."

I figured that was the way it'd play out. It had nothing to do with who was the *featured* performer. Dad just wanted Lissy to have less time to deal with any anxiety from the crowd and force her to practice dealing with it. But telling them that would lessen the benefit.

"I'm going to grab my mic," Dad said.

He nodded to Alexa, who opened the double doors, and the people swarmed in. Man, there were a lot of them! My guess was a lot more than a few hundred.

Even standing with Alex and Lissy, so many people coming toward me made me nervous, so I put on my skate guards and walked to the skate rental counter where Dad was testing his ancient wireless mic, back from the 90s when it was considered high tech. He tapped his finger on it and we could hear the *tap tap* through the overhead speakers. He gave me a grin. "This is fun, isn't it? Having so many people here?"

He was clearly enjoying it. I could never figure out how his mind worked though, because when he should have been thinking about the show he was hosting, he surprised me with, "Honey, I'm sorry I didn't think about a skating outfit for you. We'll buy you some, okay? But you look beautiful already."

Beautiful, right. The things parents have to say.

We walked back to the ice together. I saw that Alex and Lissy were slowly circling the rink, slapping hands and saying "hi" to practically every single person as they filled in around the rink. They were both so relaxed and having fun. They really knew how to work a crowd. I wondered if Alex was saying to each one as he shook their hand, "Don't forget to follow us on Twitter . . ."

The three of us met in our roped-off Kiss and Cry, and immediately the lights were extinguished in the lobby, leaving the ice looking even brighter. Some people clapped in anticipation. Dad was immediately out on center ice. "Ladies and gentlemen of Lake Arrowhead, my name is David Wilder and I—"

A big round of applause broke out which was sweet, probably recognition that he'd kept the rink open for the town all these years.

"Thank you. I have two requests. First, please no flash photography. And no videos please. Second, can I ask that you all take two steps back, just to give our skaters some extra room? . . . Thank you." Since our rink didn't have the customary hockey boards, everyone had been just inches from the ice. "Alright, we will have two performances tonight. As many of you know, at skating competitions at the highest levels, there are two performances in a competition, the short program, and the long program. We also call it the free skate. Tonight we are going to see both a pairs, and a singles, free skate."

More unsolicited applause. I did a quick guesstimate. The rink was more than two-hundred feet long and almost half as wide, so considering that people were standing three to four deep in some areas, there had to be . . . about a thousand people! I hoped no one from the Fire

Department was here to notice the "MAXIMUM OCCUPANCY: 120" sign by the door. I'd never imagined I'd be skating in front of so many people. I spotted some of the skaters from my classes and skate nights, but most everyone was a stranger to me.

Dad moved to the Kiss and Cry to leave the ice empty for Alex and Lissy to skate a couple warm-up laps. Back on the mic, "And now, introducing the reigning U.S. National champions, and World bronze medalists . . ." Man he was really punching it, like this was a boxing match, and from the faces around the rink, they were clearly loving it. ". . . Please welcome Alex Piezovvvvvv and Melisssssa Caaaaake!"

I didn't think a thousand people could make so much noise—it echoed in the rink and multiplied in volume. It was *loud*. It went on so long that Alex and Lissy actually had to get out of their starting pose to acknowledge it, then finally strike their pose again when it had quieted down. Now I knew what my dad meant about the crowd. He started the music, and Alex and Lissy were on their way.

It was four beautiful minutes set to their new music, Aerosmith's *I Don't Want to Miss a Thing*. In a way I couldn't have imagined, they were better than they'd been in any of their practice sessions. Now I knew what my dad meant when over the years he'd talk about *performance* skaters, those who were elevated by the crowd and could somehow take all that energy and have it bring out even more from within themselves. Alex and Lissy were those kinds of skaters.

The changes by Tom Dickson to their choreography, and the new music, had made a huge difference—the program was awesome now. They had to feel pumped the way their big lifts, throw jumps and twists drew *"aaahs"* from the crowd.

During their skate I'd taken a few quick looks into the faces in the audience. It was amazing how captivated they were. With all the technology available, I wondered if U.S. Figure Skating or any coaches ever video-taped audiences just to measure their reaction to a performance. When did people sit back just watching? And when did they get sucked in, sitting forward in their seats, enthralled? I'd have to ask my dad. Or maybe it was a new idea and would be my contribution to skating.

*The Katiecam.* Hey, just throwing it out there.

After they skated off the ice I gave them both a hug. "Amazing, guys!" They were beaming. They still needed more time to be fully comfortable with the new program, but they'd skated great. When the audience gave no sign of stopping their applause, Alex and Lissy skated back out on the ice and circled the rink, giving everyone a high five. The noise level finally started tapering off as they got back to the Kiss and Cry the second time.

Alex said, "Wow! That felt like overtime at the Super Bowl or something! That was amazing!"

"Our first curtain call ever!" Lissy said.

Then Dad was next to me, giving me a quick shoulder squeeze and whispered, "Ready to have fun?"

I gave him a nod and he was back on his mic. "Thank you, ladies and gentlemen, and thank you, Alex and Lissy!"

Applause all over again. Dad was really milking it, but the audience seemed to just want an excuse to cheer and show their appreciation. I think if you added up all their periods of applause it would be twice as long as Alex and Lissy's entire program.

"And now, our singles performance. Please welcome Lake Arrowhead's own . . . Kaaaaatie Wiiiiiilder!"

Wow, I got the celebrity name-stretch too.

I don't even remember actually skating out on the ice. I'd been sitting or standing for ten minutes so made a couple quick loops to get warmed up. I'm sure the applause wasn't as big for me as for Alex and Lissy, but out on the ice it sounded deafening. As I stroked I felt what I'd been waiting for, that surge of adrenaline, but with it came the tremors too. I commanded they work for me—make me jump even higher, skate even faster. I reminded myself this was my domain, the one place I fit in.

I took my starting position and spoke to the ice: *You are my best friend. Take care of me.* And then, a new feeling . . . I could literally feel the audience's energy—no longer strangers—we were linked by the ice. They wanted to see a beautiful performance and I wanted to give one. If we both willed it to be, how was any other result possible?

Charlie Puth's piano chords brought me out of my starting position. In my mind, I was a flower opening in the sun. As he started to sing that he was just *One Call Away*, I went into my first element, a triple combo: triple Lutz - triple toe - double loop. I had so much energy I over-rotated the Lutz, managed to save the landing but had to change the triple toe to a double. But after that I adjusted to the extra buzz my body was feeling. During my footwork sequences, I was a bee, darting between flowers, enjoying a spring day. In my spins I was a perfectly formed tornado, a vortex of such power the air was propelled from my body.

When it came time for where I could insert my quad, there wasn't even any conscious thought—it was the quad. And I landed it! Perfectly. I held the landing deliciously as I covered the ice to my final move, a spin: a forward illusion entry to a layback spin in a haircutter position to a Biellmann. When I finished, there was no sound. It felt like an hour, but it might have been a few seconds, then the wall of sound hit me. Just as loud as for Alex and Lissy. Maybe louder. I told myself to circle the ice as they had done and high-five the crowd, but that was too much for me. But I did bow and wave my hands in thanks. Sometimes masks are handy to hide happy tears.

# 28

As I approached the Kiss and Cry, Alex and Lissy were clapping harder than anyone else in the room. Lissy mouthed over the noise, *"A quad?! A freaking quad?!"*

They'd never even seen me do it in practice. They both gave me huge hugs, the kind where you really wrap your arms around someone and lift them up. I was a little worried about Alex's reaction. I mean . . . a quad, especially by a woman, was *huge*. But his excitement was as big and real as Lissy's. I'm sure it helped that their skate had been so sensational.

When the applause continued with no sign of abating, Alex and Lissy pulled me out with them and together we circled the ice, their third round of high fives and my first. I thought if we could bottle the feeling in the rink at that moment we could solve every problem in the world:

no war,
no hunger,
no cruelty,
no disease.

When we got back to the Kiss and Cry my dad was there, his face red and blotchy, an *I'm not going to cry* face. He had planned the whole evening perfectly—except how to end it. When he got on his mic and thanked everyone . . . no one left! As if, *This party is just starting!* Everyone wanted more of Alex and Lissy, maybe even of me.

Dad quietly asked Alex and Lissy if they would mind posing for pictures. He caught Alexa's eye and waved her over. "Let's put Alex and Lissy by the door so after people get their picture we move them right outside. Can you be right there and hustle them through? Just one picture each, and say no time for autographs. There's just too many people, But make sure *you* say it and not Alex or Lissy, okay?"

He was thinking like a true coach, wanting his skaters to be loved. It'd be okay if people got annoyed with Alexa, but you had to keep the fans loving the skaters. Dad got back on the mic, thanked everyone again, then told them they could line up at the exit for a picture with Alex and Lissy. To keep things festive, he even pulled up some music, one of my workout mixes: Rihanna-Taylor-Ellie. He was pretty adept with that remote, that was for sure.

As the audience moved off, I turned to my dad. Except for my one over-rotation, I thought I'd skated better than I ever had before, but I wasn't sure—my whole skate was a surreal blur. I just started to tell my dad what I'd felt out there when he spoke first. "You are one of them, honey. One of those skaters that gets better with an audience. That's your home out there."

Before I could say any more, I noticed that a big chunk of the audience hadn't all gone to the photo line for Alex and Lissy. There were a few hundred patiently lined up facing our improvised Kiss and Cry booth.

They were waiting for me.

First in line was a little girl with a parent over each shoulder. "Can I have your picture?" she asked shyly. Then from the mom, "We've heard you give lessons? How can our daughter sign up?" I looked behind them and saw everyone had a camera or cell phone out, waiting for a picture. I looked to my dad. He knew how I felt about pictures, but gave me a little smile. "Why not? But up to you."

I'd never had my picture taken with my mask before. What was the point? And no pictures without it either, except just Dad and me.

But with a mask, anyone could be behind it, so what were they getting out of the picture? I just didn't get it. Unless . . . maybe people didn't just see the mask. Maybe they saw the person and the skater, who just happened to wear a mask.

"Yes," I said to the little girl, "I'd love to take a picture with you."

And so it went down the line. Not one question about the mask, but once they got close, a lot of subtle looks at the sides of my face and throat. My first thought was of curious faces pressed right up to the bars of a cage in a zoo, but then I cut myself some slack. The night had been too glorious to be negative, so I thought the best of the people lined up—and the best of me. About halfway through the line I laughed at myself when I realized I was instinctively smiling for each picture, even though no one could see. So just for fun I made funny faces in a lot of them.

After a picture with me, most of the people doubled up and got in the back of Alex and Lissy's line. Alexa though, was moving people through in record pace. Most of the crowd had come in groups, so often there would be four people in one picture, and the line moved quickly. Alex and Lissy handled the whole thing as smoothly as politicians running for office, but with much better smiles.

Dad's and my side of the rink was finally empty and everyone was focused on getting their Piece of Cake, so I turned my back to them and quickly slipped my mask up just enough to give my dad a kiss. "I love you, Dad. Thanks for including me tonight. It was the best night of my life."

In the back of my mind, I was wondering if this night had really just been about Alex and Lissy . . . or if my dad, and maybe Alex and Lissy too, had also done it for me.

There were still a few hundred people waiting for a picture with Alex and Lissy and I was fading fast, so I went to my room and got my shower out of the way and into my pajamas. Whatever had happened out there—that feeling of emotionally linking with the audience—had been exhausting. So my body was saying *bed,* but I wanted to relive the night one last time. I left my door open hoping

Alex and Lissy would stop by on their way to their cabins. I finally heard their animated voices in the hallway, then they were in my doorway.

*"A quad Lutz?"* Those are the first words from Alex as he came in and held two hands up to slap. "You just throw a quad Lutz out there like it's *nothing*? Like, *Oh by the way everyone, here comes something only a few women have ever done in history . . .* Everything you did was *flawless . . .* Who *are* you?"

"You were amazing, Katie," Lissy said, giving me a smaller version of the hug she gave me earlier. "Really amazing. That quad was wicked. Wow."

The cool thing was I could tell they meant every word. Best of all, there was no masked emotion in Alex's eyes like before when I did something he couldn't do. Maybe we were past that. He was totally stoked for me. I don't think I'd ever been so happy.

I said, "Thanks. You guys skated beautifully. I was watching the crowd when you were skating, how they lit up."

Alex waved the compliment away. "No, seriously. I'm just not getting it. I mean, we've seen how good you are, but what you just did . . . that routine could beat almost any woman in the world. I am *not* exaggerating. I just don't see . . . it's just not *possible*. Like, how is it you can skate like that and *no one even knows you exist?"*

All I could do was shrug, and beam behind my mask.

"No," he said, "I mean, *I really don't understand.*" He looked to Lissy for a second, like *help me here.* "I know both your parents were skaters so you're in the lucky genes club, but . . . still, how can you be so good? You've never even competed!" He looked back to Lissy, "Aren't you blown away by this? I mean, that audience may not know it, but we were the second best skaters out there tonight."

If that was true, it wasn't bothering him. He was beaming.

Lissy laughed and put her hand on his shoulders. "Calm down, you're geeking out, dude! I agree with you. She's amazing, but it makes sense. She's been skating since she could walk, six hours a day, seven days a week. That's how many hours?" She was actually asking herself. "Ah . . . fourteen years times fifty-two weeks a year . . . times about forty hours a week, that's . . . God, that's almost thirty thousand hours! *Thirty thousand.*"

She was referring to that whole "ten thousand hour" thing. There was a theory that to be truly expert at something, you had to spend at least ten thousand hours doing it. Not just figure skating—playing the guitar, basketball, whatever. And barely anyone ever got to there, unless they were a pro and it was all they did. So, I guess I did have an edge. The top skaters in the world usually started when they were about six or seven, usually slowly at first, then more seriously years later and connecting with a top coach. Only then did they start getting in two or three hours of skating a day, and learning proper conditioning. All that didn't start until they were ten or eleven. For me, all that began shortly after I leaned to walk, top-level coach at my side the entire time.

Alex looked sheepish. "I'm trying to do the math. I think we come in at less than half that. And we're two years older!" He laughed then got a serious look. "Katie, you *have* to start competing. I know you have this thing about your fac— . . . about the mask, but look how you did tonight! Look how the audience reacted! They *loved* you. The mask doesn't matter."

As glorious as all these compliments about my skating were, even my mask couldn't hide that while Alex was talking, I was yawning. Huge, open-mouthed yawns. I just couldn't help it. I was so tired that if I were lying on the bed I'd have fallen asleep even with them in the room.

Lissy said, "Look at her Alex, she skates one of the best performances I've ever seen . . ." She faked a snooty yawn, "and she's just bored by the whole thing. Like, whatever, just another day on the ice. What else is new? Maybe tomorrow I'll cure cancer."

And then I yawned yet again, but talked through it. "I'm sorry, I'm just so tired . . . I'm just so . . ." My tank was now one-hundred percent fully empty. I thought I was going to fall down. Maybe this was why

I'd seen some athletes literally fall to the ground seconds after they finished competing.

I could dimly remember Lissy guiding me toward my bed. She said, "Alex, go. I'll see you in a minute." And when he didn't move at first, she more firmly said, "Go."

Lissy stopped our progress to the bed until he actually left, but not before he said, "Night, Katie."

When I woke up the next morning, my door was closed and I was under my covers. And my mask . . . my mask was on my bedside table, where I always put it. But I had no memory of taking it off. Did that mean . . . Lissy took it off? Is that why she made Alex leave? Or did I wake up in the night and do it myself?

# 29

Over the next few days Alex and Lissy kept talking to me about going through USFS testing so I could compete, and talked about how much fun it'd be if we could all go to competitions together. The best part though was that these conversations didn't just take place during the one session we shared each day. We'd gotten into the habit of sharing a lot of time off the ice, and sharing meals had become the norm.

My dad wasn't so pushy on the subject of testing. He knew better the issues I'd face leaving home. Competitions weren't just about the skating—that part I thought would be fun—but it was everything that went with it. There would be travel, airplanes and airports, and having to take off my mask to go through security, not to mention big cities, hotels, restaurants, and interaction with hundreds of people. This all by a girl who had basically never left home.

So my dad suggested I start small, go to some local stores and restaurants, the library, a tour boat ride on the lake. Things I'd actually long dreamed of doing but never had the courage. Alex and Lissy had invited me a couple times to go into town with them, Dad too. So maybe I'd finally say yes soon.

Dad also didn't agree with Alex and Lissy on how high to test. He wanted me to only test to the junior level. USFS testing started at the lowest level, called pre-preliminary, and moved through eight testing levels to senior skater, the highest level. Right below senior was junior. The levels had nothing to do with age. You could be a twelve-year old senior, like Michelle Kwan had been. It was all about ability. My dad said, yeah, that I could skate with the best, but entering as a senior with no prior competition had never been done. He thought not only was it too big a jump, but judges might feel it was disrespectful not to pay some dues at a lower level.

The morning after our show was just as remarkable as last night had been, although I didn't realize it until I was brushing my teeth. When it hit me, I was so stunned I had to sit down on the toilet with toothpaste running down my chin.

For the first time in years, I hadn't awakened to memories of my nightly dream. No walk in the mall trying to blend in. No hate-filled stares and cruel shouts. No falling to the ground as angry men tried to beat me to death with clubs and bats. No shouts of "Kill It! Kill it!" No need for a rescue from an alien spaceship. No need to bring me to the safety and comfort of a planet where everyone looked like me.

All that, gone. At least for last night.

Remarkable.

I made up my mind—I would test, and I'd test all the way to senior. I wanted to compete against the best.

My morning session was fast and furious. I'd slept more soundly than I think I ever had and I had energy to burn. My music was a mix my dad had made for me when I was little with his favorites: Beatles, Beach Boys, Monkees. I actually thought the songs from that era were fantastic, so fast and catchy, and innocent and fun.

When I got back to my room I checked online about testing and was bummed to see the deadlines had passed for the local ones coming up. I didn't want to wait a couple months. I got Barbara Felsdorf's email address from Dad and sent her off some questions. She answered within a couple hours.

*From: B. Felsdorf (b.felsdorf@usfigureskating.org)*
*To: K. Wilder (katiewilderskates@gmail.com)*

149

*Katie,*

*So nice to hear from you. I'm thrilled to hear you are inter-
ested in competitive skating. As I'm sure you know, you need
to be a member of U.S. Figure Skating to test. Here is a link
to download the application. We look forward to you joining
the wonderful family of U.S. Figure Skating.*

*As far as fast-tracking your testing, yes, there is a proce-
dure for doing multiple levels. From the small portion of your
routine that I saw, and from what I've heard from both
Melissa and Alex (and yes, they bring you up every time I talk
to them!), it would not make sense to slow down your ability
to develop as a skater and compete with skaters of your ability.*

*Under special circumstances, we can add a name to a test-
ing roster after the application deadline has passed. In fact,
having seen you skate, I would be happy to even arrange a
special testing session. As long as we have judges available
for the testing, it can be done at any time, at any place. When
you and your father have determined what is best for you, let
me know and I would be happy to set things in motion. For
now, get your application in!*

*Best wishes,*

*Barbara Felsdorf*
*Director, Athlete High Performance*
*United States Figure Skating*

Excellent! I went to find Dad to talk about it. After years of having no
interest in testing or competing, suddenly it was all I was thinking
about. Each of the eight levels I had to get through to senior was actually two tests, so I was looking at sixteen in total. Prior to testing for

each level I had to first pass a corresponding skills test called Moves in the Field. Each of those tests had specific patterns you had to skate, with assigned movements in a set order, almost like a mini-program.

Even though the moves were easy for me, it involved memorizing the required patterns. I'd have to start dedicating my practices to learning them. I could see why most skaters tested only one or two levels at a time. Doing all eight levels in one day would be impossible, so we decided to divide them up between two testing dates.

Barbara had offered to have judges come right to the Ice Castle and do a private testing—friends in high places—but Dad said no. Part of the reason was he didn't want me getting special treatment, but also because he knew if I was actually going to compete in the future, I had to get used to skating in different rinks, and being surrounded by other skaters.

He did accept her offer to squeeze me in after the application deadline had passed. So a few days after they'd be back from The U.S. International, I'd test for pre-preliminary, preliminary, pre-juvenile and juvenile levels at the Riverside Icetown, then a week later for intermediate, novice, junior and senior at the Center Ice Arena in Ontario. Both were down the mountain, a little over an hour away. Dad said he doubted anyone had ever tested at so many levels so quickly, but there was nothing normal about me.

# 30

I was doing homework after my late-morning session when there was a knock on the door. It wasn't my dad's knock so had to be Alex or Lissy. I quickly grabbed my mask and was tying it as I said, "Come on in."

It was Lissy. "Sorry to bother you. Can I raid your closet?"

She'd filled every leftover inch of my closet to such a degree that my small corner of clothes looked like strangers in there. And she had at least two dozen shoes and boots neatly lined up underneath. I had to say the girl knew how to dress.

"Sure, grab what you need. I'm just doing homework."

She came in and started throwing a few outfits over her arm. "Oh, I remember those days. Homework, ugh! I'm so glad Alex and I finished early and got our GEDs. Do you like doing school online?"

Most kids probably said "no" to liking anything about school, but I actually did. "Yeah, it's a really good program. We get a bunch of choices, more like college I guess. Like right now my English class is focused just on poetry. I have to write an essay on a love poem."

"Oh, I really like Carl Sandburg. And Maggie Estep is really trippy. Do you know her?"

I kept forgetting how bright she and Alex were. As much as I wanted to put them in a simple box under the *star athlete / beautiful people* category, they kept breaking out.

"I haven't, no. But I'll look her up. I'm doing my essay on a poem by R. C. Shepard.

She tossed the clothes she'd been holding on my bed and plopped down next to them. "Let's hear it."

"What?"

"The poem. Can you recite it?"

"Um, I guess." Maybe I should have felt weird reciting a poem, but I didn't. I turned my chair to face her.

"*Your Love* by R. C. Shepard," I started officiously, to which Lissy actually laughed.

*The scent of jasmine in the night air,*
*Alone on the beach. Naked. Trusting. Together.*
*Impossibly, a rainbow lighting up the darkened sky.*

*You lift me high up on your shoulders,*
*Because of you, I can touch the stars,*
*And I feel the breath of God warm me as I fly.*

*You walk to clear my path,*
*and feed me strawberries in the bathtub,*
*with gentle lust and wonder."*

"Oh, that's so romantic," Lissy said.

"Yeah, I really like it too."

She sighed and let herself fall back on the bed. "I wonder if that's what it feels like to be in love?"

She was asking *me*? I said, "You'd know better than me. I've never had a boyfriend. Obviously."

"Yeah, me either, just some dates, but they never went anywhere. But it'd be nice, wouldn't it?"

What was I missing here? "Yeah, I guess, but . . . you and Alex are a couple." When she didn't say anything, I added, "Aren't you?"

She looked toward the open door, then got up to close it and sat facing me on the bed. She took a deep breath. "Actually . . . no.

The boyfriend-girlfriend thing is just, oh, what's a nice word for *lie* that's not quite so strong?" She actually seemed to be trying to think of one and finally said, "*Misleading*, that's the word. Anyway . . . we love each other, but it's more like brother-sister. We've been together since we were ten."

I couldn't believe it. "But what about that kiss?"

She rolled her eyes skyward. "Oh that damn kiss. That's what started it all. I don't know why he kissed me like that, or why I kissed him back. It wasn't planned or anything. We'd just done the performance of our *lives* and we were so *happy*. And at the end he gave me that tender little kiss. And then I gave him one back. I know the way it looked, but it was innocent actually. Still . . . it was all anyone talked about afterward. Not our performance. *The kiss!* And within a few days we're getting endorsement offers and interview requests. No one really noticed us before. Not like that anyway."

"Wow," was all I could think of to say. "But why didn't you guys just explain that back then?"

"We did! We tried! But everyone thought we were just being shy and didn't want people to know we were in love . . . which made them believe it even more! So after a while, it seemed like if we really set everyone straight, they'd think we'd been fakes all along and were manipulating everyone. And part of competition is a popularity contest. We just can't afford to alienate anyone like that. So we're stuck."

"So you guys act like boyfriend and girlfriend when other people are watching? That's got to feel weird."

She gave me an odd look, then asked an even odder question. "So you haven't figured it out yet?"

"Figured out what?"

"You can't tell anyone. That means even your dad, okay?"

"Um, okay."

"I guess it's obvious to me just because I know, but I guess it's not to anyone else. Alex is with Bridget."

# 31

I should have figured it out, I'd never seen any romantic affection between them. And why else would Bridget have been going to see him so late that night I'd brought him a pillow? How she took it from me to give to him, knowing he was naked in his room. Her anger when Alex would choose to spend time with the world's ugliest girl, when he could be with the prettiest. And, eeeewwww, why she wanted her sheets changed every day. Gross.

I didn't know what I should say to Lissy. *I'm sorry?* But she didn't seem jealous. Really annoyed about it for sure, but just factual.

"So," I said, "they're like secret boyfriend and girlfriend?"

"Well, the *secret* part is right. But I wouldn't call it boyfriend-girlfriend. She made her play for him a few months ago. And I don't blame him. I mean, Alex is the nicest guy there is. He really is sweet. But he's an eighteen-year-old boy. You think he could turn down a body like hers? My God, she could crack walnuts with that ass."

She made me laugh, but not for long. "But she's what? Twenty-eight? And he's eighteen. That's just . . ." I made a face.

"I know! . . . on so many levels. She works for us for one thing. And she's like a semi-cougar, right? I don't even want her to stretch me anymore but if I say that, it's going to be obvious to everyone that something's up and they'll figure it out. So now it's like *I* have to cover for *them*!"

155

"Have you tried talking to her?"

"Absolutely! Right after I knew. I told her if people learned about them that it would ruin Alex and me. But she just . . . she just doesn't care. We'd go from *America's Sweethearts* to complete shams. Like either we were really together, and he was cheating on me, or we faked the whole romance thing. But she just . . . she just doesn't care."

She was right. It would affect the way people saw them, maybe pushing my dad's first skaters well off the podium with the Olympics so close. And for sure no Coke or Pepsi reps knocking on their door.

We were quiet for a while. Finally she said, "Can we stop talking about me and Alex? And especially about Bridget? My life is too depressing. How about we talk about you. And I don't mean your skating. That's all we talk about."

"Um, sure, okay." The problem was I lived here. I skated here. I wore a mask. End of story. "Not much to tell though." I waved my hands around my room as if to say, *This is all there is.*

She said, "You and your dad never talk about your mom. My mom died when I was little. Did yours? Is that too personal to ask?"

"Yeah. I mean, no that's not too personal, but yeah, she's dead." Dead to me.

"And that picture on your dresser. That's you?"

Me on a sled, going down a slope with pure joy on my face. "Yeah." I pointed to my face. "That's the day this happened. Ten minutes later everything was . . . never the same."

"And your mom, she died in the fire?"

She hadn't gone sledding with us so it was just Dad and me in the car when the accident occurred. But that was the day I lost her.

"Yeah, she died that day." Actually she stuck around a few days. Long enough to see what her daughter had become. Dad said she left because of him, but I doubt that. He just didn't want me hating her.

Fat chance.

"So, your body is okay? . . . God, are these questions too personal?"

"No, it's okay." In a weird way, it felt kind of good to talk about it with her. There had never been anyone before to ask me—to have the slightest interest. "I had some first and second-degree burns on parts of my body. But those healed. My dad had some burns too, on his shoulders. The fire was mainly in the back where my car seat was. I don't like to use the word lucky, but I guess we were. We had those wet clothes on and some cars stopped with fire extinguishers and got us out."

I ran out of steam and we sat there.

Lissy finally said, brightly, "Boy, this sure is happier talking about you!" And we both cracked up. Stopped laughing and cracked up again. "Hey," I said, "too much talking about sad stuff will give us premature wrinkles. I don't know about you, but my face is my money shot. Gotta take care of the moneymaker."

"You really are too funny," she said. "Can I admit something to you? I really didn't need any clothes. I was just lonely. Alex was *busy*," she made a hand gesture I assume meant something sexual, "and I just wanted to talk to someone. Someone nice. So thanks. I'm glad we're friends."

*Friends.*

No, I didn't hear the sound of angels singing or even a distant boys' choir. Perhaps the faint echo of an angel's trumpet, but maybe I imagined it. Definitely no spotlights shining on the word spelled out in giant letters, suspended by blimps in the sky.

But close.

To cover up my emotions I went with funny. I gave her a British accent. "So sorry, dear, spot of bother, but you are not quite sufficiently horrid to be in the official friendship circle with Katie Wilder. We are extremely selective with entry into the ultra-elite Group of Gross Disfigurement. However, worry not. With some hard work on your part you *may* qualify for the Group of the Slightly Repulsive we're forming. Yes, we've heard about your feet, dear. Should you elect to apply in a fortnight we will give your application the attention it deserves. Ever so."

She replied in kind. "I shall endeavor to make my feet and other bad qualities sufficiently horrid to qualify for entry to Katie Wilder's Group of Gross Disfigurement, but should I fail to qualify, I thank you in advance for consideration into the Group of the Slightly Repulsive."

Wow.

*Was this what friends did?*

If so, it was delightful.

I gave up on the English accent. "Full disclosure . . . I know you probably think I have tons of friends because I'm so stunningly beautiful and delightfully clever that all the cool kids want to hang out with me. I mean, the mask is like a boy magnet. But . . . I've actually never had a friend. So if I do it wrong you'll have to tell me . . . Seriously, I'm not making a joke. You'll need to tell me."

She got up and held her arms out and I got one of the best hugs of my life. My first from a friend.

She said, "Well, I'm not too far ahead of you in the friends department. I mean, I have friends, but not a lot. I tell myself it's because they're uncomfortable or jealous about my dad being a kazillionaire, or they think," she made air quotes, "*pretty* girls are conceited. And a lot of the girls are real competitive . . . But sometimes I think that's all just crap and it's me."

"I guess it's good I'm not a pairs skater then," I said, "or you'd have it in for me."

"Oh absolutely. Friendship annulled. I'd hate you with every cell of my body."

"Okay, I guess I just have to stay a singles skater."

She nodded, "It's for the best I think."

"So I guess we can stay friends then."

"Yeah," she said. "I guess so."

# 32

That night at dinner it was the five of us. Alex and Lissy were the last to walk in and just as they did his phone chirped. I watched him read a text then angrily shove his phone back in his pocket as if blaming it for the message he'd received.

When we'd all sat down and filled our plates, Lissy must have noticed his reaction too because she asked who'd been on the phone.

"My dad," he said. "Coming for a visit apparently."

I didn't know which surprised me more, how joyless Alex looked—mirrored by Lissy—or Bridget showing the exact opposite reaction.

"Your *dad?* When is he coming?"

From Alex's look I could tell I wasn't the only one surprised by her excitement. "Ah . . . Saturday, for lunch. Why? You know my father?"

She said, "I don't *know* him, but I know who he *is*. Hockey in Finland is like football to you Americans, except even bigger. All of Finland knows Boris Piezov."

"The Crushin' Russian," my dad put in. "One of the best enforcers ever."

I knew that Alex's dad had played in the National Hockey League, but I'd thought he was just a run of the mill guy until my dad had set me straight. Evidently Boris Piezov had been in the first wave of players to leave Russia for the NHL in the 90s and was one of the hockey's most famous tough guys. My dad said he still held the record for most penalty minutes, usually for knocking other players out of the game with questionable hits.

"How long will he be here?" Dad asked. "I've got to be down the mountain Saturday morning, but I'd love to get back in time to meet him."

Alex shrugged. "He probably won't be here that long. The Rangers play the Kings Friday night, then they go down to Anaheim to play the Ducks on Sunday, so he's just got a little free time on Saturday."

Usually the only person quieter than me at the table was Bridget, but talking about hockey instead of our usual figure skating had her going. Bringing up Alex's dad got her and my dad into an animated discussion about Finland's greatest hockey players. Evidently Bridget's little country had contributed some of the world's best. She and my dad went back and forth swapping names.

"Teemu Selanne," from my dad.

"Jari Kurri," from Bridget.

"Tomas Sandstrom."

"Saku Koivu."

And on they went, going back and forth past a dozen names, none of which I knew. Or cared about. I had to admit I was impressed Bridget knew so much about hockey, but surprised she clearly loved a sport that was so violent. My dad had tried to get me to watch some games on TV with him, but I couldn't get past how vicious it was, how the players would drop their gloves and have actual fist fights on the ice, continuing until one of them was bloody and semi-conscious. I couldn't understand how my sweet and gentle father could enjoy it. Even weirder that a knockout beauty girlie-girl like Bridget would.

I didn't know why Alex and Lissy seemed unhappy about the visit, but at least Saturday would be a free day for it. My dad worked with them Monday through Friday. Saturday they skated on their own but for only one session. And Sunday was a mandatory rest day. That was a pretty standard schedule for elite skaters so they wouldn't overtrain. I was the freak, out there seven days a week, five or six hours a day.

We were almost done with dinner—and the hockey talk thankfully over—when I decided to drop my bombshell. I'd been trying to find the courage to go outside the rink, and my time with Lissy today gave me the courage to do it tonight. Of course, it was a bombshell only because it was me asking the question. It'd be mundane coming from anyone else.

"So," I said. "Who wants to go out to a movie tonight?"

My dad literally choked on his food. I don't mean he needed a Heimlich or anything, but he did have a rough few seconds. He could tell I wasn't making a joke.

If I was going to start competing, I had to get used to the outside world. Plus, I didn't know how else to build a friendship with Lissy and Alex than to force myself to get outside the rink. Even I knew there was a life beyond skating.

"A movie?" my dad asked weakly.

"I looked online," I said. "They're playing a new digital version of the original *Star Wars* at seven. Does anyone want to go? Or we could see one of the new movies."

I'd actually never seen *Star Wars* and imagined it'd be amazing to see on a big screen. And if I was going to see my first movie ever in a theater, it'd be nice to start with something incredible like that. But I'd be thrilled to see anything actually. I was trying to imagine what it would feel like, hundreds of seats in perfect rows, slanting down toward a giant movie screen, and share the experience with a bunch of people, all in the anonymity of darkness. It sounded kind of magical, in a slightly scary way.

"I'm in," Lissy said. "I love the *Star Wars* movies, and I've actually never seen the first one."

"Yeah, sure," said Alex, who looked to Bridget.

"American guns and violence," she said dismissively. "No thanks."

"Light sabers, I'll have you know," Alex responded.

My dad's face was busy trying to hide his emotions. And failing. But if anyone noticed, they were too polite to let on. He didn't want to take away the casualness of the moment I was giving it, but he knew how big this was for me. I knew he wanted to share it, but I could also see him thinking I might feel scrutinized if he were there, constantly checking to make sure I was okay. So he took a leap of faith and said he had a lot of work to do and the three of us should go without him.

"If I like it, Dad, can we go another time? Just you and me?"

He nodded and quickly got up with his plate to wash it off, even though half his food remained. When everyone had left the table and I was in my room he came by as I knew he would. But he surprised me. He didn't say anything about being proud of me. He didn't say what a big step this was. He didn't give me a lecture on being careful when he knew I'd spent a lifetime doing exactly that. He just acted like it was normal for me to be going out with friends. Maybe he was afraid if he said anything, it would break the spell and I'd change my mind.

He handed me a twenty-dollar bill. Although I'd touched money, I'd never actually used it. People paid for the cabins by credit card, and my only interaction with cash was if someone left a tip in the cabin, which let's face it, they rarely did since all we did was give them a clean cabin with fresh sheets when they arrived. After that they were on their own. So tonight it was going to be such a cool experience to hand someone money, and get change back.

I was waiting by Alex's car when he and Lissy came down the path. They knew this was not a normal event for me, but I don't think they had any idea how big it was. I tried my best to act like going to a movie, going *anywhere*, wasn't a huge deal.

Lissy had a purse over her shoulder and the first thing she asked me was, "Did you forget your purse?"

As if I even owned one. "Oh, no. I'm fine."

Now that I thought about it, when I watched movies, girls always did seem to have a purse. I'd have to ask her later what she kept in there. She could share those secrets of girlhood with me.

Lissy got in the front seat and I opened the door to the back. And stopped. For some reason I didn't want to climb in. Actually, not a question of wanting. I literally couldn't move. It was as if the back seat was a dark cave with an unseen monster waiting for me. I had not been in a back seat since the accident.

Finally, Alex said, "Katie . . . did you forget something?"

God, what was with me? I could do this. I'd been psyching myself up about going out for weeks. I'd chosen a movie because the theatre was close, and once the movie started I'd be in the dark, invisible to others' eyes. But all I'd thought about was the destination, not getting there.

I forced myself into the car and put on my seat belt, if only to keep me from fleeing. It'd be so humiliating to run back into the house, not even making it past the driveway. But in the car it only got worse. At least I knew my mask was hiding the contortions I could feel my face making. I closed my eyes and willed myself to relax as the car coasted down the driveway and onto the street as Alex and Lissy chatted in front, blissfully unaware of the war silently raging in my head.

But I couldn't keep my eyes closed. When I opened them it wasn't the back of Alex's head that I saw, but my dad's. And the flames. Then the screaming.

*"NO! Noooooo! Help! Let me out! Let me out!"*

At first I didn't know it was me screaming. I clawed to release the seat belt then had a terrifying moment when I couldn't find the door handle. It's lucky Alex pulled over as fast as he did or I'd have been out the door even with the car moving. As it was, he had barely stopped when I pushed out and sprinted from the car. Even from twenty feet away I could still feel the flames lick my face, but when I tried to rip off my mask, my fingers wouldn't work right to find the knot.

Then I couldn't move my arms at all, and I realized it was because Alex and Lissy both had their arms wrapped tightly around me, making soft sounds. But as soon as it had started, it was over. The flames were gone and so was my panic. The soft sounds turned into words.

First from Alex. "It's okay . . . everything is okay. Just breathe. Yeah, like that. Don't worry. You're safe."

They must have felt me relax because I could feel them loosen their grips without fully letting go. But they did pull their heads back enough to look at me.

Lissy softly asked, "Katie? . . . Katie, what happened? Are you okay?"

Actually, I was. As quickly as the terror had gotten a hold of me—ten seconds? Twenty?—it was gone—just seconds after I got out of the car. Just in time for the embarrassment to take its place. No accident. No fire. No being trapped in a car seat as the flames enveloped me. Only shame.

"I'm so sorry," I said. When I realized I'd spoken so softly they couldn't hear me, I said it again. I'd told Lissy a little about the accident and I'm sure she told Alex. By now they were putting it all together.

"Oh, Katie." Lissy looked stricken. "It's okay. Let's just go home. We can walk and Alex can drive back."

"No, no," Alex said. "We'll all walk together. Then I'll come back for the car." He looked to me. "Okay?"

No. It wasn't.

I made myself stand up straight. "No. We're not going home. We're going to the movies. I'm fine now. I really am. And . . ." I could feel my forced bravery crumble and the truth come out. "I can't go back home, especially after this. If I don't do this now . . . I'm afraid I never will."

When they looked at each other doubtfully, I tried to not sound as desperate as I felt. "Really. *Please.*" I managed a weak laugh. "It was just the back seat. I'll be fine in the front. I promise." I held out a flat hand. "See, no shaking. Rock solid."

164

And thank God it actually was steady.

I think they had their doubts but they let me get back in the car, although for the next minute Alex didn't drive over ten miles an hour and kept stealing glances at me. It was so ridiculous that I heard a real laugh come out of me. "Seriously, Alex. We could *walk* faster. C'mon, let's go. I don't want to be late for my first movie."

They must have seen or heard what they needed because I could feel the tension in the car melt away and Alex started driving like he wasn't ninety-five years old. By the time we got to the theater we were chatting like always. It was almost like it had never happened.

Blue Jay's main road had all its businesses clustered together: a Jensen's market, a few dozen stores, some restaurants, and the movie theater. The town was lucky to have it considering the population over a hundred square miles was only about thirteen thousand. But I guess the tourists added a lot more.

As we got out of the car I pulled the hood of my *John Wilson Blades* sweatshirt up, telling myself it was a bit cool outside, but let's be real: No need to advertise the mask. There was a short line for tickets, and two teenage guys right in front of us, both of them smoking. I'd never smelled cigarette smoke before. It was absolutely gross, but at the same time, I liked it. A completely new smell, even if a bad one. It was so strange to have so many people around, all moving in different directions. Everyone seemed in a hurry.

One of the guys in front of us turned around. I watched his eyes not just take in Lissy, but move his eyes up and down her body. His friend turned and did the same. Their eyes turned to me. The hood would be covering up the sides of my face, so they couldn't see the scars, just the fact I was wearing the mask. I was used to curiosity, but they didn't look *interested* curious—they looked *mean* curious. I knew the difference.

And they just kept staring.

From Alex, quietly, but in a tone I'd never heard from him. "What's your problem? You guys need something?"

That got a reaction from the guys, almost as if they wanted one in return. Hoping for escalation. I hadn't seen Alex move but suddenly he was in front of me.

Lissy to the rescue. "Hey guys," she nodded ahead of them, and they turned to see there was no one in front of them and the cashier was waiting.

They gave a hard look back, but not at me—at Alex. I have to admit, I was scared and I could feel my body react. I thought, *fight or flight!* Exactly like my dad talked about! I felt it even more so when one of them tossed his still-smoking cigarette at our feet. But Alex just ground it out with his foot and smiled coolly. Maybe he was used to guys like that. They were clearly bad news.

I could hear the guys get tickets for a different movie. At least they wouldn't be in the same theater, maybe sitting right by us. They seemed to have forgotten the three of us and walked into the theater. Maybe their day was a long line of little hostilities, each so insignificant to them that they forgot each one and moved on to the next.

What a night! But even with all that, I still savored handing the cashier my twenty and getting eight dollars and a ticket back. We walked a dozen feet to hand the ticket to someone at the door, and he handed me back half the ticket. I put it in my pocket and vowed to start a scrapbook filled with amazing things just like it. The ticket would be my first entry.

The lobby of the theater was dominated by a long snack bar. There were two popcorn machines making popcorn right in front of us—actual popcorn popping before our eyes. The scents in the room were overpowering, nothing like the rink or forest smells I was used to. I couldn't decide if the smell was good or bad, just incredibly different.

"Do you want to get anything to eat or drink?" Alex asked.

We walked closer and I could see what must have been the world's largest display of candy. I didn't even know what most of them were. I recognized M&Ms and licorice, but the rest were a mystery.

"I've never eaten any of these things."

"No favorite candy?" Alex asked.

"Actually, I've never had *any* candy."

166

"Seriously? Jeez, I feel like we're corrupting you. I mean we eat super healthy, but we do cut loose sometimes."

"Can we try popcorn?" I asked. I had no idea how it would taste, but it was amazing the way it looked and sounded as it popped then tumbled down from the little tray at the top into the big glass case. It seemed to be what everyone was getting, and I could put it through the mouth hole in my mask kernel by kernel.

When we made it to our seats, Lissy said, "Sorry about those guys out there. They were just jerks."

"It's okay. You have to admit, it's kinda strange to see someone wearing a mask. Don't worry, I'm having fun." And I was. Being stared at was a fact of life for me. My biggest fear had actually been that Alex would get in a fight and get hurt.

I didn't own a watch so tried to look at Alex's to see how long before the movie started. He must have thought I was looking at his drink.

"You want some of my Coke?"

I'd never had a soft drink, and I was curious what the world seemed to be addicted to. "Are you sure?"

"Why, are you sick?"

*Ah, no, because your straw will be touching something hideous and any sane person would not want to put their lips on it afterwards.*

But I said, "No. It's just . . . well, okay. Thanks."

So I had my first sip of Coke.

Argh! Never again! So syrupy sweet, nothing like the smoothies I made. This was the drink that ruled the planet? I was glad I had my water. But I loved the popcorn, and it was cool the way we kept wordlessly passing the bucket around and taking a handful. Out of the corner of my eye I watched to see if Alex kept using the straw. He did, which made me absurdly happy. Better than landing the quad, actually.

Any worries about not enjoying my first movie after my mini-meltdown, then the guys in front, were gone the second the movie started. The immensity of the screen, the volume; it was all absolutely amazing. Completely different than watching a movie on my computer or TV. There were times where I was so immersed in the story that I didn't even realize I was in a theater. I was with Luke Skywalker and Princess Leah, and Hans Solo and Chewbacca, battling Darth Vader in a universe far, far away. Then something would bring me briefly back to reality and I'd notice I was gripping hands with both Lissy and Alex. I'd put my hands back in my lap and then a few dramatic scenes later notice I'd grabbed their hands again.

It was after ten by the time we were driving home. Even though I was usually in bed by eight-thirty, I wasn't sleepy at all. I could see Dad through the kitchen windows as we pulled up. I said goodnight to Alex and Lissy and literally ran inside, slipping off my mask. I'd never been more than a few hundred feet from my dad. I ran up to him and just as he turned around I jumped into his arms. He must have thought the night was a disaster because I could see the look of concern when he pulled his head back. Maybe he was imagining silent sobs. But he looked down and saw me grinning.

"It was great, Dad."

# 33

Uncle Robbie and I stood in the parking lot as Lissy, Alex and Bridget stood around my dad as he tried to fit everyone's suitcases and skate bags into the trunk. It was bad enough I was staying home—even though it was my own decision—but seeing Bridget going and not me seemed so unfair.

Dad finally gave up with one small suitcase unwilling to play nicely and fit in the trunk. "Bridget, do you mind sitting in the front seat and I can put this on the floor in front of you? Or all three of you can sit in the back, but that's kind of tight."

"Or we could just take two cars," Bridget suggested.

"I can sit there," Alex said. "I don't mind. It's just over an hour to the airport."

"No, it's okay, "Bridget said, her sacrifice now clear. "I'll sit in front. I'm shorter."

With that decided, we stood around awkwardly. I'd miss Lissy and Alex—a lot actually. But my dad? I'd never been away from him for more than a few hours at a time. I gave Lissy and Alex hugs, then a huge one for my dad. A nod to Bridget. She'd run out of abuses lately. She had been amusing herself by humming *Phantom* when she passed me if no one was around, but when I started humming it before her, I could tell it took her fun away.

The three of them climbed in the car and Uncle Robbie and I waved until they were down the driveway and out of sight.

At the U.S. International, the only member of The Big Three in attendance would be Canada's Peligrino and Maples. The two Russian teams had opted for a European competition. Now was the time for all skaters to be debuting their programs for the new season. Alex and Lissy would have tomorrow to get acclimated, then their short program was Friday, and the free skate on Saturday.

"So what's your day, Katie?" Uncle Robbie asked.

I knew today was going to be tough for me with everyone gone so I wanted to be busy. "I've got a group class and I'm teaching Dad's two privates. And my own workouts, of course."

"*What?* You're teaching?"

"Yeah, I've been teaching the groups, and while Dad's gone I'll do his privates."

Uncle Robbie put his hands to his head like he had a massive migraine going. "Are you and your dad trying to kill me?" Mister Drama.

"What are you talking about?"

"Insurance, Katie! Insurance! There's no coverage for you. Only your dad's on the policy. Why don't you two tell me these things?"

"I'm sorry, Uncle Robbie. I don't know about any of that. But no one's going to get hurt."

"Oh yeah, there's nothing possibly dangerous about people moving at high speed on sharp blades on ice . . . nothing dangerous about that."

Maybe he had a point, although we'd never had anyone get badly hurt or sue us. What could I say? "Sorry."

"Ahhh, it's not your fault, it's that crazy father of yours. He never thinks about these things . . . that's why he's got me." He gave me a pat on the back. "No worries. I'll get on the phone with the insurance company and get you covered. But you guys have to tell me this stuff."

"Okay. Will do, Uncle Robbie. But my first lesson is in about an hour, so maybe you better call now."

Before my dad left he'd bought himself a cell phone. Like me, he just hadn't needed one before, but he wanted to be easily available if I needed him—and just maybe to join the twenty-first century. Now I guess I was the last surviving person on the planet without one.

The group class went well and the two little girls who had the private lessons were so much fun to work with. I wondered if I'd showed so much joy at learning at that stage. No wonder my dad loved coaching so much. By the end of the day I'd actually put in more ice time than I had in years, close to eight hours.

When it came time to watch the short programs the next day, I was in front of my computer. The U.S. International wasn't one of the big Grand Prix events, so it wouldn't be on network TV, but nbcsports-gold.com would have it. Buy a Figure Skating Pass and you'd get both live and on demand access to every skating competition, even small events like Regionals and Sectionals. You could even see the competitors' protocol sheets.

Unlike their free skate, Alex and Lissy hadn't had to make any choreography changes to their short program, so they were already locked in on it. Their music was Justin Timberlake's *Can't Stop the Feeling*, which was pretty brave by figure skating standards. Even with the new music allowed, most skaters were still going orchestral.

When Alex and Lissy took the ice, it was so strange to now see them as my friends and training partners. Finally, I understood all those anguished parents and friends in the stands, living between exaltation and despair with every jump and lift. They skated a technically clean program except for Lissy under-rotating on their second element, their triple Lutz—a sign the early jitters were still a work in progress.

But I was happy to see on the screen what was obvious when I watched them in person every day—their presentation had improved. There was more honesty in the joy of their skating and a better connection to their music. You could really see them having fun, not just

171

acting like they were. Still a ways to go to match the older and more seasoned Big Three, but they were getting closer.

At one point the camera showed Lissy's dad in a rink-side seat with a Miss Universe-sized bouquet of roses ready for her. He had never made it to the Ice Castle, although the phone never failed to ring at 7:00 pm with his call, so I was happy for Lissy that he was there to spend time with her. After all the pairs had skated, Peligrino-Maples were in first with a 64.18, and Alex and Lissy were just a bit behind at 62.73. A German team was a distant third, with another American team in fourth. Everyone knew the battle was between the Canadians and Alex and Lissy.

That night I talked to the three of them and they all seemed very happy with the skate. The new long program still wasn't quite second nature yet, but they'd only had it a few weeks. This was early in the season, so they weren't the only skaters tweaking their programs. The new choreography had changed more than half the transitions, moved two elements, and modified their side-by-side spin combination—but the result was awesome. The long programs would be the following day, worth double the short program score. There was a draw to determine the skating order among the teams with the highest scores and Alex and Lissy had drawn next to last, with the Canadians getting the most-desired final spot.

When Alex and Lissy took their opening positions and started skating to Steven Tyler's masterful lyrics, I found myself talking out loud, leading them into each element. "K, set it up . . . set it up . . . now go big and. . . *yes!*" A perfect triple twist, Alex throwing Lissy straight above him as she rotated three times parallel to the ice then fell back into his arms. ". . . Now ease into the Lutzes . . ." They took off into their side-by-side combo, a triple Lutz - double toe. Their timing was a little bit off so they weren't in perfect sync, but the jumps had been flawless. "Okay, here we go . . . axel lift, make it big . . ." The first of their three lifts, Alex lifting Lissy directly over his head, her legs in a split above him, Lissy supported only by their locked hands, hers extending down below her legs to grip his raised above him. Alex made several revolutions, turning Lissy above him, then she changed positions into a side reverse star, before Alex cart-wheeled her gently back to the ice. Masterful.

Later in their program they did have a small problem on their triple throw, Alex tossing Lissy into a triple loop. She got tilted in the air and had to check herself with a hand to the ice to keep from falling. Most of the other pairs had multiple falls, and even Peligrino-Maples didn't have a fully clean skate. But that was what the early season was for. By the end of the season all the top teams would be scoring at least twenty points higher.

Peligrino and Maples came out on top, earning a 128.83, so a total of 192.82; Alex and Lissy in second with a 126.72, total 189.45. The third place team was double digits back. On screen they showed the point breakdown between the technical points each pair earned com-pared to the presentation score. I was thrilled to see Alex and Lissy had actually beaten the Canadians on technical points, which they'd never done before, but they were still lagging on the presentation side. I had my own idea how to help fix it, and it had nothing to do with skating—but whether or not I'd have the guts to ever tell them was another matter.

# 34

They got home just after lunch the next day. I had taped a few sheets of paper together to make a "Welcome Home" poster for the back door, which I knew was completely corny and something a nine-year old would do, but so what. I felt like it, so I did it. Big hugs for everyone not of Finnish ancestry.

I had a million questions but I forced myself to wait until they settled in and relaxed. Alex and Lissy must have been tired because they disappeared into their cabins, but not before Lissy said to give her an hour to unpack and shower, then come over to hang out. Not once in my life had anyone invited me to "hang out." I'd have to see what time it was as soon as I went inside. I didn't want to appear over-eager so I figured I should actually wait sixty-one minutes.

I followed Dad into his room. "So details, Dad! What was it like to be coaching again? Did you see a lot of your old friends?"

"Ah, nice . . . and yes." He wasn't trying to be funny in his brevity. He could talk skating all day, but ask him about himself and he became a man of few words.

I held up my hands. "Please, Dad! You are overpowering me with your excitement. Try to contain yourself."

He laughed. "Very funny. Actually, my first thought was how old all the other coaches got, then I realized . . . that was me too. I was one of the young guns back then, only thirty-eight. Now I'm fifty-four and *establishment*. Kind of depressing." He actually didn't look depressed about it, more like he thought it was funny. "It was actually great to be in the middle of things again. I kind of thought it might feel different somehow, but . . . it was like I never left. A lot of new faces though. *Young* new faces."

His suitcase was filled with balled-up clothes so he was simply tossing everything into his laundry hamper.

"What about all the people you used to work with who ignored you the last sixteen years? Did they apologize?"

He paused and looked at me, surprised. "Was that really something you were thinking about? If people would apologize to me?"

"Yeah, and they should. Don't you think?"

"Katie, it's sweet of you to be watching out for me like that, but no one owed me an apology. Surprisingly, a few did anyway, saying they should have called, or that they'd never believed any of that stuff. But . . . honey, I'm actually very grateful to Juliette for finally owning up to it all. She didn't have to do that." He resumed his laundry-tossing. "So no need to worry about your old man's feelings. All's good in the skating world."

Well, if he was okay with it, I guess I had to let it go too. I filled him in on the lessons I'd given and what I'd been working on for my testing. When I was done he gave me his thoughts on Alex and Lissy's performance. In a nutshell . . . technically very good except for Lissy still working through the early heebie-jeebies—and of course, still needing to work on presentation. Overall he was thrilled and very proud of them.

Likewise, I was proud of myself. I looked at the clock and realized it was going to be closer to sixty-two minutes by the time I got to Lissy's.

When I knocked on her door she opened it wrapped in a towel. "Sorry, I just got out of the shower. C'mon in. Give me five minutes, K?"

She closed herself up in the bathroom, but that didn't stop her from carrying on a conversation through the door about old skater friends they'd seen, and getting to visit with her dad. Earlier today he had sent the usual twice-weekly gargantuan flower display, timed to be waiting for her when she got back. I'd put them in her room and now the scent was overpowering.

As if reading my mind, her voice came through the door. "Thanks for putting the flowers in my room. Isn't my daddy so sweet?"

I could see the card propped open on the dresser, *"Missing you already. Love, Daddy."*

As we were talking I sat on her bed and accidentally bumped her open laptop. As I did, the screensaver disappeared and by reflex I looked at what came up: Lissy's credit card statement. I really didn't mean to read her private stuff, but sometimes your eyes just get drawn in and you can't turn away. What had caught my eyes was seeing the same charge over and over. About every three days since she arrived at the Ice Castle it showed: *Arrowhead Flowers, Blue Jay CA - $145.28*, right up to today's flowers. The name at the top of the statement was Lissy's, not her dad's. I could actually feel a pain in my chest for my friend.

Lissy was sending flowers to herself.

I hopped off the bed and prayed her computer was set to quickly bring up the screensaver so it'd hide the bill. Lissy's voice was still coming from the bathroom but my brain wasn't registering what she was saying.

During the entire time Lissy and Alex had been here, there had not been a single visit from the father who was supposed to be Super Dad. I'd thought that was strange, but didn't give it too much thought since it seemed he was so attentive in other ways, like his daily call at exactly seven o'clock every evening, and all the constant flowers, always with a thoughtful note—just the kind a daughter would want to show off from a loving dad.

But evidently he was around only when there was a camera and a media opp. And those "phone calls" he always made at exactly seven o'clock? Maybe just the alarm on her phone set as a ring tone. That's why whenever Alex had asked to say hi to him she always said no.

So she was just talking to the air—a fantasy father—trying to hide his apathy about her from the world, at least when there were no cameras around. It made me want to rush to her and give her the tightest hug and tell her how wonderful she was.

She came bursting out of the bathroom, full of energy. "So, what do you say? Sound fun?" She glanced at her computer and my eyes followed hers. Thank God, the screensaver was back.

I said, "I'm sorry. What will be fun?"

"The party!" She closed the laptop. "Didn't you hear a word I said?"

"Oh, sorry, I guess my mind was someplace else."

She nodded. "Testing, I bet. I remember those days. Even Alex and I got kind of nervous. But you're going to ace them. Our secret tips await." She plopped on the bed and patted the spot next to her.

I sat down. "What about a party?"

"Okay, here's the thing . . . when we were in Salt Lake City we saw one of our friends. Alan. We knew him from Lake Placid. Really a nice guy. He moved back home to train in San Diego . . . So he's having a big Halloween party, a superhero costume party! He invited us and we told him about you and you're officially invited too."

This one's too easy. Let's all say it together . . . *Halloween? Well, she already has the mask!*

Har dee har har.

"Ah, Lissy, that's really nice of you guys, but . . . I . . . I can't go to a party." What was she thinking? Me, at a party? Hours away, in San Diego? Maybe dozens of teenagers I didn't even know?

"Yeah, Alex and I figured you'd say that, but listen . . . didn't you have fun at the movie?"

"Um, yeah."

"And you're going to Riverside in a couple days to test?"

"Yeah."

"So that will be twice you've left here in about a week." She playfully poked me in the ribs. "You aren't seeing a trend here?"

There was a tap on the door and Alex let himself in. "Hey, Lissy. Hey, Katie. Have you told her about the party?"

"Yeah, she was about to say yes when you came in." She turned to me. "Weren't you, Katie?"

"Ah . . . *no*." No as in, *not in a million years*. "I mean, thanks for inviting me, but you know I can't go to something like that."

Alex said to Lissy, "Did you tell her about the costumes?"

She reached for her laptop. "No, not yet. I'll find them while you tell her."

"We already ordered you a costume," Alex said, "while we were in Salt Lake City. We got them for all of us. Captain America for me, Lissy is going as The Flash, and you . . ." He waited for Lissy to move the laptop in front of us. ". . . You are going as Mystique, from the XMen. Perfect, right?"

The screen showed a row of models in various costumes, with the Superhero names underneath, handy for people like me who didn't know most of the characters. They didn't look like kids' costumes. They were clearly pricey and well made, like for a movie studio. The Mystique costume was a blue body suit so tight it looked like skin, with a blue mask and bright red hair.

I said, "These costumes look really expensive. You should have asked me first before you bought me one. Can you return it?"

"Don't worry about it," Alex said, nodding at Lissy. "Lucky for us, we know someone who's super rich."

"Exactly," she agreed. "And besides, if we asked you, you'd say no, so we're planning to use guilt and guile to get you to come. Isn't that right, Alex?"

"Absolutely, guilt and guile."

"Well," I said, "I'm not dying my hair red."

"You don't have to." Lissy said. "It's a wig. And the mask covers your whole face."

"But still . . . it's so, um, sexy."

"Right!" Alex agreed. "Your point being? Sexy and superhero do kind of go together."

I didn't know what to say. They had really put a lot of thought into this, getting costumes that would have masks like mine. In a costume like that, I'd be wearing a mask, but no one would know the reason why. The other kids there would think I was like them. Normal. I'd never experienced that.

"You guys really want me to come?"

"She's weakening," Alex teased.

Lissy said, "Listen, we know you want to skate, like all the time, but we'd be able to do our first two sessions on Friday, then leave for the party and stay at Alex's Friday night. His family lives in San Diego, remember? So we wouldn't be driving late at night coming back, and we'd just miss one session Saturday morning. And there's a guest room you and I can share. I've stayed there a bunch of times."

I stalled. "I don't know. And I don't know if my dad would say yes."

"Listen," Alex said. "It's not for a month. It's a few days after Skate America. So there's no rush. Think about it. But just know that if you don't go, we aren't going either."

"Yup," said Lissy. "Try and handle that guilt."

"A party," Alex added, "that will just be other skaters, all really nice people. Just think about it, okay?"

Think about it? Seriously? As if I'd be doing anything but.

# 35

The next day was Saturday and Alex's dad was set to visit at eleven. I'd been out on the ice with Alex and Lissy since 9:30 just getting in some light work. Lissy had asked me to join them, I had the feeling as a buffer for when Mr. Piezov got there. I still didn't know the story. All I knew was it had been two years since Alex and his dad had last seen each other. That sounded like a lot more than just a busy NHL schedule.

It was just before eleven when I saw the man out front. I watched him try both doors, find them locked, then step back to wait. "Alex, is that your dad?"

He stopped skating and looked over. "Yeah, that's him."

He didn't make a move toward the doors though, so I said, "I'll go let him in."

As I got closer I could see he wasn't the huge bruiser with the face of an old boxer that I'd expected. Just the opposite, actually roughly handsome. He was the same six feet as Alex, but huskier, and still looked fit enough to play NHL hockey.

As I opened the door he gave no sign of surprise at the masked girl in front of him. Even forewarned, every other person I'd ever met had some reaction, even if it was faking no reaction, but he was in complete control. He reminded me of one of those elite Special Forces guys or a Navy SEAL, at least how they look in movies. One side of his mouth rose slightly, sort of a cool guy smile that he completely pulled off.

"Hi. Boris Piezov." He held out a hand to shake.

"Katie Wilder." I stood aside to let him in. He'd only said three words, but he sounded as American as me. No hint the first half of his life had been in Russia.

I could see Alex and Lissy were side by side, looking our way. I trailed Mr. Piezov as he headed toward them, stopping at the edge of the ice.

Alex gave a nod. "Dad."

His dad gave a nod back. "Alex."

When the moment had stretched out long enough to be noticeably awkward, Mr. Piezov added, "Lissy. Good to see you."

"Hi, Mr. Piezov." She gave Alex the subtlest of touches with her arm, as if to say, *go.*

And he did. I was surprised when his dad gave him a bear hug, then a kiss on each cheek. Maybe I shouldn't have been. I'd seen enough international skating to know Russians, especially the men, were big on hugs and cheek kisses. Not dainty like the French, but strong and forceful. I thought of Alex as big and buff, but he looked like a kid in his dad's arms.

I was thinking Mr. Piezov was actually acting pretty nice. Then he looked around and in the most polite tone said, "What a waste of a nice rink. No boards."

I was proud of our rink and didn't like hearing it called a waste, but kept it to myself. It was designed solely for figure skating, so it was one of the few rinks in the world without the customary hockey boards circling it to keep pucks in play.

Alex said, "You met Katie?"

He said, "Yes," but nodded to me again anyway.

I heard the back door open and turned to see Bridget walking in. Actually, more like sashaying. I'd never seen her in the skin-tight leather pants she was wearing, and the tiny top was an odd choice considering we kept the rink at sixty degrees.

Alex said, "Dad, this is Bridget, our trainer."

She got his full wattage smile, not the half-a-mouth twitch I'd gotten, and she gave it back doubled. And then she started speaking to him. In *Russian*.

I didn't even know she spoke Russian, and from the look of Alex and Lissy, neither did they. But I guess it made sense. Finland did share a border with Russia. I knew even Alex didn't speak more than a few token words.

After a fairly long back and forth between them that none of us understood, Bridget finally switched to English and turned to us. "Sorry, I know you Americans only learn your own language."

I guess it was a dig. I could never tell with her. Regardless, it was true. I'd heard people from Europe usually spoke a few languages compared to our mastery of only one.

Bridget pulled her cell phone out of her back pocket and said, "Can I get a picture? My dad will love it."

She moved next to him and put one arm around his waist, pulling him so tight one of her breasts half popped out of her low cut top, the other arm extended for a selfie. I'm not sure if it was having a fan, or the hug of a gorgeous girl, but Mr. Piezov was looking pretty happy. I stole a look at Alex, but his face was unreadable.

Bridget's attention was fully on Alex's dad. "So, I asked Alex once if he played hockey when he was a kid, and he said not too much. I can't believe you didn't turn him into a hockey player."

I don't think anyone but me could hear the sigh escape Lissy, a silent wish of, *Please don't go there.*

But Alex's dad couldn't be happier with the question. "Alex said he didn't play much? Well then, he was being modest. At nine he was outplaying the best twelve year olds. At ten he was dominating the fourteens. The best natural scorer you've ever seen." Just when I was thinking it was sweet the way he was bragging about his son, he added, "But he gave it up. For dancing."

He didn't say it sarcastically or with even a hint of innuendo. But still . . . *dancing?*

Neither Alex or Lissy bothered to correct him. I had the feeling they'd heard it before and were just anxious to move past it.

But Bridget kept it going. "He was that good?" Then she turned to Alex. "You and your dad should play some one on one or something."

Alex spoke up quickly, as if to put a stop to any thought about his dad joining him on the ice. "I was thinking we could head out to lunch now, Dad. There are some nice places right on the lake."

But his dad looked to Bridget and said, "Hey, I always keep my gear bag in the car." Then to Alex, "And I've got sticks and some biscuits. What do you say? For old times sake."

I knew *biscuit* was slang for puck.

As if it was decided, Bridget said, "Great! We'd love to watch you guys out there together."

Lissy said, "Well, I'm sure Alex would like to, but he doesn't have the right skates. So . . ."

Hockey blades were completely different than those for figure skating. For the speed and sudden stops required in hockey, the blades were short and light. Figure skating blades were longer and flatter, with a sharp toe pick for jumps. Not at all suited for hockey.

Mr. Piezov gave Lissy a mild, *Are you serious look?* Then to Alex: "Just some no-contact stuff. Some handling drills like we used to do." Then with the subtlest of sarcasm. "Don't worry. No contact."

I watched as Lissy bit back a comment and her face took on a forced blank expression—as much of a mask as mine.

Alex sighed. "Sure, Dad. A few minutes would be okay."

Lissy's head dropped slightly in resignation.

"I'll help you carry in your gear," Bridget said excitedly and followed Mr. Piezov as he went outside. I caught Alex's look of annoyance at their backs, but I didn't know whether it was at his dad or Bridget.

When they were out the doors, Lissy said with forced calm, "Alex, you said you weren't going to skate with him. I'm not going to watch this time."

He just rolled his eyes and used a sharp tone I'd never heard him use with her. "Do whatever you want, Lissy."

She locked eyes with him then without a word turned and skated off the ice. Alex moved in the other direction, moving in hockey-style, rapid, jagged cuts. When Lissy sat down to pull off her skates I sat down next to her. "What's going on, Lissy?"

She didn't say anything for a minute, like she was deciding what to say, or maybe say nothing at all. Finally, "The last time Alex skated with his dad he got so beat up it messed up our training for weeks."

"But why would he want to hurt Alex? And risk his skating?"

She looked up and watched Alex circling the ice, so much love obvious in her face. "His dad was furious when he gave up hockey. It was like rejecting *him*. And not just to give it up, but to give it up for figure skating. He's the ultimate NHL tough guy, and to him figure skating is . . ."

She trailed off but I knew where she was going. Some saw it as a sissy sport for guys. My dad had told me how the perception created a challenge to their masculinity before they even got on the ice. Gay, not gay? The sad thing was that it even mattered to people either way. The reality was figure skaters were among the best athletes in the world.

She stood up. "Anyway, I'm not going to stay here and watch."

I couldn't believe she'd just leave. "But why don't you say something? Stop them."

She took a few steps toward the door then came back. "Katie . . . guys are . . ." She sighed. "You just can't tell them what to do. Not when it's . . . something like this. He promised me he wouldn't skate with his dad. But now . . . he is. I'll make it worse by trying to stop it." As if reading my mind she added, "And if you're smart you'll keep quiet too."

Mr. Piezov and Bridget came back in, chatting in rapid Russian. He had a heavy gear bag and she held two sticks and some orange rubber cones. He pulled on his skates without changing out of his jeans, which seemed to indicate he wasn't planning any serious skating. I thought that was a good sign.

He grinned at Lissy. "How about you and Bridget be our cheerleaders. Get some noise going."

I didn't know which bothered me more . . . that he left out the ugly girl—as if I wasn't even there, clearly not cheerleader material—or, that he was reducing Lissy to such a role. Didn't he know Lissy could skate circles around him?

But Lissy just politely said, "No thank you, Mr. Piezov. You and Alex enjoy your day together." And with that she was gone.

Something told me I should follow her, but I couldn't make myself leave. I watched as Mr. Piezov skated out on the ice and dropped some pucks in front of Alex and said, "Set us up."

Then he darted off. If he was showing off, he succeeded. Maybe he'd been a hoodlum on the ice, but that didn't mean he couldn't skate. For a guy his size he was amazingly quick, moving with a controlled fury that was nothing like the skating I knew. I suddenly had a new respect for hockey players.

While his dad moved around the ice, Alex was arranging the pucks in a pattern. He made two rows of three, each a foot or two apart. He'd kept out one puck and now he maneuvered it with his stick around the pucks, left to right, up and down, then sideways. It was a pretty impressive display, especially for someone who I was guessing hadn't touched a hockey stick in a long time.

Alex stepped back when his dad skated up. Mr. Piezov did the same drill Alex had been doing, but so quickly I couldn't even see the puck move. The guy really had skills. They went back and forth a few times. I was glad to see them acting like a father and son should, exchanging both compliments and good-natured jibes as they moved the puck in different patterns. Lissy was wrong to be worried. No one was going to get hurt. They were just having fun. If they didn't have much to talk about, this was the ideal way to spend some pressure-free time together.

"Okay," Mr. Piezov said. "How about this?"

He took Alex's stick then dropped it on the ice. He moved a puck next it, then with quick little moves, popped it up and over the stick, back and forth. The puck was a blur and his stick moved so quickly it sounded like fingers on a keyboard as it tapped the ice. Wow, if an *enforcer* was this good, I wondered how good the scorers were.

When it was Alex's turn he couldn't match his dad but was still pretty impressive. I smiled at the thought that they'd done these drills, father and son, from when Alex was tiny, just like me and my dad with our drills.

When Alex lost control of the puck his dad simply said, "Not bad. You still got the great hands, kid. Lookin' good."

Alex gave his first genuine smile since his dad arrived. "Thanks."

"Do you want to take some shots?" his dad asked. Then without waiting for an answer, he said something in Russian to Bridget and she walked out with the four cones and set up two at each end where goalkeeper nets would usually be.

Alex said, "Dad, we can't take any shots in here." He indicated the wall of windows running along one wall. "We don't have any boards. We'll end up breaking a window." He looked quickly to me in apology, recognizing this was basically my house.

"No we won't," his dad said dismissively. "Let's just play a little one-on-one shinny. No contact and no roofing. And the rubber flooring is a few inches higher than the ice. It'll stop the puck. Alright?" He didn't wait for an answer, adding, "First to five. A goal is one, a miss is minus two, just like we used to play."

Bridget had placed the cones only about three feet apart. That was a lot narrower than a regular hockey net, so maybe they were only going to shoot from up close. Still, I was feeling nervous. Bridget came and stood next to me as Alex's dad finished speaking. She was evidently so mesmerized by the hockey she forgot she despised me.

She said, "Don't worry about the windows. He said no roofing."

When I just looked at her she said, "That means they'll keep the puck on the ice. They aren't going to take any shots where it goes airborne." Then she cupped her hands and shouted, "C'mon Alex!

Let's see what you can do!" Then she yelled something in Russian to Mr. Piezov. Cheerleader for both evidently.

It wasn't the windows I was worried about. Well, a little, but mainly it was Alex. They weren't wearing the padding hockey players usually wore, and a flying puck could easily break an ankle or a knee. Clearly his dad was super skilled with a puck, but still, mistakes could happen. If my dad were here I knew he'd stop it. I wanted to, but I didn't know how.

Alex's dad slid him the puck. "Home team honors."

Even in figure skates, Alex definitely looked like a hockey player out there, moving the puck back and forth as he moved toward the goal, his dad keeping pace ahead of him, moving backwards and taking little pokes at the puck. Just as Alex got close enough to where I thought he was going to take a shot, his dad somehow knocked the puck back through between Alex's legs, then darted around him and raced to an easy goal, Alex helplessly trailing him by ten feet.

"One," said Mr. Piezov. He slid the puck to Alex.

They moved down the ice as before, but this time Alex faked out his dad. He somehow spun in a complete three-sixty giving him an open shot at the goal. And . . . yes! He scored! Alex even gave a whoop. I think even he was surprised.

Bridget jumped up. "Yes! Take that Crushin' Russian!"

I didn't think egging on Alex's dad was a good idea, not matter how good-natured. "Um, Bridget . . . I think we should just watch."

Maybe Alex's dad didn't like getting scored on—or perhaps it was the leather-panted, boob-flashing Finnish beauty to impress—but when it was his turn with the puck he wasn't messing around. He faked sharply to each side then with Alex off balance, charged right through him. As Alex tried to get out of the way he lost his balance and ended up on his back, his dad easily skating past him. More like, over him.

"Two," he said.

Alex did a few knee bends to take the sting out of his fall, his dad making tight little circles as he waited. When Alex moved forward with the puck, his dad effortlessly stole it off Alex's stick, three-sixtied, planted a shoulder hard enough to send Alex to the ice, then sent a shot between the cones from thirty feet. "Three."

Bridget was on her feet. She was whooping, her arms high in celebration. Then she switched her loyalties to Alex. "C'mon Alex! Man up. Get it back."

I couldn't believe she was literally goading him. I know Lissy had said Alex and Bridget had only a friends-with-benefits thing, not love. Still, even as their physio she should be protecting him. Was he just a paycheck, with the bonus of being her bedwarmer? The reality was if he got injured and was out for the season, she could have a new job within a week. And maybe one she'd like better than being stuck out here in what I could tell she considered the boonies.

I jumped when I heard someone yell, "Stop it!" It was loud and it was angry.

It took me a second to realize it was me. I don't even remember walking out on the ice, but suddenly I was planted in front of Alex's father. "What are you *doing?* You said no contact! He's got Nationals coming up! And the *Olympics!* You're risking all that."

But his dad just gave me the same little half-smile he'd given me at the door. He looked over to Alex who was finally on his feet. "Seriously, Alex? How many mommies do you have?"

I could see the slow rage build on Alex's face. He skated over, so angry I was afraid he was going to take a swing at his father. But his anger wasn't for him. He stopped in front of me.

"Shut up! What are you even doing out here?"

I was too stunned to move. Or speak. It had taken every bit of the courage I had just to go out there. Now I just stood frozen like an idiot. He moved closer so only I could hear and I thought he was going to apologize, or secretly thank me for rescuing him. Instead, with a quiet intensity, he said, "Just get off the ice. Now."

*What was happening?* Why was he mad at me? His dad had put him down—twice—the last time clearly on purpose. How hard would the next one be? And he had to know that one puck hitting him above his blades could end his season. And not just his. My dad and Lissy's hopes would be gone as well. Those were the things I wanted to say.

But *damn it*. What I did instead was cry. No one in my life had anyone ever yelled at me in anger. Or even told me to shut up. Even with the mask, it was obvious to everyone I was crying, like a pitiful kid. Even Bridget was out on the ice now. Alex's dad seemed to consider me a joke. Alex no longer looked angry; he just looked miserable. Bridget was the annoyed one. She took my arm as if to move me off the ice. "Will you just let them play? God, Katie, what are you doing? They're men, not children."

But I shook her off. Somehow I got the words out, even if they came out in sobs. "No! No more hockey!" In my head I was shouting; that Mr. Piezov was his dad, that Bridget was his physio. Their job was to take care of him. Protect him. And if they wouldn't, I would. As they all stared at me I realized I might have actually said all that out loud. I was too upset to know.

What I did know was they still hadn't moved. I said, "It's my rink, and I said no more hockey. Not unless my dad says it's okay." God, that made me sound so spoiled. *My rink. My daddy.* But I didn't care.

Alex threw up his hands. "Screw it. I'm outta here." He turned to his dad. "I . . . I don't really feel like lunch. Okay? So . . . thanks for coming up."

Mr. Piezov held his arms apart as if to say, *"What? Seriously?"* But Alex was already skating off the ice, then out of the rink, without waiting for a reply from his dad.

That left me with his dad and Bridget. They acted like I wasn't even there and started talking in Russian again. I heard a few *Katies* in there, and some nods and laughs in my direction. I wanted to tell them both to leave but my reservoir of bravery—or stupidity—was exhausted. So, feeling completely lame, I just left them there. Alex was off the ice and that was all I cared about.

# 36

I sat in my room rehashing what happened. Every single way I relived it was better than the way it had actually happened. I still didn't know if what I'd done was right or wrong. The only sure thing was Alex was once again mad at me. Not hidden resentment like before, but full-on anger.

I couldn't talk to my dad about what happened. That would just make Alex madder. But Lissy I could talk to. Actually, had to talk to. There was no one else, and she knew Alex better than anyone. And I wasn't going to say it to her, but what happened to me was partly her fault. Why had she just left?

I checked the rink to find it empty, and when I was back in my room I heard Alex's car start up and drive away with an angry squeal of tires. So I knew the coast was clear and headed to Lissy's. She was sitting in the Adirondack chair on her little porch reading a book.

"So, are they at lunch?" she asked.

"Um . . . no. They never got that far. Alex's dad left."

She sighed. "Figures. What happened?"

I didn't say anything, but even with my mask she could tell I was upset.

She said, "Oh, no. What did you do, Katie?" But before I could answer: "Never mind. Later. Let's get out of here. Have you had lunch yet? Do you want to go into town?"

I shook my head. I couldn't handle more interaction with strangers. I was already on people overload. Not a good day for my first-ever lunch in town.

She stood up. "You know what? How about a hike? I used to love taking hikes when we trained in Lake Placid. Are there some trails near here?"

She couldn't have come up with a better idea: away from here, no people.

I said, "I love hiking." I told her there was an easy trail through the woods to the lake that only took ten minutes. My dad and I had walked it hundreds of times since I was a little girl. That was a benefit of living in a forest. You could just take off from your back door. Lissy stepped off her porch and we were off.

We were a few minutes into it when she said, "Okay. Spill."

And I did—everything—ending with Alex looking like he hated me and Bridget egging them on.

"Bitch," she muttered. "And what was with that top? I mean . . . Nipple Alert! I thought she was going to take out somebody's eyes."

If I referred to someone as a bitch my dad would take away my internet for a week. But I agreed with Lissy. And she didn't even know about Bridget's secret campaign against me. Since I'd taken away her *Phantom* fun, she'd started giving me "compliments" when no one was around. She made it an art form, just the slightest nuance turning them into insults:

"Wow, did you put that outfit together by yourself?"

"I love the way you pronounce your s's."

"Oh, you have to tell me where you bought that sweatshirt."

"That top really makes your breasts look bigger."

"I think it's so great that you're so brave and don't just give up."

She'd even delivered one right in front of my dad. When she'd left he said, "That was very nice of her, wasn't it?" Guys didn't have a clue. Even my dad.

But I didn't want to talk about Bridget. All I was thinking about was Alex—how he'd looked at me; the way he'd spoken.

"So, Lissy . . . I get that his dad is . . . well . . . kind of a jerk. But I don't understand why Alex would take a chance like that. And why he got so mad when I made them stop."

We crested the hill and could see the deep blue of Lake Arrowhead through the trees. There was a big, flat boulder right off the path and when Lissy took a seat, I sat down next to her.

"So," she said dryly, "You're asking me why Alex . . . a six foot, eighteen-year-old guy . . . got mad that a fifteen year old girl *rescued* him? In front of his dad . . . and the girl he's sleeping with? Ah, is that what you're asking?"

Oh. "Well, when you say it like that . . ."

She laughed. "Well, at least you stopped them. Sounds like it could have gotten worse."

No kidding. "Lissy . . . I don't understand why you left. I mean, especially if you knew something like that might happen."

As much as I didn't want it to, it came out like an accusation. I might have lost Alex as a friend; I didn't want to lose her too. But luckily she didn't seem to take offense. She leaned back and moved her arms behind her so she was staring up at the clouds, watching them slowly drift overhead.

Finally, "When I was . . . I think thirteen? I saw two of my friends, Adam and Will, get into a fight. Really hitting each other, and Adam was getting kinda beat up. So I ran over and stopped them. I never did find out what they were fighting about . . . Anyway, a few days later, they were buds again, but Adam barely spoke to *me* ever again. Like, it was okay for him to be friends with the guy who beat him up, but he couldn't forgive the girl who *saw* him get beat up . . . and worse, rescued him." She waved a hand as if dismissing the entire male gender. "It's all totally whack."

No kidding. I was learning that boys were ridiculous. And judging from his dad, some of them never changed.

She went on. "So I should have known better, but I made the same mistake again with Alex. He and his dad were literally slamming each other into the boards and everything. With pads, but still. So when I yelled at them to stop . . ."

I was already getting it. I'd been the second girl to "rescue" Alex. Now I knew why his dad's crack, *So how many mommies do you have?* really set Alex off.

"Anyway," she went on, "Alex didn't speak to me for a week. Not that it mattered because he was too beat up to skate anyway. That's why this time I left. I knew if I stayed and said something, Alex would just fight his dad even harder. But hey! You actually got them to stop! You did better than I did."

Yeah, but at what cost?

"But Alex hates me now. You should have seen his face."

She shook her head. "He doesn't hate you. He hates how you see him now. At least how he *thinks* you see him. And how he thinks his dad sees him. Weak." She laughed. "It's such a joke. People say women are the weaker sex, but *we're* the stable ones. It's men that are fragile. If *we* ran the world, there wouldn't be any wars. And nuclear weapons wouldn't even exist. No testosterone and ego and male pride making us act all crazy. We'd actually *talk* things out instead. But guys, they stuff all their emotions down . . . until it boils over and they punch someone. Or launch a missile."

My dad had said some of the same things. Evidently everyone knew these things but me. Lissy pushed herself up off the rock and stood in front of me. "Hey!" she practically yelled, her tone making it clear she was wanted to change direction. "Enough about Alex. Did you ask your dad about going to the party?"

Seriously? How could she be thinking about that now?

"Um, no. But there's no way Alex would want me to go now anyway. So . . ."

She just gave me a look. "Didn't you just hear me say, *Enough about Alex?* Besides, he'll be over it by then." She shrugged and made a face. "And if he's not, we'll take my car. He can drive by himself and think about Bridget in those ridiculous leather pants."

It was so obvious Lissy more than liked him, even if she wasn't admitting it to herself.

"Well . . . okay," I said, but evidently without much conviction.

"No, Katie, I mean it. Promise me you'll ask your dad tomorrow. He'll need time to think about it. And I'll help you fix things with Alex. K?"

I only needed a few seconds to make up my mind. "Okay. I will." And this time I meant it.

She reached out a hand to pull me up. We'd only walked a little ways when she said, "Jeez. I just remembered, you're testing tomorrow. All this wasn't very good timing. You going to be alright?"

Wow, I'd completely forgotten about testing. Actually, that was the only good thing about today. I'd been so focused on everything else I hadn't had time to get nervous.

# 37

Dad and I got in the car for our drive to Riverside just after six a.m. I hadn't had to go down the mountain for a doctor visit in years, so it was almost like seeing it for the first time. It was hard to adjust to all the cars. We hit the valley by seven but before we even got on the freeway, cars were backing up. There were hardly any trees and a lot of smog. I liked home more.

I still didn't have a fancy skating outfit, not that I needed one for testing anyway, but I did polish my boots. Dad and I didn't talk about testing on the drive. We'd been over it and both of us knew I'd do fine, even doing four levels in one day. The question was going to be off the ice. Dad had told me there would be about thirty kids testing and a bunch of parents there as well—so a different rink for the first time in my life, and a lot of people. I was hoping no one would see the mask and make a crack: *Hey, Halloween isn't for another month.*

"Hey Dad," I said, "Alex and Lissy invited me to a party."

Eyes on the road. "Um hmm?" Kind of, *Where is this going?*

"They saw one of their friends when you guys went to Salt Lake City, and he trains in San Diego now . . . Anyway, this friend, Alan, is having a costume party and Alex and Lissy already ordered costumes, even for me. Theirs have masks too, like mine would. So . . . um, I don't know. I'm just telling you they asked me."

A nod, then another. "So . . . are you asking me if you can go? Or just telling me they invited you."

Good question. "Ah, I don't know actually. I guess I'm just telling you so . . . so we could talk about it?"

"Okay . . . Well, San Diego is a long way away. Almost three hours. I assume this party is at night?" Bless him for not sounding shocked I even brought it up.

"I think so. But Alex's family lives there, so he said we wouldn't have to drive far at night. And they have an extra bedroom that Lissy and I could share."

We finally made it to the freeway, but the cars were now moving even more slowly. Where could so many people all be going?

He said, "So, when is this party that you may, or may not, want to go to?"

"The Friday after you all get back from Skate America."

"Okay . . . well, that's a month off. Why don't you think about it, and I'll call Alex's mom and learn more about all this, and we can talk about it later."

Wow, not an immediate "no." Part of me had almost hoped for one, just so I wouldn't have to keep thinking about it. I couldn't make the wrong decision if someone made it for me.

About thirty minutes later we passed the accident causing the slowdown. We got to the arena with only ten minutes to spare for check-in. I grabbed my skate bag and we hustled in and found the check-in table. The lobby was filled with skaters. Everywhere I looked there were clusters of kids or parents. Most of the skaters wore brightly colored sweatshirts or warm-up jackets from their skating clubs. I was about the only one without one.

Dad and I walked up to the elderly woman behind the check-in table. "Hi, my name is Katie Wilder. Is this where I check in?"

She'd been looking down at some paperwork and when she looked up she literally jumped in her seat and let out a startled little scream—loud enough that I think everyone in the lobby heard. Luckily my back was turned to them, and the hush behind me slowly turned back into the murmur of conversations.

"For heaven's sake," she said crossly. "You scared me half to death. Why are you wearing that mask?"

Didn't she have eyes? She couldn't see the scars? I could sense Dad by my side, getting ready to intervene, when I reached out my hand. "It's okay, Dad." And to the lady, "I'm sorry if I startled you. I have burns on my face and I just feel more comfortable with a mask on. So . . . Katie Wilder, checking in? I don't know where to go or what to do. Can you tell me please?"

Hopefully I'd removed any extra paths of conversation. She looked down at her roster, now looking embarrassed. "Oh . . . well, you're number fourteen. We'll call your name."

As my dad and I moved off, he sounded impressed, "Wow, that was good. Short and simple, and . . . so confident." Then gently, "Do you have to say that very often? It sounded like you say it a lot."

Although we were both within a few hundred feet of each other all day, every day, he wasn't with me when I usually encountered people, like the cabin guests or on the ice on public skate nights. Even the best and most involved parents don't really know the world their child lives in.

"Thanks, Dad. That's just what I say to get the whole thing over with and move past it."

Now that my back wasn't turned to everybody I was getting some stares. Some fleeting and some fixed. Either way, usually following it was a whispered question or comment to the people they were with. I could feel my dad bristling.

"It's okay, Dad," I said. "It's natural that people stare. I'm used to it. It doesn't bother me." A half-truth—I *was* used to it. And actually, I guess it didn't bother me that much. After a while it was just the norm.

"When did you grow up so fast?" A little crack in his voice.

The testing was actually easy and went faster than I thought it would. They quickly cycled through everyone testing for each level, gave the results, then moved to the next. I passed all four easily. On the way home before we hit the freeway I got a whiff of something delicious.

"Dad, what's that smell?"

He nodded toward to a place we'd just passed. "In-and-Out Burger. Best hamburgers around."

I was really hungry. "Dad, can we eat there?"

*"Really?"* This was like his dream come true. Not the hamburger, but seeing me actually go into a restaurant. That was the main reason I'd said it. That and the fact it *did* smell amazing. He said, "You mean, eat inside?"

"Yeah, why not? Can we turn around?"

Dad and I were super healthy eaters at home—no red meat, no deep-fried foods, virtually no sugar—but this was a delightful diversion. I had a cheeseburger—well, half of one—fries and a vanilla shake. Incredibly good. I could see why people ate at places like that, not that I was going to turn into a red meat carnivore.

But better than the food was Dad trying to hide his pride just sitting inside with me. I wasn't stressing that much, even eating. After so many meals with Alex and Lissy I'd found it was easier to just lower my face and tilt my mask up a little than turning away. Yes, someone could get a fast, partial view of my face if they were really intent on seeing it, but I wasn't going to let it bother me.

# 38

The testing at Ontario the next week went fine as well, and I was officially a senior skater and eligible to compete in local competitions, and go to Regionals as the first step toward Nationals. Beyond the concept of competing, I hadn't wanted to talk specifics with my dad. But now I was ready.

"Dad, I want to try to go to Nationals with you and Alex and Lissy. What do you think?"

We'd just finished my second session of the day and were stretching. My question got a big smile. "Honey, that'd be fantastic. I'd love to have you come along. I think you'll really enjoy it."

"No . . . Dad . . . I meant I want to go . . . to compete."

His smile shrunk. "You want to compete *this* year?"

"Yeah."

I thought he'd be thrilled, but he wasn't.

"Well," he said, "You know you've got to qualify through the NQS or a Regional, then a Sectional, to be eligible for Nationals . . ."

U.S. Figure Skating's route to be one of the best and compete at Nationals started at the National Qualifying Series. The top six advanced to Sectionals. Or, if you didn't make top six at the NQS, you could try again at one of the regional competitions around the country. The top four skaters advanced from each Regional to one of three Sectionals. And the top four again advanced to Nationals.

"I know how it works, Dad."

"I know you do. But honey, NQS is over, and our Regional is only what . . . a week away?"

"I know. I checked. It starts October second. I've got a week. And I emailed Barbara. She said we can get around the late registration. They've had two withdrawals and they only have thirteen senior ladies in our Regional."

Barbara had made it clear she wanted me competing and was doing all she could to make it happen.

Dad came out of his stretch and gave me all his attention. "I don't know what to say . . . If I'd known you wanted to start competing I wouldn't have taken on Alex and Lissy. But I did, and I have a duty to them. I can't disappear for days to go to Regionals and then again for Sectionals a month later." Then, his voice almost pleading, "You understand that, don't you? There's still so much they have to work on."

Team USA skaters like Alex and Lissy were exempt from having to go through Regional and Sectionals to qualify for Nationals, so they'd be training instead. If I gave them the chance, they'd probably insist on Dad going with me, and just practice on their own. But there was no way I'd do that to them, or put my dad in that position.

"I do understand. I know you need to stay here. . . but couldn't Uncle Robbie just take me? I don't have to have a coach with me, do I?"

He blew out a breath. "Technically, no, it's not required that you have a coach, but almost everyone does. And you should, especially since you've never done it before . . . Darn it, Katie, I just wished you'd told me before."

"I know, Dad, but you need to be here with Alex and Lissy." If he still had his staff of coaches like in the old days, things would be different, but he was a one-man show now. "But if I advance, and I think I will, then you'll be with me at Nationals, Dad. With all of us together. Don't you think that would be amazing?"

I could tell I almost had him. Not there yet, but leaning.

"Jeez, Katie, when you make up your mind to do something . . . You're just moving so fast."

"But that's good, Dad, right?"

He nodded. "Yeah, good." Then he gave me a real smile. "Very good." He said he'd talk to Uncle Robbie to make sure he was even available, then he'd talk to Barbara about the late registration. "You've already got some long programs to choose from, but we've never had a reason to do a short. We're going to have to come up with one . . ." he laughed, ". . . a week before you perform it."

When I told him I'd already been working on it, he laughed again and said, "Why am I not surprised."

"I didn't want to show it to you until I felt good about it, but I think it's ready. I'll show it to you this afternoon, okay?"

"Fine. Any other surprises you have for me? Like . . . you're leaving for college in a few weeks? Getting married . . . ?"

Focusing on testing had helped me not worry too much about Alex. Not that he made his feelings obvious. Even the day after his dad's visit, Alex at least *acted* friendly, like nothing had happened. We still shared a session every day and some meals too. But I could tell there was a wall between us, even if visible only to us. Lissy told me to just let time do its thing.

But . . . I didn't listen. It had been a week, and the wall was still up. I wanted my friend Alex back. I knew that my dad and Lissy knew so much more than me about how the world worked—particularly about boys and the whole weird thing about not talking about their feelings—but I had to listen to what my heart was telling me.

I always did my maid duties when Alex and Lissy were skating, so unless Bridget blabbed, they still didn't know it was me cleaning their cabins every week. But today I went to Alex's when I knew he was there.

When he opened the door I could see his eyes widen at the sight of me with my cleaning supplies.

"Hi Alex. Is it okay if I clean your cabin now?"

"What? Wait . . . *you* clean our rooms?"

For once, Bridget acting like I didn't exist had paid off. "Been my job since I was thirteen."

When he just stood staring at me uncomfortably, I said, "Ah . . . can I get started?"

"Oh." He moved to the side. "Um, Oh, sure. Sorry."

The cabin was too small for him to do anything but watch me work. I went straight to the bathroom. First I wiped down the counter and shower, cleaned the mirror, put in a full roll of toilet paper, then got down on my knees and scrubbed his toilet.

He literally groaned. "You know . . . you really don't have to do all that. I can do it."

I just gave him a smile and kept working. I moved to the shower, and again on my hand and knees scrubbed the floor tiles. I was putting my humility on full display. I moved over to his bed and stripped off his dirty sheets. *Are you getting this, Alex? Please, are you? I'm not shamed by you watching me at my most humble: cleaning your toilet, changing your sheets. No ego. I can be humbled in front of you, and not be ashamed. Because I have that much confidence in myself. And in you. Trusting you as my friend to accept me like that.*

"Be right back," I said. "I've got your clean sheets ready."

Alex was looking even more uncomfortable by the time I came back from the laundry room, my arms full of bedding.

"So," he said. "Um . . . you clean everybody's cabin? Lissy and Bridget . . ."

I was busy making his bed. "Of course. And the guests. Who did you think cleaned them?"

He tried to help by going to the opposite side of the bed, reaching for the fitted sheet, but clearly confused by the elastic edges misshaping it. I gently moved him aside so I could finish.

He said, "Ah . . . I don't know. I guess I never thought about it. I just didn't know it was you all this time."

I gave him a bright smile. "Oh. Well. It is."

I fluffed up his comforter and arranged his pillows nicely, then put all my cleaning supplies back in the caddy. But I didn't leave. I walked up to Alex and stood right in front of him. "I owe you an apology, Alex. I never thanked you."

He looked even more confused than when he'd first opened the door. "What do you mean? Thank me for what?"

"That day we went to the movies . . . and . . . what happened in the back seat. You and Lissy were so nice to me. The way you took care of me and made sure I was okay. It's just . . . I was so humiliated that you guys saw me like that. So . . . pitiful. I just didn't want to ever think about it again. About myself in that way. And if I thanked you, I'd have to admit it happened. But that was wrong of me . . . I should have thanked you."

"Oh, no. Katie, you—"

"And then when we got to the theater, and those two guys were looking at me that way? I was so scared I was actually shaking. But you were so brave. The way you stepped in front of me. Even though there were two of them, I knew I was safe. That you wouldn't let anything happen to me. So . . . thank you for that too. I should have said it then but . . . same thing. I was just embarrassed. I get tired of being so . . . vulnerable. So, thank you, Alex. Thank you twice."

I looked up at him, hoping. *Do you see? It's not weakness when friends are there for each other. Just the opposite—it makes us all stronger. It bonds us. Please, Alex, give me a sign you can see what I'm saying.*

For the first time ever, I saw his eyes well up. And I could tell he wanted to say something the way his lips parted—but just as quickly the moment was gone, and he blinked his eyes dry. He looked to the floor. "Um, well . . . Thanks for cleaning up my room."

# 39

No Alex or Lissy for dinner that night, and Dad had gone someplace with Uncle Robbie, so I ate standing at the sink then headed out on the ice. I only turned on the perimeter lights so the rink was barely lit. After a short hour of easy skating I laid down on the ice. My ritual. I never thought of it as praying when I talked to the ice. But God made the water that made the ice, so maybe it was. I just knew the ice heard me.

When I heard the door into the rink open I assumed it was my dad, but when the footsteps reached me, I looked up to see Alex standing above me. I smiled behind my mask.

If he thought it was weird to see me laying on my back in the center of a darkened rink he didn't say anything. Maybe I was strange in so many ways that it didn't even register with him any more. Without a word he laid down next to me, so closely that our bodies were touching side to side from our shoulders all the way down to our feet. The silence stretched into five minutes. Ten.

Finally he barked out a laugh and practically shouted, *"God, this is cold!* Seriously, how can you *do* this? And what exactly are we *doing* here anyway?"

I couldn't help but laugh too. I was sure that as ridiculous as I looked laying out there alone, it was doubly so with the two of us. But I wasn't about to tell him about talking to the ice, and I *absolutely* wasn't going to tell him that tonight I'd been talking to the ice about him. Even though his jacket was thicker than mine I could feel him shivering next to me.

But he stayed.

"So, Katie . . . I wanted to apologize for yelling at you when my dad was here. That was stupid. I know you were trying to help me. And you *did* help me. It's just, my dad really pushes my buttons. He's such an asswipe. He's a crappy dad and he cheated on my mom like three times and he . . . well, he's just an asshole. Anyway, it could have ended kinda badly for me if you hadn't stepped in. So . . . thank you."

We turned our heads toward each other at the same time.

"Do you forgive me?" he asked.

"I apologized to you first. Do you forgive me?"

"Katie, there's nothing to forgive. You—"

"Yes, there is. Do you forgive me?"

"Yes, I forgive you, Katie."

"Thank you, Alex. I forgive you too."

I could feel him shivering for another half minute before he finally shouted toward the ceiling, *"Okay then!* Now, can we *please* get up off the ice? *'Cause I'm freezing!"*


At our shared session the next day I told Alex and Lissy about my conversation with my dad about Regionals. They were thrilled I'd made the decision to go, but started to argue with me when I got to the part about my uncle taking me instead of my dad. But there was no negotiating that at my end. When they accepted it, I got to the subject of my short program, which was where I wanted their input. The idea of planning a program with friends my own age was just so cool.

"What are you thinking for music?" Lissy asked.

"I was thinking Rhianna, *This is What You Came For*. I like the way it builds and I've never heard anyone use it. What do you think?"

"Love it!" Lissy said, to Alex's agreement.

He said, "Can't wait. You're going to show it to us today?"

"Yup."

"And you choreographed it yourself?"

"Yeah, but I want your ideas, 'cause I'm not sure about a couple things."

"Our brains are at your disposal," Alex said, "such that they are."

Dad rotated our sessions into hard, medium and light days. Today was a light day. When it was finally time to wrap up the session with our short programs, Alex and Lissy did theirs, then it was my turn to show what I planned for Regionals.

There's a lot more to a program than spacing out some "tricks" to music. Each element needs to flow into the other with seamless transitions, as well as sync with the music, so a lot of thought goes into it. I was excited to show what I'd come up with.

I queued up Rihanna and skated it once through: triple Lutz - triple toe loop combo, triple Axel, flying sit spin, my step sequence, change of foot combination spin, triple flip jump, and ended with my layback spin.

"Nice!" Alex said, "You're going to blow them away."

Lissy nodded enthusiastically and said, "You know the transition into your sit spin? How about you do your Ina Bauer there instead? Yours is as amazing as Arakawa's."

An Ina Bauer was a glide across the ice, body sideways with the toes of your front foot facing forward and back toes facing backward. It was a pretty but common move, but years ago Japan's Shizuka Arakawa did it while bending over so far backwards her head was practically behind her knees. She won the gold in the 2006 Olympics, and that was the move everyone was talking about. I'd shown Alex and Lissy last week that I could do it too. Thank you, Ashtanga yoga.

I did the program again with Lissy's suggestion and everyone gave it a big thumbs-up. I felt one-hundred percent ready for Regionals, and had a few more days to get even better.

When we stretched afterwards the conversation was so natural and easy. I could tell Bridget noticed by the way her lips tightened. I'd been on the outside the past week, but actually so had she. Alex's dad's visit had been like an earthquake, shifting teutonic plates under the Ice Castle. And we were still sorting out the aftershocks.

When Alex had bailed on lunch with his dad, Bridget had evidently gone with Mr. Piezov instead. Then the following day he invited her to the Ducks game. I'd heard her car pull into the lot when she got back. At three a.m.

Like the rest of the world, Mr. Piezov thought Lissy was Alex's girlfriend, so he would have felt no compulsion to not make a move on Bridget. And evidently she felt the same as a few days later Lissy told me she'd heard raised voices from Alex's cabin and, "We never said we were exclusive," shouted by Bridget.

So maybe I shouldn't have been surprised that after our workout, when Bridget finished stretching Alex and Lissy, that she gave them her two-week notice. I was surprised she did it in front of me, but then to her I didn't exist anyway. She said she'd been offered a position as an Assistant Trainer with the Rangers. Even as an assistant, the NHL was a big move up for her. And I was guessing she was going to be very, very happy, a locker room full of buff hockey studs to take care of.

When she left, I was glad that Alex didn't look sad, instead almost relieved. By comparison, Lissy was fighting to keep a smile off her face. I could grin as big as I wanted since no one could see it. But it melted away when it hit me that Bridget might throw me under the bus on her way out the door: Peeper Katie. So I got up the courage and right then told Alex and Lissy about accidently seeing him naked right after he'd showered. I admit I didn't share the part about staying and staring—no need for *too* many details. The funny thing was Alex just laughed and could not have cared less. And Lissy laughed even harder.

She teased him by raising her eyebrows at me. "Well, you've seen more than me. We *have* to talk."

Suddenly Alex's eyes literally went wide. "Um, Katie? It wasn't a Wednesday or Friday was it?" He sounded almost panicked.

I told him I actually couldn't remember. It had been a while. When Lissy asked why it mattered he said, "Because on those days I take *really* cold showers." He looked at me, then Lissy. "Just so you know. *Ice cold* showers."

Lissy found it hilarious but I didn't get the joke.

# 40

Phoenix, Arizona would be a six-hour drive. Uncle Robbie and I could have flown, but adding my first airplane ride to my adventure would have been too much. So we were off in Uncle Robbie's cherry-red Ford Escape. This time, when everyone gathered by the car, it was me leaving and all of them staying. I was afraid my dad wouldn't be able to hold it together, but it was me who cried. It wasn't over missing my dad. It was seeing not just my dad, but two true friends, there to say goodbye.

It wasn't that long ago that having a friend and leaving the Ice Castle were things I could not have even imagined. And the trip even came with a present—Dad bought me a cell phone. I was going to spend the drive playing with it and practicing all the things Alex and Lissy had taught me.

I don't know how other people feel about long car rides, but I loved the drive to Arizona. Front seat, of course. Once we got out of SoCal, I couldn't fathom all the empty space, especially in the desert. I fell asleep for the last couple of hours and I didn't wake up until I felt the car braking when we exited the freeway.

I had my own room and Uncle Robbie was just down the hall. My first hotel room, my first mini-fridge, my first time getting room service. I texted home that we arrived, and felt very much the official teenager. My phone rang just a few seconds later. It was Dad, who asked about the drive and the hotel, then passed the phone to Alex and Lissy. They were all at the dinner table. It felt funny to imagine them all there without me. Regionals were broadcast on nbcsportsgold.com but on tape-delay, so they demanded a promise I'd call them the minute my scores came up. Dad didn't know any better so handed the phone to Bridget as well, who had to go along with the farce and wish me good luck in front of everyone. I smiled knowing how that must have killed her.

We left the hotel at ten the next morning and it was already almost a hundred degrees. There were three rinks in the arena, two for competition and one for practice. There were so many kids wanting practice time that I'd have to share the ice with ten other skaters. Uncle Robbie and I got there an hour before my scheduled practice time so I could register and check the place out. Skaters were everywhere, most of them in their skating club jackets, all proudly wearing their colors.

Skaters always joined their local skating club, so Alex, Lissy and I registered with the newly reborn Arrowhead Skating Club, which now had all of three members. But I was wearing my dad's old Ice Castle jacket. It hung on me, but it was so cool. I loved it. It even had "Wilder" embroidered on the back. He said Dorothy Hamill had been visiting once and had borrowed it one night when it turned cold. How amazing was that?

When we registered I got a lanyard with my name and picture on it. I'd dreaded sending in the picture, imagining people I didn't know looking at it and making mean comments—but Barbara had told me that for security reasons they couldn't let someone submit their picture with a mask on. I understood it, but didn't like it. At all. My dad and I had cheated a bit and took the picture in the worst possible lighting, dark with backlighting, which softened the horror. Still, I had been worried about walking around with my face visible in the picture until my dad pointed out that once I'd shown it to get into a restricted area I could just flip it over, which was what I did.

Still, I'd been dreading it being scrutinized every time I went into a skater-only area, but I knew there would be costs to my journey into the world. I just kept my eyes straight ahead when I had to show my lanyard, so I wouldn't see the person's reaction to my picture. Thankfully, none of them made me raise my mask—either kindness, or maybe word had come down from Barbara Felsdorf.

There was a food court that had nothing I'd ever want to eat, and a locker room where I'd never think of getting naked in front of people. There were also booths set up where skaters could get their hair and makeup done before they performed. I wondered at the reaction I'd get if I sat in one of the beauty chairs, took off the mask and said, "Do what you can . . . and maybe bring out my eyes a little."

Yes, even the disfigured can have a wicked sense of humor.

All three rinks were in constant use, with loudspeakers blaring and music coming from the two competition rinks. Every few minutes you'd hear a skater announced, and later their scores. The rinks were built for hockey so there were bleachers, but not too many people filled them, less than at our Ice Castle show. It looked like mainly family and friends.

I was wearing my first official skating costume. Lissy and I had fun looking at costumes online, but they were so expensive and it was hard to choose from a picture what would actually look good on me. So Lissy went through some of her old skating costumes and she showed me one she thought I'd like, white with lavender trim and a two-tier georgette skirt, which I loved. Lissy was a little more shapely than me but the same height, so it fit fine—that was one good thing about stretchy spandex. So I felt pretty blessed with good karma, wearing an outfit from Lissy Cake, and over it the jacket of David Cole Wilder, as loaned to Dorothy Hamill. The outfit was so loaded with talent, it could probably skate without me.

There was no fancy digital scoreboard like for national events. Instead, on a wall in the lobby there were sheets of paper, one for each level with the list of participants. The novice and junior skaters had all finished their short programs, so there were updated sheets posted for them. For now, the senior list was just a row of names. Still, it was a thrill to see "Wilder, Katie" up there. Years ago, Alex and Katie, and all my heroes like Michelle Kwan, Tara Lipinski, Jason Brown and Nathan Chen, had started at this level.

By random draw, the fourteen senior girls were divided into two groups of five and one of four. Then they did another draw to determine the order within each group. I would be second to skate in the middle group. I knew most skaters didn't watch their competitors before they skated, thinking that seeing either an unbeatable program, or one filled with falls, would get in their head, but I watched the first five girls skate.

What amazed me was how slow most of them were. It was like they were in slow motion, at least compared to Alex, Lissy and me. Their programs were easy compared to mine, yet most of them still made several mistakes. The highest score of the first group was only a 33.78, but none of these girls had been blessed with my ice time, or my father as a coach.

I got a tingle when I heard my group called. "Ladies senior skaters six through ten on the ice, please," came the voice through the overhead speakers. "Ladies senior skaters six through ten. Six minute warm-up."

I wasn't used to sharing the ice and couldn't do my full program, so I just tried to find clear patches to do an element at a time, although one girl in a pink costume and matching pink gloves cut me off twice. I recognized Pinky's outfit from when I was shopping online: a Jan Longmire. That was a two-thousand-dollar costume. We left the ice so the first girl in our group could skate. When she was done and waiting for her scores, I was next up so was allowed to take the ice alone while they reviewed her scores. That gave me about two minutes. I took deep, slow breaths to relax and went through my yoga mantras. My heart was beating hard and the adrenaline flowing. I told myself to welcome it. Embrace it. Channel it. Unlike our Ice Castle show, I felt no energy from the crowd. They were here for other people and most weren't even looking at the ice.

They announced the last skater's scores, then "From the Arrowhead Skating Club, Katie Wilder." I had no one there to applaud except Uncle Robbie, and thank goodness he didn't applaud all by himself. That would look sadder than complete silence. As I moved into my starting position, I talked to the ice: "*You are my best friend. Take care of me.*"

As my music started I disappeared into my own little world. I visualized myself as a flower opening when I came out of my starting position, then I accelerated quickly and into my triple Lutz - triple toe loop combo. I moved through my program effortlessly, savoring the Arakawa Ina Bauer when it came, and finishing with my three-variation layback spin, where after each eight revolutions I slightly altered my arm and head position.

Nailed it.

As I skated off the ice I saw everyone in the bleachers was watching and quite a few skaters had moved to the boards. Word spreads quickly when there is somebody worth watching on the ice. Or maybe it wasn't my skating. Maybe it was, "*Let's check out the freak in the mask.*"

But the applause seemed warm and real, and I'd gotten the crowd's attention. They announced my score: 57.21. That put me in first place by more than sixteen points, a huge lead considering the free skate was still to come tomorrow, but the score was still less than I'd anticipated. I'd be interested in seeing my protocols and see what the judges found. After my scores were read and I was taking off my skates, half a dozen giggling girls came up to me.

"Are you the Katie Wilder that trains with Piece of Cake?"

"Is your dad David Cole Wilder?"

"How often do you get to eat with Alex?"

"Do you make him smoothies every day?"

"What's his favorite sandwich?"

"Is he as yummy in person as on TV?"

"Lissy's hair is so beautiful. Do you know what shampoo she uses?"

And so it went. It was ridiculous, but it was also fun. It was nice to get the attention, even if it wasn't really me they were interested in. Alex was going to be thrilled to know the reach of his tweets and that thirteen-year-old girls desperately wanted and needed to know his favorite sandwich. The best part was no one asked me about my mask. I could see several of the girls' eyes take in the damage, but to their credit they didn't see a need to ask what they already knew.

I texted home with my scores and found Uncle Robbie in the stands. "Katie! You skated beautifully! Congratulations. I was going to walk over but you had a bevy of admirers around you."

"Actually they were just asking about Alex and Lissy, but it was fun. I want to watch the rest of the skaters. Would that be okay?"

He held up his Dean Koontz book as if to say, *Take as long as you like.* The best part of watching was seeing the joy most of the girls had in skating, whether they did well or not. Dad got so frustrated when someone's goal was to be a champion and anything less wasn't worth their time. You should skate because you love it.

The girl who had skated two after me made it a point to find me in the stands afterward. Her name was Tracie Quintano, and she was from right there in Phoenix. She had the second best score to mine, 53.77. She was a rule-breaker too and had watched me skate and we traded compliments. Her coach, Leslie Deason, came to sit with us and I was amazed when she told me Tracie had only been skating seriously for four years after switching from gymnastics. When Pinky strutted by, now in a designer warm-up suit, Leslie told me Pinky was the local star (actual name, Isabelle Bestagio), and had gone to Nationals last year and finished twelfth.

She was the last up in our group and I had to admit she was an excellent skater. Her program wasn't as difficult as mine, but she skated beautifully and got the highest score, 58.93, dropping me to second and Tracie to third. After the final group skated we were still the top three heading into the free skate tomorrow. The top four would advance to Sectionals so I'd come with a top four finish as my goal, but now that I was here, I realized I wanted to win.

# 41

The next morning there was another draw to determine the skating order for our long programs, but this one was based on where we finished after the short. Those with the highest scores would skate in the last group. Tracie, Pinky and I were all in the last group, so shared the final warm-up. Again, Pinky kept cutting me off.

The etiquette of sharing the ice was if you could see a skater was about to enter a jump, you gave them their undisturbed piece of ice and didn't make them pull up short, which was a good way to get injured. But that didn't stop Pinky from skating right in front of me several times right as I was getting ready to jump. I think she'd pegged me as her chief competition and was trying to unnerve me—that or she just didn't like me.

When I talked to my dad last night I asked him about my low scores. He'd said, "Judges don't want to give you high scores if you're a fluke. It might make them look bad later. Those judges have never seen, or heard of, Katie Wilder . . ." In the background I heard Alex, who must have been overhearing. He shouted, "Yes, they have! She makes my sandwiches!"

Dad didn't have any idea what nonsense Alex was yelling, so he tried to get his train of thought back. "Sandwiches? What? . . . Anyway. So for all they know, that was a once-in-a-lifetime performance for you. They're going to unconsciously reward the ones who have been there, done that. So you're laying down your rep starting now, every time you skate in competition. When they see you skate just as well in the free, they'll trust that you're really that good, and your scores will go up. But, hey . . . your score was high for a Regional! Cut yourself some slack. It's your very first competition."

I watched Pinky skate a perfect long program, receiving a 114.24, so with her short program score she was at 173.17. Tracie was in second with a 109.02, total 162.79. I made up my mind not to do the quad. I still didn't have the confidence to do it away from my home ice, and I didn't want to risk a fall. The reality was my program was already more difficult than the other skaters. No one had a triple Axel or a triple combo, or level four spins and footwork. My level of difficulty was actually higher than any of the other girls, so lots of points for the taking, especially at the Regional level.

As I circled the ice waiting for my name to be called, I went through my mental steps. I welcomed the adrenaline I could feel filling my body. I commanded it to make me skate faster, jump higher. And the crowd was bigger and paying attention today, so I pulled in their energy. As I took my ready position: *You are my best friend. Take care of me.*

Charlie Puth's opening piano notes sent me into my first move, going big with my triple combo, the triple Lutz - triple toe loop - double loop . . . perfect . . . savor the landing . . . a triple Sal . . . into my step sequence . . . stags and Russian splits transitioning into my triple toe. By the time I hit my last element—my layback spin into a sit spin—I knew I'd won.

And I had. For a Regional, it was a big number, 125.47, total 182.68, beating Pinky by nine points. I felt bad that I felt good about that.

I'd forgotten that there was a medal ceremony at the end until they called me over. They didn't do it at center ice like for big events. Instead, they had a podium set up in the lobby and we took our places there. I had the center position, Pinky to my right with the silver; Tracie to my left with bronze; and next to her, Alison Long with pewter. They took a photo of us, then positioned us for the traditional photo where the other girls would join me on the top stand and all hold up our medals up.

*I'd dreamed of that picture!*

But when we all put our arms around each other I felt Pinky pull away. At first I thought she was bitter over not winning—which maybe she was—but then she moved around to be next to the fourth-place finisher and put her arm around her. I got it then—she didn't want to touch the scarred, disfigured girl.

When Uncle Robbie and I pulled into the driveway the next day, I knew Alex and Lissy would be on the ice with my dad, but there was a homemade "Welcome Home, Gold Medalist!" mini-poster on the door, like I'd done for them—maybe a new Ice Castle tradition. I ran, not walked, through the apartment and into the rink. Alex and Lissy were in the middle of their short program and I stayed by the door to not interrupt them. I loved being a singles skater, but there was some-thing extra thrilling about the big throws and lifts that pairs could do.

At times, Lissy's body must have been twelve feet in the air. The fact that the moves were actually incredibly dangerous made them even more thrilling. The trust a pairs skater must have in their partner had to be off the charts. When they finished I ran up to the ice just as they spotted me. I was even okay that in our group hug my mask got pushed aside a little and some of my grosser body parts briefly flashed.

And yes, I was wearing my medal around my neck.

Later, when I had the ice to myself for my session, I told the ice about the competition—not out loud like when I was little, but I did communicate with my thoughts. I never told anyone—even my dad—that I talked to the ice. A trip to a psychologist I didn't want. But I really believed the ice had life, just like I believed that when a tree was chopped down to make a table, some life force remained in it. The ice had been my only playmate as I was growing up. There had been times I'd curled up in a ball at center ice, just to feel it embrace me. But whether I was crazy, or I knew something no one else did, the fact remained that I believed the ice gave me magical powers—and it was that belief that mattered.

I was the last one to get to the dinner table. Happily for me, Bridget was absent. Evidently she was off for a couple days to visit a friend in Los Angeles. Lissy had brought her laptop, which seemed to violate my dad's "no screens at dinner" rule, so we could focus on each other, but he didn't say anything.

Lissy asked me, "So, have you been online in the last few hours?"

"No, why?"

"Well, your favorite website just put up your picture." She started typing to bring it up.

"Oh, cool, the podium shot!" I said.

You'd have to go through several clicks to get to it, but FanZone showed the medalist ceremonies for all the Regionals. Pinky's move wasn't going to ruin it for me.

Alex laughed gleefully and Lissy turned the screen to face me. I could see the FanZone logo at the top of the screen.

She said, "Yeah, they have your award picture, but look. They did an article on you . . . right on the home page."

It took me a minute to make sense of what I was seeing. There I was, a photo of me—airborne in one of my jumps, arms nice and tight, no air to be found—right at the top of the page. And she wasn't joking. The picture took up almost the whole screen. The headline under it said: "Mystery Skater Stuns at Regional."

Oh, my God. I looked up first at my dad, then Alex and Lissy. Alex held up a hand to give me a high five, which I lamely returned. Everyone at the table was excited about it—everyone but me. I scrolled down to find the article.

> *Get ready for a shocker. Three-time Olympic gold medal-winning coach David Cole Wilder has a daughter. Yes, that David Cole Wilder, back from the dead after Juliette Francine's*

*stunning admission she wrongly caused his banishment due to her false allegations. Katie Wilder is fifteen, and has been skating since she was eighteen months old. Yes, eighteen months. Even the Russian skating factories don't start them that early!*

*Wilder stunned at the Southwest Pacific Regional with a 125.47 in her free skate, the highest score given at any of the Regionals this year. Considering the program's level of difficulty, and how cleanly it was skated, even that score could be considered low due to lower-than-deserved GOEs and component scores, but maybe even the judges couldn't believe a skater like this could come out of nowhere and dominate a Regional.*

*Besides her talent, what distinguishes Wilder is that she skates with a mask due to suffering severe facial burns. Until the arrival of Team USA's Alex Piezov and Melissa Cake last month to train with her father, it appears Wilder had virtually no contact with the outside world. There is no record of her ever skating in competition before. Her free skate included a flawless triple Axel, a triple Lutz - triple toe - double loop combo, and level four spin and footwork sequences. Her short program featured a breathtaking Arakawa Ina Bauer, rarely seen in competitive skating since its debut at the Torino Games in 2006.*

*Tracie Quintano, who finished third to Wilder, said that Wilder trains for six hours a day, seven days a week. Her off-ice regimen is just as demanding. Piezov and Cake declined comment, except a short statement from Alex Piezov that Katie Wilder "is not just an incredible skater, but one of the nicest people Lissy and I have ever met, and we are really happy that now the world will get to know her, too."*

*Katie Wilder's first-place finish earns her entry into the Pacific Sectionals starting October 12. She may have chosen to hide away the first fifteen years of her life, but all eyes will now be on this exciting new skater, who will no doubt soon be advancing to compete against the best in the country at Nationals.*

When I looked at my picture on screen all I saw was the scars around my mask. The curse of high definition, now frozen in eternity. I could just imagine people around the country looking at that picture and asking themselves how horrific was it under the mask. Yeah, I dealt with it face-to-face, but now people I didn't even know could look at me, maybe saying terrible things I'd never know about, making fun of me from thousands of miles away.

Lissy could read my body language. "Katie, I'm sorry. We thought you'd be thrilled. Everybody is going to be talking about you, and what a great skater you are."

"Isn't that a good thing?" Alex asked. "We didn't want to say too much when they called this morning until we knew what you wanted us to say. So we kept it really short."

"What you said was nice," I said. "Thanks."

I'm sure Tracie had looked at it like they did. When the reporter called her, she likely assumed I'd be thrilled that they'd asked her about me for the story. They must have called Pinky too, which would have bugged her to no end. At least that brought a tiny smile to my face.

# 42

I felt bad, like I'd ruined an evening everyone else thought would be a celebration. I wished I had a skill like poetry or painting, where I could create something amazing and put it out there to give people happiness and joy, but I could stay out of sight. I didn't have those talents though—my one gift could only be shared one way. I was saved from further beating myself up by Lissy's distinctive knock on my door.

"Come in, Lissy."

She came in and closed the door behind her. "Hey," she said.

"Hey."

Silence.

I finally said, "I'm sorry I left the table early. Sometimes I'm kind of a baby. I shouldn't be so upset about . . . just some article." The picture actually.

I was sitting at my desk, so Lissy took her usual spot at the end of my bed. She said, "Actually, I was thinking about it, and I think I understand. I mean, I've been doing competitions since I was seven. And at first I'd just get my name mentioned, then I started winning and maybe I'd get my picture in the local paper or online. It wasn't until I was sixteen and Alex and I started doing really well that we started getting a lot of attention. So I had like ten years to get used to it." She laughed. "You got there in one day."

She had half of it right. It turned out she had the other half as well. She said, "Katie, I know you worry about your face, but . . . sometimes do think you worry maybe . . . too much? Like with Alex and me. We're your friends. You know that, right?"

I nodded. "Yes, I know. Thank you."

"You don't *need* to say thank you. You're an amazing person. You are one of the nicest and funniest people we've ever met. Do you think when we think of you it's of a girl with scars on her face? We just think of our friend, Katie, a super cool, smart and funny, nice girl who also happens to be the best skater we've ever seen."

I could feel my eyes welling up. I knew that was how they saw me, and that was why I was so grateful for their friendship.

She said, "And we never talked about it, but you know I've seen your face . . . that night I put you to bed. And Katie . . . I'm still here. I consider myself lucky to be *your* friend."

She got up and stood right in front of me and reached around behind my head. "You don't need this anymore. Not around me."

And I let her untie my mask and gently pull it from my face. She looked me full in the face. I started to cry and she did the same. I don't know if she was weeping for the reality of what my face was, a burden she now shared as my friend, or for the trust I was giving her. I'd wanted to take off my mask in front of someone other than my dad and uncle for so long. To have someone love and accept me, who didn't have to because they were my family.

I didn't want the hug she gave me to ever end. I'd never felt so accepted, even more than from the applause after I skated. It was at that moment that I realized why I even wanted to skate in front of other people. Yes, I wanted to share something special that I created, but I wanted their acceptance in the only way I knew how to get it.

A knock on the door and Alex's voice came through. "Hey guys, can I come in?"

Lissy looked at me, my mask in her hand, as if to say, *It's okay.*

She was right. I braced myself and said, "Come in."

Alex walked in, then at the sight of me, quickly pulled up. A natural reaction. First just to take in that I wasn't wearing my mask, then the actual horrors of my face. But to his credit he found a way to push the shock off his face.

"About time," he said, and moved forward to give me a hug, not caring that my grotesque face was pressed hard into his chest and neck.

This was the best day of my life. I couldn't wait to tell my dad. Actually, I wouldn't tell him. I'd just walk out without the mask for my sessions tomorrow. An evil thought occurred to me. Bridget was due back and I'd do it even with her there. She was the type of person I wore the mask to protect myself from. And her from me. Seeing the real me would likely haunt her shallow soul for years.

The second best part of the day was the conversation Alex and Lissy and I fell into after the hug. We didn't even talk about my face. The subject was done. I could see Alex struggle, as anyone would, to keep his face neutral, but I loved him for the effort he was putting into it. Lissy had seen me the night she took my mask off, and who knew how long she'd stood above me as I slept, absorbing the real me. I knew Alex would need time too.

We talked about my program at Regionals and how good it had felt. This was the conversation I'd been so excited to have at dinner before seeing the FanZone article. I told them about what it was like for me to compete for the first time and how I'd gone into a zone for both performances, lost in my music and my skating.

Lissy said, "That *zone* you talk about? Do you know a lot of even the best skaters never get there? You are so lucky you can do that. You were born to skate, Katie. Don't let this attention coming your way make you stop competing."

Before they left, Lissy reminded me tomorrow was her fashion show. She'd be leaving after the first session to drive to Los Angeles so we were moving up our shared session to the morning. All the Olympic winter sports teams were taking part in a huge fundraiser for breast cancer prevention, and I assume to pique interest in the Winter

Games. So Lissy was excited about a day of glamor in L.A. with all the other big names in figure skating. The women from the U.S. Ski Team were going to be there too. It sounded like one big party and a lot of fun.

The next morning I didn't chicken out, although I came close. The relief of taking off my mask last night was gone, and it was going to feel like doing it for the first time all over again today. So for the first time since it was just Dad and me, I left my mask in my room and headed to the rink. Minutes later, I was on my stomach, face down, doing my stretches when I heard Alex, Lissy and Bridget come in. They called out "hellos" and I could hear them laying their mats next to mine.

At the exact moment I sat up from my stretch, Bridget looked at me and caught the new maskless me, full face. She was squatted down, getting ready to stretch Alex and Lissy, and when she saw me she literally cried out and fell backwards on her butt.

She popped up, embarrassed and angry. *"Oh my God!* Where is your mask? You're *hideous!* Have some respect for other people!" She looked to Alex and Lissy for support, but they just looked at her dumbfounded. Bridget wasn't wrong, I was hideous, but she'd let *her* mask slip, the inner evil overcoming the shell of beauty.

She was still making sputtering sounds of outrage when Alex said very quietly, "I think you should leave, Bridget."

She stood up straight. "Yes . . . yes. This has been very upsetting." She gave me a glare, then gratefully to Alex, "Thank you."

He said, "No, that's not what I meant." He walked with her to the door, where they talked for a moment, Lissy and I not bothering to hide the fact we were watching them. Then Bridget turned quickly and slammed the door behind her.

After Lissy had told me about the truth between her and Alex, I'd come up with *Operation Help Alex and Lissy.* Step One had been to

224

get Bridget to show Alex her true colors. It didn't matter as much now that she was leaving soon, but the sooner she was gone, the better.

He slowly made his way back to us. "I'm sorry, Katie. That was so wrong. I can't believe she'd act like that . . . She's not coming back."

I said, "You didn't have to do that for me, but thanks."

"Oh, but I did have to. That was . . . horrendous."

Lissy said, "It's no loss, Alex. We didn't need her sticking around another couple weeks. Besides, she was never a very nice person. You just couldn't see like everyone else."

He looked genuinely hurt. "Well . . . I guess I owe you an apology too. Why didn't you say anything? She was your trainer too."

Lissy gave a little shrug, but looked him in the eyes. "I was just waiting for you to see what's been right in front of you."

Was he that blind? Couldn't he see she was talking about herself?

# 43

Since today was set to be a light practice day, and Dad had some errands scheduled for the afternoon, Alex asked me if I'd like to go into town with him for lunch and to walk around by the lake. Both sounded scary and wonderful, so I said yes. Lake Arrowhead has two shopping areas. There is the official town of Blue Jay, where we'd gone to the movies, and about two miles away, today's destination, Arrowhead Village. It was a peninsula extending into the lake, filled with stores and restaurants. So I masked up and we headed out.

There was a grass median and wide sidewalks between the shops and cafes, and the lake wrapped around each side. But the nicest part was Alex holding my hand as we walked. I'm no dummy. I had no fantasies of him as a boyfriend. Some things were just impossible. He was holding my hand because we were friends, and he knew leaving the Ice Castle was still a major event for me.

Still, holding his hand was magical. It was something I thought I'd never get to do—walking and holding hands with a boy. I could feel his annoyance at all the stares-then-lookaways I got, but it was just human nature. We chose a restaurant with a nice view of the lake and got a table on the terrace. I felt amazingly adult and independent. We took chairs on the same side of the table so we could watch the boats bobbing in the harbor. I'd been trying to find the courage to say something to Alex and it was finally the right time.

"So Alex, when are you going to tell Lissy you're in love with her?"

That probably wasn't the lunchtime conversation he was imagining.

*"What?"*

"You heard what I said. When are you going to tell Lissy you're in love with her?"

He gave me a patient look. "Katie, Lissy is my best friend. If you mean that *kiss* thing, that was just us being . . . I don't know, just overcome with the emotion of the moment. We're not in love with each other."

I shook my head. "No. I see how you guys are every day, how you are together. You both keep saying you're best friends, like that's how you explain your emotions to yourselves. But it's not friendship . . . it's love."

He tried to laugh off the subject. "Hey, no offense, but aren't you the girl who told me she's never had a boyfriend?"

"Obviously."

"Well, don't you think just *maybe* you're misreading what you think you're seeing?"

I wasn't going to let him talk his way out of it. *Operation Help Alex and Lissy* wasn't going to be denied. "First off, that kiss you gave her? The most beautiful kiss I've ever seen by the way . . . You didn't fake anything. You *had* to kiss her. Your heart made you. But you chickened out afterwards and left Lissy hanging. How do you think she felt when you said you didn't mean it? Of course, she had to say the same thing."

Alex was no longer taking my words lightly. "Wait, did Lissy tell you that? What did she say?"

"She didn't say anything to me. But she did to you." When he looked confused I spelled it out for him. "She kissed you back! Even from a thousand miles away on a screen I could feel the love in that kiss. Are you telling me that you couldn't?"

He looked out over the water. "Oh, man, you just don't know—"

"Alex, can't you just trust me like I've trusted you?" He knew what I meant. I'd trusted them with the most private thing about me. "You and Lissy are the first friends I've ever had. Won't you please let me really be a friend? Can't you just be honest with me?"

He kept staring at the lake, but finally looked down and sighed. "Okay . . . Yes, I'm in love her. I've been crazy in love with her for years. And I finally kissed her. I just couldn't stop myself. But as soon as I did, all I thought about was what could go wrong . . . She's been the main person in my life for so long. What we have right now is . . . safe. But if we let ourselves fall in love and something goes wrong, what then? I'd lose my best friend . . . maybe my skating partner too."

At that moment I thought Lissy was the luckiest girl in the world, to have this beautiful boy loving her. "But you just said it, Alex. You said *if* you let yourselves fall in love . . . but you're both already *in* love. You're just denying it. Don't you think that could destroy you too?"

His head fell in resignation. "Maybe. I don't know."

"Isn't that why you were with Bridget? To take away any chance of being with Lissy?"

"You knew about me and Bridget?"

I just nodded. Eventually he said, "Katie, do you really think I should tell her? And that . . . she's in love with me too?"

Boys can be so dumb. "Alex, she told you that when she kissed you back. Seriously, that kiss didn't tell you what she wanted to hear? . . . For you to say you love her?" When he didn't say anything I said, "And she told you again yesterday, that she's been right in front of you, waiting, this whole time."

He looked almost panicked as I could see him replaying her words from yesterday in his mind. Finally, he collapsed back in his chair. "Oh, I'm so . . . oh, man. So do I tell her now?"

I think he was asking himself, but I answered anyway. "You can't tell a girl you love her right after you were with someone else. No girl wants that. But when the time is right . . . tell her. She's waiting to hear you say 'I love you.' And she'll say it back."

He stared out to the lake, thinking his own thoughts, but I had one more important thing to tell him. "Alex, don't you think this is what's missing in your skating?"

"What are you talking about?"

I really believed what I was about to say. "The way you guys are so technically excellent, but have a hard time presenting the emotion?" My dad thought it was their youth, but he didn't know about the scam romance like I did. "Don't you see? You're both so busy trying to *not* fall in love with each other . . . how can you show any real emotion on the ice? Doesn't that make sense?"

Not all pairs skaters were couples off the ice, but a lot of the best ones were.

He gave a long sigh. "Katie, wow . . . I think . . . I think you're right. We've been fighting it this whole time."

He leaned over and put his arms around me then shocked me with a gentle kiss on the side of my face—his lips on skin so creased and scarred that I thought he'd recoil when he realized his lapse in judgment, but he didn't. He kept one arm around me as we sat side-by-side and stared out silently over the water. I wondered how so many seagulls had found their way here with the ocean over a hundred miles away—and if they felt like me, so out of place but grateful to be here.

It was such a perfect moment, something I'd never thought I'd get to have. I didn't even notice when my head fell to his shoulder, but when I did, I left it there. It was so wrong of me but for just a moment I allowed myself the brief fantasy that this imperfectly perfect boy was mine and his love was for me.

"Katie, this is going to kill me. I've locked it away so long. Now all I want to do is tell her. But you're right, it's too soon after . . ."

Yeah, the never-to-be-spoken-of-again Bridget. I knew one thing—whenever Alex did decide the time was right, I bet I'd be the first person Lissy would come to tell, so I'd know when it happened. And I knew that hearing about it would be the closest I'd ever come to ever being loved like that.

# 44

The two weeks of training before Skate America were gone in the blink of an eye. Alex's feelings for Lissy remained his secret and their performances hadn't changed. They were still technically excellent, but lacking the maximum emotional spark. If anything, though, I thought they worked even harder than before, maybe picking up a sniff of Nationals, now just six weeks away.

They didn't replace Bridget. They continued their gym work in town every other day on their own, and my dad found them a new dance coach. He enlisted me to help with their footwork so for the first time they were joining me in our exercise room.

As I led them into the nondescript door at the back of they rink, they looked around with interest.

"Wow," Alex said. "I didn't even know this was here."

The room was about the size of half a basketball court with the wood flooring to match. Painted on the floor of one side of the room were the equivalent of long ladders. Ladder drills were not only great for cardio, but tied in directly with good footwork on the ice. There were four ladders side-by-side, allowing races between skaters from back in the days when the room was full of athletes. The yellow painted lines were faded after all these years, but the history of all the great skaters' feet wearing them down kept us from repainting them.

On the other side of the room were four workout stations with re-sistance bands hanging from different positions. I thought it was funny that I'd see ads for exercise classes featuring resistance bands like it was a new thing. My dad had been using a version of them since before I was born. He thought they were superior to weights and exercise machines. If you were used to big, shiny equipment and mir-rored walls it wasn't a very impressive room, and indeed, Alex and Lissy didn't look too impressed.

"So," I said, "Do you guys do any ladder drills?"

"Used to," Alex said a trifle dismissively, "when we were kids."

"Okay, well, my dad has me do them every other day." I moved to the bottom of one. "You've probably done ones like this . . ." I quickly moved my way up and back, dancing lightly through the squares like you see in football drills.

Alex didn't answer. Instead he danced up the ladder as quickly as I had. "Yeah," he said, "we've done it. So you do a lot of that?"

"Oh, not that one. We stopped doing that one when I was six. I do them like this now." This time I did a much more intricate footwork pattern, not just moving forward but side to side, sometimes spinning as my feet moved, similar to what I did on the ice. Then I did another one even more complicated. Then another. "Like that."

Okay, I was showing off. I admit it. But I loved footwork, and my dad told me to push them. He needed their footwork to jump from level three to level four. We both thought Alex could handle getting humbled again. Besides, they didn't have a lot of time so it was now or never for this season.

"That," Lissy said, "was *amazing*." The room didn't seem like such a joke to them anymore. She turned to Alex. "Did you see what she was doing? Can you imagine doing those patterns on the ice. We'd kill it."

Alex said to me, "Do them again."

And I did. Lissy was right. The patterns were intricate, but basi-cally tied in with what a skater could do on the ice.

He shook his head. "Man, you've got maybe the best footwork I've ever seen. And I don't just mean in here. Judges would love that."

My dad was a nut for footwork. Partly because he felt it was one of the most overlooked arts of figure skating, but also because it was something you could work on off-ice; there was only so much time you could spend in skates. It was, as Alex was saying, also a way to enhance your scores.

His competitive juices were flowing. "Teach us that first one," he said, as he took a position at the bottom of a ladder, and Lissy went to another.

So we went through one of the patterns slowly a couple times, then a bit faster. They really were remarkable athletes and picked it up faster than I would have thought possible.

"Race?" Alex asked me.

"Absolutely! Up and back four times." They nodded, ready to have some fun, but wanting to win, too. "Okay, go!"

I didn't go easy on them and was done when they were just past halfway through. Not exactly a fair competition—I'd been doing these drills for hours every week for more than ten years.

"My God," Lissy said after we'd caught our breath. "What other super powers do you have?" Then to Alex, "I think our training has a big hole in it."

"No kidding," he said. "That was embarrassing." But one look at his face told me there were no ego problems this time. His grin was real and he truly wanted to learn. "We want a rematch in a couple weeks . . . and we want you to teach us how to do that."

Was he kidding? I'd pay to do it. "Deal."


It was ten days to my Sectional. I had my two routines down, so I didn't feel any pressure, even though the skill level of the other skaters was going to go way up—the top four from each of the nine Regionals. The only problem since Sectionals had been more unwanted attention. Our local newspaper, *The Mountain News*, did an article on my success at Regionals, and a few bigger newspapers from down the mountain called as well. Maybe having the highest score of all the Regionals would be a story regardless, but I was afraid it was all about the mask.

Dad said I was "in training" and couldn't talk, my lame way to try to keep my name out of print. Regardless, there had not only been the FanZone story, but one in *Skating* magazine, and talk in a lot of the skating blogs. It was both funny and sad to read people ask and answer questions about me, when none of them knew what they were talking about. One "insider" said I was so focused on skating that I'd never attended school, and I spent so much time training that I'd never learned to read. But I have to admit, most were complimentary and almost fun to read. There was a real nice one on Golden Skate. I wasn't as bugged about the whole thing as I was before. The media was just one more person staring at me.

Since I was now an experienced world traveler (one trip to Arizona), I'd thought about going to Detroit with Alex and Lissy for Skate America, but decided to stay home again. I didn't want to cancel the group lessons, and two cabins were scheduled to turn over while everybody would be gone. Plus, they'd be flying there and I wasn't ready for that.

Skate America was a Grand Prix event and would be on network TV. The Canadians wouldn't be there, but another of The Big Three would, defending world champions Romanov and Ludnova, as well as a young pair from Italy who had won their first event of the season a few weeks earlier. Just as Alex and Lissy were striving to catch up to The Big Three, others were trying to catch up to Alex and Lissy.

I gleefully plopped into one of the big easy chairs off the kitchen to watch the two-hour broadcast, treating myself to a half-bar of chocolate so dark no one could call it candy. Alex and Lissy's short program was excellent; no mistakes and better emotion, a 68.92. The best part was seeing no sign of anxiety from Lissy: the first elements had been flawless. Romanov and Ludnova topped them with a 70.91. The rising Italian pair, Rizzo and Bertolucci, had a catastrophe on their third element, their triple throw. Bertolucci lost her center axis and came down at a terrible angle, her knee bending on impact in a way knees weren't meant to be bent. Every skater watching knew it was either an ACL or a meniscus, but either way, they were out for the season. Just like that, with one bad landing, a season's effort was washed away, their chance to compete at the Olympics gone.

The next day, everyone knew the competition was the U.S. vs. Russia. Romanov and Ludnova drew the first skate, and they turned in not just a clean program, but a touching one as well. Skating to the haunting theme from *Schindler's List*, the camera captured all their emotions. If Oscars were awarded for the night, they would have won one. Their score was almost unmatchable: 147.17; total 218.08. Alex and Lissy skated a glorious program with no indication they'd made significant changes only a month ago. It was technically even more difficult than the Russians', but didn't match their emotional artistry: 144.56; total 213.48. So Alex and Lissy finished second once more, but it had been close and they had to be happy with their performance.


After dinner on their first night back, as Alex and Lissy were getting up to go, I heard Alex ask Lissy if she'd like to skate with him. His eyes caught mine just before they went out the door, saying, *Tonight's the night.*

I didn't have actual experience, but in the movies when a boy told a girl he loved her, the first thing she did was tell her girlfriends. Lissy had other friends, but as far as I knew none of them knew the secret of the fake romance, so I was the only one she could tell that it was finally real.

I was in my room alternating between doing my homework and watching the clock. By eight o'clock I was thinking, *How long does it take to skate around and tell a girl you love her?* Finally, just before eight-thirty, I heard their voices approaching, and laughter. I could tell that they stopped at my door—and yes, I moved right behind it to listen. I heard what was clearly a kiss. Then Alex, softly, "I love you," before I heard his footsteps fade away.

Yes! After Lissy's tap on my door I forced myself to wait at least a split-second before I opened it. She was beaming as she came in.

"Oh, Katie . . . I'm so happy. Alex finally told me he loved me . . . That he's been in love with me since we were fourteen." She gave me a huge hug. "And he told me you gave him the courage to finally tell me. You're absolutely . . . you're the best friend I ever had."

I should have been embarrassed that tears came like a faucet. I mean literally. I practically needed a bucket. I was so happy for her, and so happy for me. And it was kind of like the movies, but better, as she told me everything, from what he said to how he touched her and the look in his eyes. When she left she practically skipped out the door.

It was a perfect note on which to go to bed, but instead I moved my mouse over my Gracie Gold mousepad—showing her mid-air in one of her gorgeous jumps in her glorious 2016 season—and clicked to my least favorite Facebook page—the one I couldn't stay away from. Once a month or so I tortured myself with a visit to update myself on the new life of Gloria—aka my mother—and her twin daughters. My secret sisters. Half-sisters actually.

I was too young to remember anything about my mom leaving— I'd only been three. But I did remember a couple years later when Dad had told me she wasn't coming back. It wasn't until I was twelve that I got curious. You can find about anything online if you know how, and I'd become pretty proficient. It had started with accidently finding the divorce papers in Dad's desk. It showed my mom going back to her maiden name: Larsson. The two "ss"s were a blessing when I did my search on Facebook. She was easy to find. Her account was private so I went to YouTube to find out how to see someone's page when you were not a Friend. It was simple.

So there she was. Sweet mommy.

She was still beautiful, like the old pictures I'd seen. She was in her late-forties now but she looked in great shape. Now her name was

Gloria Larsson-Benning. The "Benning" came from her second husband, a dentist. They lived in Portland, Oregon. The identical twins, Jeanette and Maddie, were clearly their pride and joy. Every post and picture was of them. Easy to love a beautiful child evidently. They had Gloria's light blond hair, fair skin and athletic build. They looked like young clones of their mother. My mother. I wondered if I had a face if I'd look like them. They were beautiful. Blue eyes like me. They were nine years old.

And they were skaters.

From the pictures, they looked like they might be pretty good ones too. I guess I shouldn't be surprised Gloria got them into skating, and was probably coaching them. With her new name, and never getting successful enough to be famous from her skating, no one would think to identify her with my dad. Or me.

She'd never made any effort to contact Dad or me since she left, almost thirteen years ago. A while after the story broke about Juliette, I asked Dad if he ever heard from her. I thought maybe she'd say she was sorry she'd doubted him, if that was even why she left. I always knew her leaving was really about me and the lifetime burden she imagined. Since I knew her daughters were active in skating, I thought maybe she'd see the stories about my success at Regionals and contact me. Not that I wanted her to, but I wanted the chance to reject her as she'd rejected me.

At least I think that's what I wanted to do.

# 45

For pretty much all of my life, my least favorite day was my birthday. It's not that I didn't want to grow older, but it was a day when it felt painfully obvious that I didn't have any friends. Kids were supposed to have birthday parties with friends and kids from school. But no friends, no school, Dad's parents were deceased and Uncle Robbie never married. So I always told my dad I didn't want a party. It would just put a spotlight on my loneliness.

My sixteenth birthday was going to fall three days before I was to leave for Sectionals. After years of ignoring my birthday to the extent of pretending it didn't exist, things were different now. Dad and I were making lunch when I said, "Dad, can I have a party this year?"

My "no birthday" rule had probably been harder on him than me so he beamed. "A party? I think that's a great idea."

The difference was now I had friends. Good ones. Maybe to some people having two friends would not be a big deal. Actually, I would have been thrilled to have just one. One is really all you need. And I had two.

Alex and Lissy had just walked in. Alex said, "What's a great idea?"

"Having a birthday party for Katie," Dad said.

"What else would we do?" Alex said. "Of course we're having a party. I assume we *are* on the invite list." Funny, funny. They knew they were my only friends.

Lissy said, "Katie, when is your birthday?"

"Tomorrow."

*"Tomorrow?"* Alex looked at Lissy. "Nothing like giving us a lot of time to plan it! How are we going to even have time to get you some presents?"

I said, "I don't want any presents. Really." I wanted to say they were the world's biggest presents but that would be disgustingly gooey.

"Do you want to have it here?" Dad asked. "Or do you want us to go someplace?"

I already knew where I wanted to go. "Okay, so I know where I want my birthday, but everyone has to promise not to laugh." I got their solemn nods and said, "I want to go to Chuck E. Cheese."

It was famous for the preschool and grade-school set, with arcade games, those little rides you drop a quarter in and move up and down on a horse or something, and a wall of Chuck E. Cheese and his mechanized animal pals that played instruments and sang songs. Oh, and there was pizza.

Both Alex and Lissy started laughing. Couldn't be helped, promise or not.

"Chuck E. Cheese?" Lissy asked. "Really?"

"Where a kid can be a kid!" Alex shouted, their motto from the TV commercials.

My childhood fantasy had always been to go to a party at Chuck E. Cheese. It didn't even have to be my party. It could be anyone's, but of course the party invites hadn't exactly been rolling in. I said, "I just always thought it'd be a fun place for a party, and I've never been able to go. So . . ."

"Actually," Lissy said, "I've never been to a Chuck E. Cheese, so it'll be fun."

Alex said, "I've never been to one either." Then to my dad, "So coach, what time is this party tomorrow? I say we cancel all our practices and make it just a birthday day. After Chuck E. Cheese, we can take Katie to get that back tat she's been talking about."

Dad laughed. "I don't think so. Katie, what time would you like to go?"

"There's one in San Bernardino, so we could do our morning sessions then go. We could eat lunch there and play some games for a little while, then come home. Would that be okay?"

So the four of us were off by eleven, visions of Chuck E. Cheese on the horizon. Well, down the mountain, actually. I'd asked Uncle Robbie to join us, but he said something about dozens of screaming little kids and "When pigs can fly."

It was a Tuesday, so I thought it wouldn't be too busy, but it was full of happily screaming kids, most of whom were aged in single digits. We found a table and ordered a couple of pepperoni pizzas and it came with a bunch of tokens. Dad divided them up and Alex, Lissy and I headed to the games. I could tell even they were having fun—everyone liked arcade games. I'd never played one, so I watched Lissy and Alex just so I could see how the games worked and where to put the token in so I wouldn't look like a complete moron. After we'd all played a few, Alex moved us to Skee-ball. There was a whole wall of them so we got three in a row. I yelled for my dad to join us and he took another one. It was so much fun. When Lissy won the first game, I said, "Let's play again." And we played four times. When I finally got the high score I was ready to try something new. So much for telling myself that I'm not competitive.

We shot mini basketballs, and played air hockey and pinball. The games spit out a string of little tickets that you could bring to a prize counter. A little boy came up to me and asked me how many tickets my mask cost. I thought he was being sarcastic at first, but he really seemed to want one.

When we saw the pizzas had been delivered to our table we sat down. Dad had ordered pizza to be delivered at home a few times, so I'd eaten it before, but never in a restaurant. "Isn't this the best pizza you ever had?" I asked.

Everybody laughed, even my dad. "No," Alex answered for the group. "One day we'll take you for some real pizza. But this is good too."

Chuck E. Cheese and his animatronic band came to life and they started singing, *If You're Happy and You Know It.* Alex grabbed my hand and pulled me up to dance, then Lissy did the same with my dad. Even the pre-schoolers looked on us with pity, but that was okay. As we left we made one little boy very happy, giving him all of our prize tickets, although I did keep one for my memory book.

But my best birthday present came on the drive home. We were just heading up the mountain when Alex said to my dad, "Hey coach, you remember we've got Jordan coming out to film us tomorrow, right?"

Jordan? Film?

I cut in before my dad could answer. "Wait, Jordan as in Jordan Cowan from On Ice Perspectives?"

On Ice Perspectives was my favorite on Instagram and YouTube. And probably the favorite of every figure skater and serious fan. Jordan was brilliant, a USA team skater turned cinematographer. I could still remember when he broadcast his first videos a few years ago. Instead of filming a skater's program from off-ice as was the norm, he was right beside them, circling around them, giving you a perspective like you were literally on the ice skating next to them. It was completely different than the usual TV broadcast and gave people a better idea of how amazing figure skaters really were. He travelled all around the world, and didn't even charge the skaters to film them. He did it because he loved doing it. I was proud to be one of his Patreon supporters to keep his videos going. Well, it was my dad's credit card, but it was my idea, so I'm giving myself the credit.

I must have been gushing because Alex laughed. "I thought we told you. Yeah, he's coming tomorrow morning. You'll like him. He's a really nice guy."

Lissy gave Alex a nudge. "Hey, you know you're big-time legit baby if Jordan is coming out to film you."


So even though it was the day after my birthday, I'll always think of the day On Ice Perspectives came to the Ice Castle as my best birthday present ever. Of course, he was there for Alex and Lissy, not me, but still.

He must have met up with Alex and Lissy in their cabins because they all walked in together. When he said hi to me I could tell he was shy, which was endearing considering he was so young to be so famous at what he did, not much older than Alex and Lissy. But what I really liked was that he looked right into my eyes, like the mask wasn't there.

At first I was surprised to see him get on the floor and stretch with Alex and Lissy, but then I realized he was a skater too, and what he did on the ice had to be incredibly physically challenging. Not just keeping up with world-class skaters, but doing so while skating with a full camera rig.

After they all did a warmup on the ice, Jordan skated off-ice to watch as Alex and Lissy went through their usual work with my dad until they were ready for him. After a while he walked over to me.

"So Katie, Alex and Lissy tell me you're the world's best kept secret as a skater. They said you can skate circles around them."

Wow, they'd said that? I found I couldn't meet his eyes. "Uh, hardly. But thanks. I mean, that's nice of them."

He didn't say anything, just gave me his shy smile, and we stood silently for the next forty minutes watching Alex and Lissy. Normally I'd feel totally uncomfortable standing next to someone I didn't know, but he had a good vibe, like one of those people who walks outside and wild animals come up to eat out of their hand. At least, that's the weird image that popped into my mind. Maybe all great photographers have that and that's why they get such good shots; they generate complete trust.

When my dad gestured that they were ready, Jordan grabbed his camera rig and went out on the ice. The four of them conferred for a minute, then Jordan positioned himself just a few yards away as Alex and Lissy took their starting positions. He had an odd contraption for his camera, a bar about two feet wide with grips on each side, and the camera positioned above it.

If Alex and Lissy were distracted by him as they skated, it didn't show. To the contrary, his presence seemed to inspire them to be at their best. It was incredible to watch as Jordan constantly moved around them, seemingly reading their movements before they made them. He was a performance all by himself. Sometimes he got so low to the ice he was almost on his knees, other times the camera elevated above him, all while in constant motion.

When the program was over they all exchanged high-fives, knowing they'd all just combined to do something pretty cool. I'd assumed it would be like a movie with several takes, but evidently it only took one. Or at least with pros like Alex and Lissy it did. They all skated over to me.

Lissy said, "Jordan is joining us for lunch, then he's going to stick around for the afternoon session."

Oh, so evidently he wasn't done with them after all.

"To film you," Alex said.

*What?*

To me, being on On Ice Perspectives would be bigger than being in an Oscar-winning movie. I didn't belong in either of those worlds. I turned to Jordan.

"Are you serious? But I'm not famous. No one even knows me."

My few minutes of anonymous fame as Little Skater Girl was a fun memory, but I hadn't known anyone was filming me at the time. Jordan filming me would be terrifying. Plus, watching him buzz around Alex and Lissy looked pretty dangerous, to both him and the skater.

Jordan gave his shy smile. "I think Alex and Lissy know a great skater when they see one." Then playfully, "You're not saying they are lying to me, are you?"

No. They wouldn't.

And I was. A great skater, that is.

But the idea of being on On Ice Perspectives was too much. That was for the elites. He'd filmed Hanyu, Medvedeva, Papadakis and Cizeron, Kwan and . . . too many to list. Me? I hadn't even been to a Sectional yet. Besides, it would be embarrassing. Some of his videos got millions of views. Mine would have about a hundred, that is if my dad, Alex, Lissy and I all watched it about twenty times each. So I thanked him for the huge compliment, but said no.

But somehow by the end of lunch, my no had become a yes. Alex talked about how well I'd done at our show, and Lissy chimed in that it would be good to help establish myself as a skater now that I was competing. Plus, I told myself the reality was that Jordan would likely never post it anyway. He was probably just doing it to be nice. Still, I found myself wanting to impress him.

When we were back in the rink, Jordan said he'd just watch until my dad and I felt the time was right. And if I changed my mind and didn't want to film, that was cool too. No pressure.

So when the time came, I thought I was ready. But . . . no. There were four false starts. I kept seeing Jordan out of the corner of my eye and popping my first jump. It wasn't his fault. All mine. Every other skater in the world was used to sharing the rink with other skaters as they practiced, and tuning out the distractions. I'd spent my life skating in an empty rink.

But if Jordan was getting tired of my amateur act, he didn't show it. To the contrary, he kept joking with me and seemed to have all the time in the world. Thankfully, on the fifth take, everything changed. Suddenly he wasn't a person filming me, but someone lifting me up. It sounds corny, but it was like those movies where a fashion photographer is snapping away and saying all those corny things, *"Beautiful, baby! You're perfect! Yes! Yes!"* Jordan didn't say those things, or anything at all actually, but somehow I felt his encouragement, and his joy in what we were doing. Together. When I landed the quad, I could feel him celebrate with me, and over and over again, through each element of my program. And when I finished, it felt like I'd shared it with someone, which I guess I had.

It was later, as Jordan was leaving, that I asked when he'd send us the videos. But it was Lissy who answered with a laugh.

"He won't. We don't get to see them. Not in advance anyway."

Alex said, "Yeah, we get to see them when the public does. He's kind of famous for that. You'll know it's up because your phone suddenly explodes."

That was the only sad part of the day. I would look forward to seeing Alex and Lissy's video when Jordan put it up. I knew it'd be great. But I was bummed to know that would mean I'd never get to see mine, since I couldn't imagine him ever posting it.

# 46

Sectionals were in San Francisco. Uncle Robbie and I drove again, although he'd suggested we fly instead. He said it was going to be even further than Phoenix, and instead of desert, there would be a lot of traffic. But the first time I braved airports and airplanes, I wanted my dad with me.

Even though I'd done fine with just Uncle Robbie at Regionals, Dad wanted me to have a coach for Sectionals. When he'd found out one of his old friends, Tom Zakrajsek, was going to be there with two of his skaters, he talked him into filling in as my coach.

I already knew about Coach Z. He coached at the Olympic Training Center in Colorado Springs, and his skaters had won a bunch of National Championships. Not to mention I was always seeing him on TV in the Kiss and Cry with his skaters at the Olympics and Worlds. Talk about finding someone over-qualified to babysit me! He was known as a jump specialist, so of course I decided that I'd play a trick on my dad and come home telling him that his friend told me my jump technique was all wrong.

Uncle Robbie and I checked into our rooms and I went straight to bed. Tomorrow was going to be just a practice day, and Dad had arranged some ice time for me at a local rink since the Sectionals arena could only give each skater twenty minutes of practice time. The short programs would be the following day.

The next morning, Coach Z called to set up meeting at the arena. He said he'd be in a Broadmoor Skating Club jacket with two skaters a few years older than me, a boy and a girl, and they'd be waiting right by the check-in table. I thought that was pretty modest of him, as if I didn't already know what he looked like from seeing him on TV.

Walking into the arena, it felt like a blown up version of Regionals, a lot of noise and action with countless skaters milling around. The lower levels were already competing and I could hear the announcer giving the scores of the boy who had just finished.

One thing was different the second I walked in—how people were looking at me. Living behind a mask made me an expert at deciphering looks, and these weren't the usual, *There's a weirdo in a mask.* Every skater here was like me, addicted to nbcsportsgold.com, FanZone and *Skating* magazine, and checking out the big skater sites like Golden Skate. So a lot of the fish in this very small pond recognized me as the girl in the mask from the recent articles.

From the moment I entered the rink, quite a few of the skaters who walked past me either nodded and smiled, or actually said "Hi." With some it was even, "Hi Katie," as if they knew me. Before I even got as far as the registration table where I saw Coach Z waiting, a young boy in a Seattle Skating Club jacket ran up and asked me for my autograph. My first autograph! I was almost disappointed when he realized he didn't have a pen or even anything to write on. He ran off saying he'd be right back. As he moved off, I could tell that one leg was a little shorter than the other, causing him to run awkwardly.

Coach Z was as friendly as I'd hoped and he introduced me to his two skaters, Tiffany Zhong and Nick Woolard, eighteen and twenty, both senior skaters like me. They had never been to the arena before, but Coach Z had, so he gave us a tour. It sounded like he'd been in every rink in the country. He even told us which food to avoid at the snack bar if we ate there. I thought, *Now that's coaching.* We walked over to the wall where they had sheets up with every skater listed for their level. I saw they'd done the draw and I was number three out of twelve. There would be two groups of six and I would be third in the first group, Also in my group was Tiffany, who would skate last. Tracie Quintano from Regionals was in the second group, as was Pinky. Tracie and I had done a lot of texting back and forth since we'd met, so I was looking forward to seeing her again.

Coach Z said they were headed out to lunch and asked me along. The novelty of someone asking me out to eat with them had still not worn off and I was thrilled each time it happened. Tiffany, Nick and Coach Z all seemed super nice and I decided I wanted to make an effort to get to know them better. That, and the fact I was starving and my twenty-minute session wasn't for two hours, helped me to say yes.

Before we could finish our lunch plans the little boy came back, not just with a pen and paper but with two other kids, a boy and a girl about his age, all in their matching club jackets. I learned his name was Erik, he was ten and was a singles skater at the juvenile level. He told me his two friends wanted autographs too. Evidently I was big in Seattle! They told me this was their first Sectional and they'd competed earlier today.

Seeing me signing some autographs must have sent a signal because soon there were half a dozen skaters my age around me. At first it was almost scary to see a bunch of people heading toward me, particularly having spent every night of my life until recently dreaming of people doing just that, but wielding clubs. But I was slowly pushing that dream into my past. Besides, everyone moving toward me had a smile, and it's hard to be frightened of people wearing sequins. Some just said congratulations, saying they'd seen the video of my Regionals free skate, and others wanted to talk serious training and skating. No questions about Alex and sandwiches. A bunch of them asked for pictures and I said that'd be great. And it was. Maybe being a teeny-weeny bit famous wasn't a bad thing.

"So, Miss Popularity," Coach Z said when the group had wandered away, "unless you have another autograph session scheduled, the rest of us are hungry." He turned to Uncle Robbie. "We invited Katie to join us for lunch. Would you like to come along?"

Uncle Robbie passed, thrilled I had someone to eat with so he could head back to the hotel and read his book. Coach Z knew a good restaurant and we had a great lunch talking about what anyone over-hearing would have thought was a foreign language, all skater-talk about "flutzes," "back outside edges" and "cheated landings." It was interesting to compare training and conditioning ideas with Tiffany and Nick. This was Tiffany's second year as a senior skater and Nick's third. Like me, it was her first trip to Sectionals but it was old news to Nick, who had made it to Nationals last year and finished tenth. Re-gardless how Tiffany and Nick did here at Sectionals, Coach Z would be at Nationals as he coached one of the best male skaters in the country.

We headed back to the arena for our practice sessions. On-site practice was always important because it gave us a chance to get a feel for the ice, which was different in every arena. Double good news for me: I liked the feel of the ice, and Pinky was not in my session.

I traded phone numbers with Tiffany and Nick before I left for the hotel, and that night Tiffany sent me a link to some really funny skater bloopers. Lissy texted me a picture of her and Alex with comically sad faces with the message, *Missing you! Good luck tomorrow!* I was starting to understand why people were always looking at their cell phones.


I got a great night's sleep, did a full stretch in my room, and was in the arena at noon. Tiffany's and my group was set to skate at 1:30. I found Coach Z and Tiffany in the skater area. Tiffany and I got in our twenty-minute session with our group and our short programs would start as soon as the Zamboni finished cutting the ice.

I knew the juveniles had done their programs that morning so the final results would be posted. I wanted to see how that boy, Erik, and his two friends had done. I found the *Juvenile Men's* list and found his name. Unfortunately both he and his friend had finished outside the top four. I moved to the *Juvenile Ladies* sheet and tried to remember the name of his girl friend, but stopped halfway down. There was a name I never expected to see—desperately didn't want to see.

Larsson-Benning.

Not once but twice: Larsson-Benning, Jeanette and Larsson-Benning, Maddie.

My half-sisters.

That meant my mother was here.

# 47

I didn't even know what happened, but suddenly Tiffany was by my side.

"Are you okay?" she asked. "You just kind of went down to your knees in slow motion."

No, I was not okay. "Oh, thanks. I'm okay. I just got a little dizzy or something."

*"Dizzy?"* Tiffany said. "Katie, you skate in less than an hour! I'm going to find Coach."

"No, no. I didn't mean it like that. Really I'm fine. See, I'm standing."

She didn't look too sure but let me walk away by myself. I had to know if Gloria and her girls were still in the arena. They lived in Portland, so they'd been at a different Regional than me, but Gloria had to have seen the articles and know I'd be at this Sectional. I couldn't go on the ice not knowing. I didn't even know if I could go on at all.

I walked quickly through the arena, scanning the bleachers at each rink. No sign of them. Their long programs were done so there would be no reason to stay. Maybe she knew her girls skated hours before me, and thought she could keep an eye out and avoid being seen. She had no idea I'd been cyber-stalking her, so she didn't know I knew her last name or that she had kids, much less that I even knew their names and what they looked like. They were probably flying back to Portland now, her thinking I'd never know they'd even been here.

"Are you alright, Katie?" It was Coach Z. Tiffany must have sent him over.

I made my voice bright and confident. "I'm fine, Coach. Really. I was just sort of composing myself." But I'm sure I looked zoned out, still staring into the stands.

"Hmm. Well, okaaay." He guided me over to a sofa. He pointed to my hand and said, "May I?" I had no idea what he meant but I nodded. He took my wrist in one hand and with his other he pressed two fingers against my wrist. He was taking my pulse. Now that he made me think of it, I could feel my heart beating wildly. I must have looked pretty shaky if he could spot that just looking at me, or maybe he had that coaching mind reader skill like my dad.

He nodded. "Um hmm . . . okay . . . so, you were relaxed when you walked in . . . how about we get you back there. Okay?" Close your eyes . . . that's it . . . just breathe in and out . . . as slowly and deeply as you can . . . good, just like that . . . and with each breath imagine you are breathing in calmness . . . you can literally see it in front of you like a magical fog . . . As you deeply breathe it in you know it will slow your heartbeat . . . you can feel it slow down right now with every . . . single . . . breath . . . And feel how your body is so relaxed that you are practically melting . . . your head is falling to your chest . . . your arms are too heavy to lift from your lap . . . It's so delightful where you are right now . . . a place of perfect peace . . ."

I think ten hours went by, with his voice a gentle metronome. Okay, maybe not even ten minutes. He said, "I'm going to count to three and I want you to open your eyes, and when you do, you're going to be calm and full of energy and ready to skate your best. Ready? One . . . two . . . three."

The funny thing was that when I opened my eyes, Coach Z wasn't even looking at me. He was casually looking across the room. I know I didn't just imagine the whole thing. I said, "That was really, um, relaxing. Thanks. Was that hypnosis?"

He laughed. "Hypnosis? I don't know how to do hypnosis. That was just helping you relax. Nothing more complicated than that."

Well, I was relaxed, and my brain was on target again. Gloria had left and I could focus again. I'd deal with thoughts of her later. I moved to a clear spot of floor to stretch just as Tracie Quintano walked up.

"Hey," I said, "I was wondering where you were."

"Yeah, I just got here. I'm in the last group and I get nervous waiting, so I wanted to get here as late as I could. I saw you're in the first group. Hey, skate like last time and win this thing!"

"I wish. You too. I've got to do a quick stretch. How about you?"

"Yeah, great."

She and Tiffany had met at another competition last year so they already knew each other. When our stretches were done I put my skates back on and Tiffany and I headed to the ice for our group's six-minute warm-up, then waited while the first two skaters did their programs. As soon as the second one finished, the ice was mine. The judges were running about two minutes between skaters to get the scores in, so I had that time to loosen up. Usually a skater goes to the boards for a last word with their coach so when my time was about up I skated up to Coach Z. But my dad must have told him I had my own way to prepare mentally, so like a good coach he just gave me a confident nod and let me do my thing: deep breaths, feel the adrenaline, welcome it, use it to make me stronger, faster. Take the energy from the crowd and—

From the speakers overhead: "From the Arrowhead Skating Club, Katie Wilder." Coach Z gave me a gentle but confident fist bump and I skated out to center ice and took my ready position. As I waited for my music, I talked to the ice: *You are my best friend. Take care—*

And then I saw them.

The twins. My sisters. As identical twins they were easy to spot, sitting in seats just behind the judges' table. But where was Gloria? I came out of my starting position and slowly turned and scanned the room. I could hear my music start—but I couldn't stop looking. If the girls were here, she had to be as well. So I just kept turning, looking. Even over the music I could hear the discomfort and murmur of the crowd as they watched me, still at center ice. I could see the judges looking at each other too. Even if they wanted to, judges couldn't stop and restart the music unless there was a technical malfunction. A malfunctioning *skater* didn't count. Ten seconds must have gone by. Maybe more. Finally, my brain said I had to skate. If I could just push off, my muscle memory would take over.

I was finally moving. I had up to two minutes and forty seconds to complete my seven elements. The only way to catch up to my music was to skip my first element and start with my second—my layback spin. Somehow I did it, but I couldn't stay stationary and felt myself traveling across the ice. Next up was my Ina Bauer transition, but I just stroked across the ice instead. When I got into my flying camel spin, I managed it. For my triple flip I under-rotated and fell. Up quickly. My triple Axel was next, fell again. I think I made it through the footwork sequence—I just knew I was still standing. My final element, the change of foot spin . . . done. Then even though my music had stopped, I did the first element I'd skipped, my triple Lutz - triple toe combo. I doubled them both, managed to save the landing on the first, fell on the second. I'd get a point penalty for going over my time, but still get points for the last jump.

At first there was only silence, then an attempt at pity applause. I skated with my head down to the gate. My score would be minuscule, what few points I'd earned reduced even further by the negative GOEs. I wished I could skate straight to the hotel and skip talking to anyone and avoid hearing my scores. There was no Kiss and Cry at Sectionals like at big national tournaments, so I just put on my guards and walked to the designated area. There was nothing to say so Coach Z just gave me a hug. I'm sure he was asking himself why he volunteered for the job of filling in as my coach.

They announced my score: 16.92. I would not be joining Alex and Lissy at Nationals. But that wasn't my main concern at the moment.

I looked to where I'd seen the twins but they were gone. I had to know if Gloria had been here. I turned to Coach Z.

"Is there any way I can see who a skater's coach is?"

It was an unbelievably strange question to ask at that moment, but he'd just heard I'd semi-fainted, then watched me turn aimlessly out on the ice when my program started, followed by completely mangling my performance, so he probably figured he'd better just humor me before I had a seizure or something. He pointed out a lady in a USFS blazer with a clipboard.

"She could tell you."

He stayed with me as I walked over to the lady he'd indicated. He said, "Susan, hi . . . can you check something for us please? We'd like to know the name of the coach for . . ." He looked to me to fill in the name.

"Jeanette and Maddie Larsson-Billings. They're sisters, in the juvenile division."

She flipped through some pages on her clipboard. "Their coach is Linda Notarangelo. Is that all you needed, dear?"

Thank God, not their mom. Maybe that meant she hadn't come. "Um, is there any way to know who they came with, like their mom? Or just their coach?"

"Well, as a matter of fact I do know since I was at the desk when they checked in. It's hard to forget seeing identical twins. They checked in with their father. Is . . . is there a reason you're asking? Is anything wrong?"

"Oh, no. I just . . . I thought I might know them. Thank you."

So maybe Gloria had stayed away, knowing I'd be here, whether to save herself, or me, I'd never know. Certainly she'd never told her daughters about me. What would she say? *See that deformed girl over there? I'm her mother but I abandoned her when she was three because I couldn't handle how hideous she was.* And she probably kept the secret from her husband too. So her daughters must have asked their dad to stay and watch the girl in the mask they'd heard about, not knowing I was their half-sister. Part of me actually wanted to know them, but it was never going to happen. It would have been easier not to know they existed.

So even from a thousand miles away, Gloria had found a way to hurt me again. A ruined performance, Nationals gone, and the knowledge I had sisters I could never know. And it'd get worse when I got home because I'm sure Coach Z would be sharing all this with my dad, right down to me asking about the girls with that last name, and he'd figure it all out. In my dad's desire to protect me, he'd make it worse.

I turned to Coach Z. "Is there such a thing as skater-coach confidentiality? You know, like with doctors and lawyers?"

"Ah . . . *noooo*. What is it you don't want me to tell?"

"Well . . . I know my dad is expecting you to tell him how I'm doing and everything, which obviously isn't very good. But . . . would it be possible for you to forget the questions I just asked that lady? I mean, go ahead and tell him all about how badly I skated, but just not about . . . that." Then, "Pleeeease?" I admit it. I was playing the *Pitiful Girl in the Mask* card.

He was obviously worried about me and concerned he didn't know what was going on. But he smiled and said, "Actually, I'm so forgetful I already forgot the names you were asking about, so there's nothing to tell."

I gave him a hug. "Thanks, Coach."

*"But,"* he said, "you know he's going to see the video of your program, and I do need to tell him about you feeling a little faint, or whatever it was, before you skated. I don't think you were honest saying you were fine, because something is clearly wrong. In fact, I want to talk to your uncle before you leave, okay?" He was speaking kindly, but firmly.

That was fine—that I could handle. I just didn't want the ugly specter of Gloria raised, which I was afraid would hurt Dad even more than me. We walked over to Tiffany, who was a skater away from getting on the ice. Neither she nor Tracie had any idea how badly I'd skated yet. They all had their earbuds in and were keeping their eyes off the monitors so they could stay in their mental cocoon. I gave Tiffany a thumbs up and went to sit with Uncle Robbie in the stands. I could tell he was really alarmed and didn't seem reassured when I told him I'd been feeling weak and then got overcome by the moment. A lame lie but it was the best I could do.

My shot at Nationals was gone, but I was going to be Tiffany and Tracie's loudest supporter. When they were done, Tiffany had a 55.28, putting her in second. Tracie had skated well but fell on her triple Lutz. She was sixth with a 41.73. Pinky had the top spot with 58.16. The girl holding down the fourth spot for Nationals had 44.34. By far the lowest score was my 16.92. I headed back to the skater area knowing that by now Tiffany and Tracie would know my score, and that some kind of disaster had occurred.

I felt almost embarrassed to join them. Tiffany's parents were there, along with Tracie's and her coach, Leslie, as well as Coach Z. Eight pairs of eyes filled with pity when I walked up with Uncle Robbie. I was no longer the highest-score-in-years-at-Regionals phenom. I was back to just being a freak in a mask. But when they saw me walk up, Tracie was the first to give me a hug. "Oh, Katie, what happened?" And there was more of the same from Tiffany. I gave the same lame excuse that I'd given to Coach and Uncle Robbie.

I didn't want to go back to my room and order room service and brood about having blown my opportunity. Without giving myself a chance to weigh the risk of rejection, I did something I'd never done before: I asked the girls if they wanted to go out to dinner. In my recent entry into the world, I'd been asked out to eat several times, and always took it as such a compliment, but I'd never been the inviter. I wished Uncle Robbie wasn't standing right there to see it if everybody said no. Rejection is so much worse when it's witnessed.

But I got quick yeahs, and Tiffany's dad knew of a good local place. When we got there we were told there were no open tables big enough for us all, so we divided up into a kids' table and the adults, which was actually more fun. I was so grateful to have these girls with me. For them to hang out with me after that embarrassment meant a

256

lot. I did my best to focus on them instead of me—and the fact they both had solid shots to go to Nationals, especially Tiffany sitting at number two.

But Tiffany said, "You know, Katie . . . you've just got to be in the top four to get to Nationals, and fourth right now is a forty, so you're twenty-four points behind. For any other skater, you'd be out of it, but if you skate your free like you did at Regionals, it's possible you could still make it."

"Yeah," Tracie said. "I know the competition here is tougher, but you could do it."

I really appreciated what they were saying, but from what I'd seen of the other top skaters, it didn't seem possible. Regardless, I'd be doing my best even if I didn't have a chance.

When I was back in my room I saw the missed calls and texts from home. The video of the performances probably wouldn't be available on nbcsportsgold.com until later, but Dad, Alex and Lissy would have all seen my score posted, so they had to be freaking. I knew if I called my dad it would be a difficult conversation so I texted him:

> *Dad, I skated really badly today. I'll tell you about it when I'm home. Tomorrow I'll skate like Katie Wilder. I love you. Please don't be upset that I don't want to talk about how badly I did yet. Let me fix it myself. I'm okay. Really. Love you.*

But Lissy, I did call. I had to spill to someone and she was my best friend. She answered before the first ring had finished, as if she was staring at the phone waiting for me to call. I told her everything: that my mother wasn't really dead, about finding her online, my half-sisters, seeing them here. All of it.

Lissy knew what to say and what to leave unsaid. I felt so much better talking to her, although maybe part of it was just sharing the secret. Secrets could be exhausting. And Lissy must have felt the same way, because she told me hers—the secret I already knew about her father's fake "devotion" to her. That had to be unbelievably hard, to admit she'd been sending herself flowers and faking calls from him—but she did it for me, to let me know all of us have our share of heartbreak.

I guess we all wear masks.

# 48

As I got ready to take the ice for my long program, hearing my name over the loudspeaker as next up to skate was becoming a Pavlovian moment: "From the Lake Arrowhead Skating Club, Katie Wilder." It was the trigger to acknowledge and welcome the adrenaline. Channel it into speed and power. As I did my quick warm-up laps I heard the applause and pulled in their energy and good wishes. And from no-where my mind pulled up some Greek mythology: *You are a Phoenix, risen from ashes, stronger than the fire that tried to consume you.* I moved into my starting position and spoke to the ice: *You are my best friend. Take care of me.* Words I'd never finished yesterday.

There was no repeat of yesterday. I moved through my routine flawlessly, my mind finding that still and perfect place. My opening triple Lutz - triple toe - double loop was huge and perfect. Then I landed the Axel like a marshmallow. Not doing the quad was not even a question. And when I hit it, landing as gently as if on a pillow, the feeling was so glorious I wanted to hold the landing all the way around the rink. Then even though it was only a transition, the Ara-kawa Ina Bauer drew huge applause. When I finished I knew I'd skated the best I ever had in my life. My score was tremendous: 139.24. With its level of difficulty, it actually could have been an even bigger number, but the memories of yesterday's skate was surely on the judges' minds. So my total was 156.16. I'd moved ahead of the two skaters who'd skated before me, but the better skaters were all ahead. All I could do was wait.

Tracie was in the second group. She skated well but stumbled on one landing and fell on a triple, 90.31; total 132.04. She was in third but her score wasn't big enough to stand up to the skaters still to come. I hope she felt as good as she deserved though. It was her first year with her new coach, who'd done a great job with her. I could see her going to Nationals next year.

Tiffany and defending Sectionals champ, Pinky, had drawn the two and three spots, with one skater after them. By the time Pinky finally took the ice, with two skaters left to follow her, I was in second. She skated a clean program and deservedly took over first place: 118.81; total 176.97. I was knocked to third.

Even though her success could mean my failure, I rooted with all my heart for Tiffany. She was the opposite of most of the skaters here, who focused so much on technique they forgot about presentation. Tiffany did a great job of sharing with the audience that she was having fun. She two-footed a landing and turned one of her triples into a double, but everything else was clean: 106.94; total 162.22. She moved to third and knocked me down to fourth.

One skater to go, Tammie Runyon. She took the ice knowing she had to skate a great program to get into the top four and make Nationals—and she felt the pressure. She under-rotated on her first two triples and popped the third. There was no way she'd make the top four.

Fourth was mine and I was going to Nationals.


I was still floating on my *Nationals* high when one of the USFS officials came up to me with a letter-sized envelope.

She said, "Katie, one of the skater's dads asked me to give this to you. He was very clear he wanted me to give it to you only after you competed." She smiled. "I'd guess this is the first of a lot of fan mail you'll be getting."

I thanked her and took the envelope. There was no indication who it was from, just my name in precise printing. The letter got hot in my hand as I realized there was only one "skater dad" who would want to contact me. Luckily, Uncle Robbie didn't think much of it and I told him I needed a last trip to the bathroom before we hit the road.

I closed myself in a stall and ripped open the envelope. My eyes skipped to the bottom and saw it was signed *Alan Benning*.

My mother's new husband.

Father of my half-sisters.

> *Dear Katie:*
>
> *I know you have chosen to not reply to any of your mother's letters. As sad as this makes her, she understands, and she will continue to respect your privacy. But I am begging you to reconsider.*
>
> *She told me about you, and her life then, as we began dating, one of her twelve steps. We have not told our daughters, and now she's ready to, but not without your permission.*
>
> *I beg you to allow her, and your half-sisters, into your life. No one could hate her more for the mistakes she made than she hates herself. There is still a hollow spot inside her. Maybe there is in you too.*
>
> *In case you threw away her letters, I'm listing all the ways to reach her below. A letter, an email, a call - but please accept her reaching out to you.*
>
> *Alan Benning*

The letter was shaking in my hands.

*My mother's letters?*

What letters? She'd never sent me any letters. But clearly she had. And he mentioned my half-sisters as if I knew about them, so she must have told me about them in one of the letters. And what did he mean about *twelve steps*? My dad might know.

Wait.

Why hadn't I got any of her letters? There could be only one reason. The person I trusted the most.

My father.

# 49

"Uncle Robbie? Tell me about my mother."

I'd been able to hold my questions for the first hour of our drive home, intending to save them until I saw my dad, but my guts felt like they were going to bust open.

He'd been rambling on about my great skate and going to Nationals. If he was aware I wasn't listening he wasn't letting on, probably just guessing I was tired.

"What? Your mother? What . . . ?

And then he seemed to notice the letter I was clutching tightly in my hand. I hadn't let go of it since I'd read it.

"What's in that letter, Katie?" he asked. "Something about your mother?"

I didn't answer. Instead, I opened the letter and read it to him. Then I said nothing, forcing him to speak. But instead, all I got was a sad sigh and silence.

"Uncle Robbie, it says I haven't responded to her letters. But I never *got* any letters." I felt the intensity rising inside me. "Has she been writing to me? Did Dad take the letters before I could see them?"

I felt bad for putting him in the middle, but if he knew, he was equally to blame.

"Oh, Katie . . . this is something you should talk about with your dad." I could hear the anguish in his voice but at the moment I didn't care.

I wasn't going to be put off. "No. If you knew about it, you're responsible too." I could hear the anger in my voice and it scared me. "I want to know. *Now*. Tell me."

He was quiet so long I thought he was just going to refuse to speak all the way home. Maybe he was fighting a battle within himself about what was the right thing to do. When he finally spoke, the words came out torturously slow.

"Yes. Your dad does have your mother's letters. She sent some right after she left. Then none for a long time. He told me they started coming again recently."

I couldn't believe it. Since right after she'd left? *Twelve years ago*. "So why didn't Dad give them to me?"

Uncle Robbie turned to look at me and we locked eyes for a moment, the desert highway empty of cars to worry about. "You have to talk to your dad about that, Katie. Whatever he did, he did because he loves you."

It didn't sound like love to me. I could tell I'd pushed Uncle Robbie as far as he would go, about Dad anyway.

I said, "Okay. But why does the letter say something about twelve steps? What does that mean?"

I could imagine Uncle Robbie telling himself I could just google it, so why not answer. He said, "There is a recovery process that alcoholics and drug addicts go through. It's called the twelve st—"

"My mom was an *alcoholic?* Or a *drug addict?*"

"What I was going to say is, I don't know all the steps, but they involve doing things like admitting your problem . . . your addiction . . . and being honest with others about the mistakes you've made."

"You didn't answer my question. Was she an alcoholic? . . . a drug addict?"

He took a minute. "Her problem was alcohol. Your mom . . . was a very, very nice person. A person who . . . had some serious problems and had a tough time solving them." He took a deep breath. "And that is the last I want to say on the subject. This is a conversation between you and your dad, Katie. Please."

And those were the last words we spoke for the next six hours.

When we pulled into the driveway I grabbed my skate bag and headed inside. No "thank you" to Uncle Robbie for all his time in taking me to San Francisco. I was mad at the world and the only people I could strike out at were those closest to me. On my way inside I paused only to rip down the "We are going to Nationals!" banner taped to the door.

I could hear my dad's voice from the kitchen, excited. *"Katie?"*

But I went straight to my room and shut the door. Six hours of silence on the road and I hadn't come up with what to say to my dad. He knocked and came in, arms out to hug me and a big grin on his face. A father-daughter dream come true. Nationals. A celebration sixteen years in the making.

"Honey! Congrat—"

"Where are the letters, Dad?"

His arms dropped, as did his smile.

"What? What letters?"

"My *mom's* letters. The ones she's been writing *since I was three.*" I realized the letter was still in my hand. Had I clutched it all the way from San Francisco? I held it up like evidence. "I know about them, Dad."

Lissy must have seen me drive up because she appeared in my doorway, but she looked confused at the sight and sound of me. I'd never spoken to anyone this way, especially my dad. But I literally hated him at that moment. The emotions I'd held in for the long drive were coming out and I could feel my body shaking.

I said, "Lissy, please . . . will you go away?" I didn't want a dad or a friend at that moment. I wanted the letters. And I wanted to suffer alone for what I'd missed.

My anger broke and I started to cry. Both Dad and Lissy moved toward me but I literally shouted at them to stay away. I could tell I was scaring them, so I forced myself to speak calmly.

"Lissy, I'm sorry, but please, can you come back later? I just need to be alone right now. And Dad. I don't want to talk about it. I just want you to . . . Give. Me. My. Letters."

Lissy had to be so confused. She'd walked in to celebrate us all going to Nationals. Instead I was between furious and hysterical and talking about letters she knew nothing about. But she backed away out of my room, hurt on her face, but worry too.

Her pain didn't come close to matching the pain on my dad's face, but I didn't care. He still hadn't moved.

I said again. "Please bring me the letters from my mother. They belong to me. You have no right to keep them from me."

I heard a sharp intake of breath from the hallway. Lissy, still there, out of sight.

Dad finally turned away and I slammed the door behind him, even though Lissy was in the hallway. I threw myself on the bed and sobbed. All the emotion I'd held in on the long drive home was coming out. Or maybe it was a lifetime without a mother.

I heard the door open but didn't have the strength to even lift my head. I felt a hand on my back and knew itas was Lissy. That's a friend. Knowing when you're needed, even when being told to go away.

"I'm sorry," I sobbed, not raising my head.

She laid next to me, wrapping her body around me, like she was protecting me. Thankfully she said nothing. It took me a minute to realize she was crying too. For me, and maybe a bit for herself too, for the mother she lost and the father who couldn't find the time for her.

I heard Dad clear his throat from the door and I felt like I was coming up from under water. His hand held the envelopes. He walked up to the bed and started to sit down.

"No," I said. "Just give them to me and go away. I want to be alone."

At least I wasn't shouting anymore. But he could hear the resolution in my voice, and without a word he handed me the letters and turned away, the remnants of his pain staying behind.

Lissy stared at the envelopes in my hand. "Do you want me to leave?"

I felt bad, but actually I did. I wanted to be alone. Somehow she knew it so without waiting for me to answer, gave me a hug and softly closed the door behind her.

Leaving me with my letters.

I spread them in my hands. There were four. I looked at the postmarks and as Uncle Robbie had said, there was one dated just months after my accident, and another a few months after that. Those envelopes were neatly sliced open, the letters read by my father. Neither one had a return address. There was a gap of twelve years before the next letter was sent, just a month ago, then another one two weeks later. Both were still sealed. I didn't know why my dad opened them twelve years ago but not now.

My hands were shaking as I pulled out the first letter.

# 50

I felt like I was opening the history book of my life. But I was disappointed.

It took me only a few sentences to realize she must have been drunk when she wrote it. It was rambling and almost incoherent. It was filled with self-hate and guilt. It read more like a confession to a priest than to a letter to a young child. It was beyond painful to read. The second was more of the same.

As mad as I was at my dad, I could understand him not giving them to me, at least not then. But there was no excuse to hide them for so long, especially the new letters. I wanted to rip them open but I forced myself to get some scissors to do it neatly. These would not be the drunk ramblings of the early letters.

The first envelope held three sheets of lavender stationary filled with beautiful handwriting.

*Dear Katie,*

*I've started this letter so many times, over so many years. I just can't find the words. Maybe this one I'll finish.*

*I can't believe you are about to turn 16, and I can't believe that I am not with you. Making it hurt all the more is the knowledge that I caused our family to fall apart, and that I let you go. No, I'm lying to myself. I didn't let you go. I did some-thing much worse. I left you. But it wasn't your mother that left you. It was a damaged human being that didn't know what she was doing.*

*Knowing your father, he has likely given you a kind view of me and not spelled out my every mistake. Yes, there were plenty. Even before I met your dad, I had problems with alco-hol. My father was an alcoholic so maybe there is a hereditary trait. If so, be smart, and never take that first drink. I mean it. But I'm making excuses if I blame heredity. It was my fault I refused to admit I had a problem for so long.*

*When I got pregnant with you I managed to stop. You don't know how much love that took. But I was secretly drinking again the day after you were born. It's amazing what an ad-dict can hide from the world, even from a husband. The biggest wakeup call was when I got in a car accident with you in the back seat. You were eight months old. Luckily, no one was hurt. But I'd been drinking and I lost my license. I also lost your father's trust. And maybe a big piece of his love too, putting you at risk. That led to my first stay in a clinic.*

*I had a relapse and was back for round two, and it took, at least for almost a year. The final straw for your dad—and even for myself—was the afternoon he came home to find me drunk while I was caring for you. Actually, NOT caring for you. I was passed out and he found you wandering in the woods behind the rink. Even at age three you were smart enough to put on your own jacket and carry your little chair to reach the doorknob. You were looking for help because mommy fell down and didn't wake up.*

*He was so furious, and left with you to cool off. He called one of my girlfriends and told her to come and get me—that he didn't want me in the house drunk when you and he came back. I don't blame him one bit. I was a danger to myself, and more importantly, to you.*

*Katie, here's the hard part if your dad has not already told you. That was the day you had the accident. Do you see, Katie? It was all my fault. I wasn't driving the truck that hit you, but I might as well have been. You were out sledding with your dad to get away from me.*

*I can never ask you to forgive me. I don't deserve it. But that doesn't mean we still can't know each other. You can even tell me how much you hate me, just so you also give me a few minutes to say how much I love you. The fear of standing before you, hoping for forgiveness, has terrified me. But I'm ready to accept any judgment you give.*

*There is something important I need you to know. Katie, I remarried, and my husband and I have two daughters. That means you have two sisters. I've told them so much of my past, and my many falls, but I have not talked about you. First it was imagining the shame of telling them about leaving you, but as they got older, I realized that if I told them, they might contact you, and you may not want that. So I feel I need your permission to tell them.*

*Please don't let any hatred of me get in the way of getting to know your sisters. And I so want them to get to know you. If you don't want us in your life, I will understand. But Katie, you can never have too many people love you, even if that love is from a flawed person like me.*

*I love you with all my heart.*

*Mom*

I read the letter over and over, maybe ten times, finding new things each time I read it. Finally, I slit open the newest one. It was short, only a page, almost apologetic about writing again since I hadn't replied to her first letter. But since then I'd skated at Regionals, and she'd seen the stories and the video. She went on and on about what a great skater I was and how proud she was of me. She asked if I'd be willing to meet her in San Francisco when I was there for Sectionals. And as she did in the last letter, she listed her phone number, email and mailing address.

As I put the final letter back in the envelope, I was amazed at how I felt. *Good.* Amazingly good. Was that what a mother's love felt like? Instead of the sadness of my past dragging me down, I suddenly felt lighter than air, like rising for a jump and never coming down. I'd always believed she'd left because of how repugnant I looked after the accident, surely looking at me as a lifetime burden. But the person she'd found repugnant and without value was herself. Reading her first two letters I couldn't imagine living with that much self-hate and pain.

It was almost like she left to protect us.

And the sisters, who yesterday I thought I could never know, were a call away . . . my mom—our mom—wanting to bring us together. I even realized how thoughtful she'd been. In her last letter, knowing I had Sectionals, she didn't tell me her daughters' names or that they were skaters. She didn't want me to be uncomfortable if I knew they were there. She'd just made it sound like a halfway point between her home and mine to meet. And when I didn't respond, she'd stayed away. Even her husband, not delivering his letter to me until after I'd skated, not wanting to do anything to distract me from my performance. It wasn't their fault that I'd been cyber-stalking her and knew all about the twins and their skating.

I found my dad in the kitchen sitting alone at the table, staring into space. When he saw me his eyes lit up, then tempered back down as he remembered my anger. He looked like he was bracing himself for more. Instead I walked right up to him and held my arms out.

"I don't hate you, Daddy. I'm sorry I said that." Did I even say it, or just think it? I couldn't even remember.

My dad was such an emotional man. I could see him struggling to keep a calm face, but it looked like it could crumble at any moment.

He got up and held me and we stood like that, still as statues, for a long time. When we finally sat down, I put the letters in front of me.

Luckily, he spoke first. "I'm sorry, honey. It was wrong to keep the letters from you. I . . . I'm sorry."

My anger was gone—almost—but I still didn't understand.

"Why, Dad? If you didn't want me to have them, you'd have just thrown them away. So I know you were planning to give them to me. But, how long were you going to wait? I'm not a little kid anymore."

"No. No, you're not. I just . . . I . . . ." He took a breath and started over. "You were only three when the first two came, so of course I opened them. But how could I give them to you? You saw what they were like. Even for you now, they've got to be . . . troubling. And to be honest . . . I'm ashamed of it . . . but back then, I was still angry at her. For leaving . . . and for things that led up to it. But I should have done more. I think about that a lot."

I had a mother and a father, both wracked with guilt about the other.

"But what about the new letters? Why didn't you give me those? Or open them like you did the other ones and see she's okay now? . . . And how did you even know they were from her?" I'd noticed she hadn't put her name of the two recent envelopes, just her address, maybe afraid I wouldn't open them if I knew they were from her.

He looked at me hopefully. "She's okay now?"

I nodded and he looked truly happy for her. "I recognized her handwriting, so I knew they were from her. But I didn't open them because . . . they belonged to you. It wasn't like you getting a letter when you were little. But the first one came right after Alex and Lissy got here . . . and you were doing so well, even with everything changing. I was just so afraid of anything that might mess that up. Then you started competing, and now going to Nationals . . . such *huge* events in your life. I wanted you to get through all that first. I was just . . . trying to protect you from maybe getting hurt. But I'm sorry. It wasn't my decision to make."

Even the best of parents screwed up. Yeah, he hadn't been honest with me, but I realized I'd lied to him too. I'd kept it secret that I'd found my mom online years ago, that I had sisters, and that I'd seen them at Sectionals. And why didn't I tell him? Because I wanted to protect him, like he'd been trying to protect me.

"It's okay, Dad. I was actually hiding something from you too."

That got me a curious, and worried, look. "Oh?"

So I laid it all out for him, from my mom's Facebook page, to why I'd been so messed up for my short program, the sight of my sisters, and the letter from my mom's new husband.

My poor dad. To see his daughter's life change before his eyes, and a way that might lessen his role. To learn I suddenly had a family separate from him.

"Dad, so mom was an alcoholic?"

"She told you all that?"

I nodded. "She said we were sledding because you were mad and we left to get out of the house because she was drunk."

"I'm so sorry, honey." He said it like he was to blame.

"*Dad.* It wasn't your fault."

He shook his head. "But it was. She was sick. I don't know. I just . . . I should have done something different. Something *more*. I've learned a lot about alcoholism since then. But back then, I just . . . gave up on her. The truth is maybe she'd still be here if I'd done a better job. That's why I always told you she left because of me. You just never believed me."

I'd had no idea he had such guilt. And my mom's guilt, reverberating through her letter. Maybe my mom's resurrection would be good for all of us.

He wiped the tears that had suddenly sprouted from his eyes and asked, "So, are you going to call her?"

The answer was yes, but my anger of just minutes ago had transformed into worry for my dad. Both he and my mom had such vulnerabilities I'd never known about. I wanted him to feel part of my decision.

"What do you think I should do, Dad?"

He didn't even pause. "I think you should call her. Soon. Tomorrow." He smiled, "And tell her hi for me."

# 51

I'd planned to go tell Lissy everything after talking to my dad, but I was so exhausted I went straight to bed. And the next day we were all into our individual sessions, so it wasn't until lunch that I shared everything with Lissy and Alex.

Lissy's comment was, "And I thought *my* life was complicated."

Alex didn't say anything, but looked like he was thinking the same thing.

I guess we all believe we're the only ones with problems in our family, but maybe we all have them. It's just that we keep them secret. Maybe if everyone shared all their problems, people wouldn't be so ashamed and think they were the only ones.

I had already started on a reply to my mom—an old-fashioned letter like she'd written to me. But it was harder than I thought it would be, and so far I had about ten balled-up pieces of paper in my waste basket. I'd keep at it and get it right. It wasn't the kind of thing I wanted to rush.

I was just glad that life was back to normal. With all the Mom Drama, we hadn't even talked about Sectionals, or the news of the century, that we were all going to Nationals together. Somehow that momentous fact got buried yesterday. At least by me.

At dinner that night, Dad said Barbara called him, all excited about my performance. That was cool, but my favorite part of dinner was watching Alex and Lissy together. They'd give each other little touches and smiles without even knowing they were doing it. They were so sweet and so right for each other. That tenderness they now shared, open and free for the first time, had to find a way into their skating.

The next morning, I was so anxious to get on my home ice I was up and in the rink by five-thirty, a half-hour early. I played around with an idea I'd had of inserting a unique Biellmann into one of my spin sequences—a Pearl variation. It took tremendous flexibility and no one else was doing it. Instead of taking the Biellmann position when I was upright, I caught my blade over my shoulders while I was bent over, then slowly straightened. I liked the way it felt, and it added even more difficulty in the continuing quest to pack a program with more base value points. I felt no pressure about Nationals—so it was pure fun getting ready. Unlike others there with dreams of the Olympics, just getting to Nationals had been my goal, so I felt like I could experiment with my program all I wanted to.

When Alex and Lissy took over the ice, I stuck around to watch their entire session. They looked great. Even though it had only been a few weeks, thanks to their hard work on the ladder drills, they'd added some complexity to their footwork sequence and it flowed right into the rest of their program. They'd keep progressing and judges would have to notice it and reward them. Skating in front of an audience was the real test, but Alex and Lissy looked so relaxed as they skated, even in their most demanding lifts and throws—something that came not just from relentless training and practice, but one-hundred percent trust in your partner. And the joy my dad kept asking for . . . it was there. It was there for each other, so it was there in their skating. The world didn't know it yet, but The Big Three had become The Big Four.

Even with my mind focused on skating and my mom, my thoughts kept drifting to the party coming up. Alex and Lissy had asked me a few times if I'd made up my mind. The costume was hanging in my closet and I'd put it on at least twenty times and looked at myself in the mirror. I had to admit I looked really good. It was skintight and hugged me like a wetsuit and looked really sexy. That's one word I'd never have associated with myself. And with the mask and wig I looked like everybody else. I'd be an imposter in a room full of normal people, but I wanted to feel what that was like. The party was only a couple days away, so if I was going to ask Dad, I couldn't put it off.

When he joined me for my second session I showed him my spin change. He said, "Wow, that Pearl is incredible, honey. No one else is doing it. If they could give it more than level four, they would." Spin and step sequences were graded for difficulty and level four was the highest. "You are really packing on the points," he said.

He meant the base value and he was right. I'd definitely be bringing the technically most demanding program to Nationals. "Thanks, Dad. Um . . . can I ask you about something else?"

"Sure." He smiled like he knew what I was going to ask about. "Your mom?"

Now I felt stupid that my question was going to be about the party.

"Oh, yeah. Well . . . I'm working on a letter. But I decided maybe to wait a little while to actually meet her. I want to do it at the right time, and in the perfect place and . . . I don't know when that is yet. Or where. But I want it to be special, and not just squeezed in before Nationals. So . . . maybe you can help me think about that?"

He gave me such a big smile. "Thank you, honey. I'd love to." He'd been walking on eggshells since yesterday and I wanted us to move past it.

"Okay, great. And . . ."

"What?" I'm sure he was expecting another Mom question.

"You know that party I told you about? I've decided I'd like to go . . . I know it's all the way in San Diego and it's overnight at Alex's house, but . . . I've already been away from home for even longer at Regionals and Sectionals, and I've been going out to do a lot of things . . ."

His face turned a little tight, a battle between pride that his daughter was growing up, and despair over the risks that went with it.

He said, "Well . . . when you mentioned it before, I did call Alex's mom. And she gave me the phone number of the parents of the boy who is having the party. So I talked to them. Then I called the F.B.I. and—"

"Daaaad."

"Alright. I like Alex's mom and she speaks highly of the family where the party is going to be, and the parents seemed nice when I called them, and they're both going to be there . . . And I trust Alex as a driver, so . . ." I wasn't sure if he was giving me an answer or talking himself through his decision. Finally, "So, yes. You can go." He rattled off a few conditions like how late we could stay and when we had to be back the next day. All reasonable. So yes! I was going to my first party! I ran off to tell Alex and Lissy.

# 52

Dad did a double take when he saw me in my costume, and I think half considered changing his mind. He said, "Wow, that costume is . . . tight."

"No different than a skating outfit, Dad."

A sigh. "Yes, I guess so."

Alex had given me one of my favorite compliments. When we'd all put on our Halloween costumes together for the first time, he'd said he thought Lissy's and mine were *wicked sexy*. And to him, he was just stating a fact—a fact I'd never attribute to myself. But after that I looked at my body differently, not just as what carried around a deformed face.

As my dad was getting ready to say more, luckily Alex and Lissy walked in. Dad had never seen their costumes either. We looked like we just stepped out of a movie screen. Dad said, "So, Captain America and . . . ?"

"The Flash," Lissy said, modeling her uniform. It was pretty sexy too, but she wasn't my dad's daughter. "A female Flash."

"Yeah, I can see that," he said dryly.

I knew Alex and Lissy were doing one of their many acts of kindness. It would make more sense to wear our usual clothes to Alex's house then change and go to the party, but that would leave me, as usual, as the only one in a mask. So they'd said it would be fun to wear our costumes on the way there, so when we stopped to eat we'd all have them on. It *was* Halloween, they'd said.

As we walked to the car, Lissy said, "Katie's got shotgun!" conceding me the front seat.

I don't know why, but driving with friends was completely different than driving with my dad. It was like an adventure. When we got to the valley and stopped at a few traffic lights, almost everyone did a double take at the three fully costumed superheroes in the car next to them. I was used to stares, but this was fun and completely different. The costume mask was bigger than my kabuki, and with the wig, it completely covered the real me. We got a lot of honks and laughs and thumbs up. When Alex announced we were halfway to San Diego he got off the freeway in a town called Temecula.

Lissy said, "Oh, I can guess where we're eating."

"You bet," Alex said, "I've been without Rubio's for months. It's the one thing Arrowhead needs."

"What's Rubio's?" I asked. "Italian food? "

Alex said, "No way. It's sort of . . . Mexican seafood. They've got these great deep-fried fish tacos."

Lissy said, "He's addicted to them. Don't get him started."

I'd never even heard of a fish taco, and it didn't sound particularly attractive to me, but I kept that thought to myself. I handed Alex some money. "This is from my dad. He said to treat you guys to lunch."

"Excellent," Alex said. "Fish tacos and I'm not even paying."

When we walked in, everyone turned to look at us. Alex took in all the looks and struck a superhero pose: "No fear! We are here to protect you while you eat! Now, go back to your fish tacos and enjoy!"

I don't know how Alex could do that stuff. If I did it, which I couldn't, people would just stare at me. When he did it, half the room cheered and even applauded. I guess he was a born performer. When we got to the counter he turned to me and said, "Okay, the evil Flash over there is going to try to talk you into a salad, but I really want you to try the fish tacos, okay?"

280

I looked to Lissy who said, "I'm getting a Baja Salad with grilled salmon, but the tacos *are* good."

Alex was already ordering. "Can I have the two fish taco especial plate, chips and beans. And can you put the fish on top of everything?" He turned to me. "The fish doesn't get soggy that way."

Lissy went with her salad and I decided to follow Alex's advice and go with fish tacos.

"Fish on top," Alex said to the counter girl over my shoulder.

She gave us a number and three cups. We grabbed some iced tea and found a table under an umbrella on the patio. It was a perfect SoCal day. Even though it was late October, it was sunny and warm. It was glorious just relaxing in the shade with my friends. When our food came I checked out my first-ever fish taco, filled with cabbage, salsa, guacamole and some white sauce, with a piece of fish so big I wondered how anyone fit the taco into their mouth. But I managed.

"So, what do you think?" he asked.

I gave him a thumbs up since my mouth was full. "Delicious," I could finally say. I didn't know how so much weird stuff could combine together to make something so good. When we got to the car I was both full and sleepy, so I reclined the front seat in hopes of a nap.

It was after four o'clock when we made it to San Diego. I had actually fallen asleep for about an hour. Alex saw I was awake and said, "We left early so we'd avoid the traffic, but the party's not until seven. You've never been to San Diego before . . . What do you want to see?"

I had no idea, but then I did. "Can we go to the beach? I've never been to the ocean."

From Lissy in the back seat, "Great idea. Alex, let's go to Pacific Beach."

"You got it," he said.

As we parked, the sun was just starting to go down over the water. It was breathtaking. We left our shoes in the car and walked barefoot in the sand and into the waves just enough to get our feet wet. What an incredible feeling. I got so mad at myself that I would get emotional at weird moments. Like then. My eyes got all wet and I had to make an effort not to cry, but how could you not—seeing the ocean for the first time, feeling sand and the Pacific on your feet. The beach was mainly empty but there were a few people still riding the waves on boogie boards, or just stretched out on the sand, catching the last rays of the sun.

I said, "Do you guys think we could come back someday? And even go in the water?"

"Sure," Lissy said, "The water is kind of cold this time of year, but if you're game, so are we. Why don't we do it after Worlds? We could come down for a couple days . . . maybe go to the San Diego Zoo. I always like going there."

Before we left, Alex asked someone to take some pictures of us doing goofy poses. Actually, in our costumes, with the ocean behind us, they were really cool pictures. I decided I'd post my first funny picture on Instagram. Amazingly, after my name was out there in the skating world, people started following me @KatieWilderSkates. My quad and triple Axel combo at Sectionals had brought a new round of articles. Even *International Figure Skating* magazine, which doesn't usually cover Sectionals, had done a really cool article on me. Most of the people were skaters, but there were quite a few who weren't— both kids and adults facing challenges of some sort and I guess they identified with me. The messages they sent were touching. So far, my only posts had been my favorite inspirational quotes, but with Alex's help, my first picture went out with the message: *Alex Piezov, Lissy Cake and Katie Wilder fighting evil in San Diego . . . and around the world!*

# 53

We pulled up in front of Andy's house at seven-thirty. If it weren't for Alex and Lissy, I'd be terrified of the idea of going to a party. But with them, I felt pretty safe. Alex said all the kids were from the San Diego Skating Club, where he'd started skating. He still had a lot of friends there that he liked to hang out with.

The music was loud and I was excited before we even made it inside. A song I liked was playing, Sia and Sean Paul's *Cheap Thrills.* Through the windows I could see there were about fifteen or twenty people already there and Alex had told me there would eventually be around fifty. The front door was open and when we walked in a guy our age came over, who Alex introduced as Andy, our host. Not only was everyone in a costume, but everybody was some type of super-hero, even though I didn't recognize who most of them were. I did recognize obvious ones like Spiderman, Iron Man, Batman and Cat-woman, but the rest were kind of bizarre. Andy said he was Nite Owl, which was sort of a scary Batman.

His mom came over to say hello, then disappeared into the kitchen. My dad would be glad to know a parent was present as promised. There was a table full of food and two big TVs. One was playing some figure skating without sound. Andy said, "I put together some video highlights of everybody. It took forever."

"Everybody?" Lissy asked.

"Yeah." He indicated me. "Even Miss Quad here." To me, "Nice job by the way, that was solid at Sectionals."

And then to Alex, "Hey, I hope you don't mind, but Anton is coming. He still comes out to skate sometime and I didn't want to exclude anybody."

"Oh," Alex said noncommittally. "Okay. That's cool."

I turned to Lissy and she whispered, "Alex's older brother. I'll tell you more later."

I didn't even know he had an older brother. We got some drinks and Lissy went into the kitchen and came back with a straw for me. There was a second TV with a video game on the screen, with a couple guys—Deadpool and Black Panther— intently driving cars while shooting people. I preferred the Donkey Kong at Chuck E. Cheese. By eight o'clock the whole house and back patio was filled with superheroes. I got brave and moved around by myself, safe in my costume. My anonymity didn't last because as soon as I started talking to someone and I said my name, they'd say "Oh, Alex and Lissy's friend," then start talking about my program at Sectionals. But even if they knew what was under the mask, I still felt deliciously anonymous among all the other costumes.

A few couples started dancing to Pharrell Williams' *Happy*. Unless dancing by myself in front of my bathroom mirror counted, I'd never danced. I moved over to the food table, and when I felt someone come up next to me, I looked up into the eyes of Thor. At least, that's who I thought he was supposed to be. Long blond hair and big muscles, not that those came with the costume. He had an open leather vest and a chest that showed serious gym time. I realized I was looking at Alex's brother. They looked remarkably alike, but Anton was taller and bulkier. I'd guess a hockey player, no chance a figure skater.

"Hi, I'm Anton. I saw you with Alex and Lissy. You've got to be Katie. Am I right?"

"Hi, yes. I'm Katie. You must be Alex's brother?"

"Yeah. I'm surprised he mentioned me. He's pretty much just into himself these days."

I didn't want to admit that I didn't know he existed until a little bit ago. As I'd mingled, my default conversation starters had been "Do you skate singles or pairs?" then "What level are you?" I could have been a recording each conversation was so similar. But those lines wouldn't work with Anton. He was just a boy at a party. It was my turn to say something and the silence was stretching out. Finally, I said, "So, do you play hockey?"

He grinned, "Well, I sure as hell ain't a figure skater . . . But I've seen *you* skate. And I saw all those pictures of you on FanZone. I was hoping you'd wear your regular mask. I think it's pretty trippy. Kinda geisha, you know? Geisha gangsta. Very cool."

"Oh . . . well, thanks."

He took a little appetizer off his plate and put it on mine. "Try one of these. Really good."

It was too big to put in the mouth hole in my mask so I tilted it up just enough to put it in my mouth as he watched me intently.

I said, "Yeah, good. Thanks."

He was standing closer to me than most people did, close enough that I realized he smelled like Alex. But I knew Alex didn't wear cologne, so . . . fraternal pheromones? Maybe what I'd learned in biology was true, like big jungle cats exuding a scent.

He said, "So, what's your training routine? When you skate . . . man, I've never seen a girl with that kind of definition in your legs. It's like the world's greatest racehorse getting ready to run. All those muscles rippling. You see runners like that, but not skaters. It's incredible to see."

Was that a compliment? Comparing me to a horse? But it felt like one. I was having a tough time coming up with something to say. Finally, "So, you're into weight training?" Stupid question with his bare, sculptured chest right in front of me.

"Yeah, that's why I was seriously asking you, what's your routine? 'Cause, please don't think I'm being rude, but your body is like, amazing. You're so slender, but I bet you're made out of steel." He playfully held up an index finger. "Can I touch your stomach?"

The first time anyone had ever asked me that. "Ah . . ."

He didn't wait for an answer and gently pushed his finger into my stomach, then looking me in the eye, changed it to the palm of his hand. "Just like I thought. You're hiding the twelve-pack of all twelve packs. I so respect that. So what's your training program?" His hand was still on my stomach. It made me nervous and part of me wanted him to take it away, but another part of me was thrilled a boy wanted to touch me.

I wasn't going to tell him I walked around all day tightening muscle groups. That sounded so geeky. Alex and Lissy had caught me doing my butt clenches, but I constantly did different ones all day: shoulder blade squeezes, stomach tightening.

I said, "I do a lot of work with resistance bands. So I do that every other day. And I do isometrics . . . and I skate about six hours a day. And I do Ashtanga yoga. Do you know what that is?"

He seemed really interested. "No, but I hope you can show me before the party's over. Maybe we can find someplace not so crowded."

"Um . . ."

Out of the corner of my eye I could see Alex and Lissy approaching, and they seemed to be moving quickly. Anton saw them too and took his hand off my stomach.

"Anton," Alex said, putting a hand on his brother's back so hard I heard the slap, "How have you been?"

But Anton ignored Alex and stepped forward and gave Lissy a hard and long hug until she extricated herself. Then he turned to Alex. "Hey little brother. So, not fair, you brought two hot girls and I came alone. So like you, dude."

Alex's smile was the same patient one I'd seen when we were in line at the movie theater and the two guys in front of us were giving us a hard time. But his brother hadn't acted badly. Alex said, "Yeah right. So . . . I hear you hooked up with a team. Congratulations." He turned to me, "Anton plays hockey."

"Just semi-pro," Anton shrugged. "But Katie and I already covered that, didn't we?"

Lissy took me by the hand and said, "C'mon, Katie, let's dance. All the guys are too wimpy to get out there."

"Later," Anton said as we moved off.

I didn't want to dance in front of people, but luckily that's not where Lissy led me. We walked past the dancers and into the back yard, where it was quieter.

She said, "Katie, we didn't know Anton was going to be here or we would have said something. He's . . . kind of a bad boy, and I don't mean in a good way. I don't mean that you shouldn't talk to him, but . . ."

"He was actually being pretty nice to me."

She sighed. "Yeah, I'm not surprised. He can be a smooth talker. But you don't have a lot of experience with boys, and . . . sometimes it's tough to know which ones are actually nice guys . . . and which ones want something else."

"What are you talking about?" Then I realized what she was referring to. "Wait, are you talking about *sex?*"

When Lissy's expression told me that actually she was, I had to laugh. "Lissy, no boy would ever be interested in me like that. He even told me he'd seen me skate, so he knows what I look like around my mask." When Lissy didn't say anything, I asked, "What did he do anyway?"

She looked toward the door, maybe to make sure he wasn't on his way out. "In high school he got kicked off the hockey team for using steroids, and selling them too. Then he and some other kids were caught breaking into houses and stealing stuff. He ended up going to juvie for a few months. He hasn't been arrested since then, but I'm just telling you, he's . . . Well, personally I think he's kind of a creep to be honest. Did you see the way he hugged me and wouldn't let me go? Like he was copping a feel, or doing it just to bug Alex."

I felt like an idiot—had he been nice to me? Or creepy? I didn't even know. "Okay, thanks for telling me. I'll just stick close to you guys, okay?"

"Sorry. It was our fault. We shouldn't have been dancing and left you alone."

The unspoken words, *You don't know anything about the world off the ice.* But she was right.

"Okay," I said, trying to make it sound light. "I promise not to be alone with him so he can put a drug in my drink." Assuming he had a fetish for girls without faces.

"Good," Lissy said, pulling me behind her. "C'mon, I really do want to dance."

So we did, over and over—and it was fun. Everybody out there was just goofing around and acting stupid. We were still dancing when I saw my Sectionals program get its turn on the TV. As with all the other skaters, it got a round of whistles and applause from the people watching. I felt a hand on my waist and assumed it was Alex but it was Anton. His hand slipped down a little to my hip and he put his mouth close to my ear. "You're going to be a big star, Katie. Get ready for it."

I didn't see any alcohol at the party but Anton seemed to have found some, because his words were slurred. Alex heard it too and that seemed to be our signal to leave. When we left, Anton gave Lissy another uninvited long hug and I noticed how he turned his face into her hair, breathing her in. Gross. I didn't know how to decline a hug so got the same. I felt completely powerless and I didn't like the feeling. I could see Alex's conflicted face, but he was right to let it go. Two black eyes at Nationals would not be a good thing. As we turned to go, Anton said to Alex, "Drive careful now, Tutu."

*Tutu,* as in worn by ballerinas.

But Alex seemed immune to it and just turned us toward the door. I wondered if Alex had grown up with that, cracks about his masculinity as a figure skater in a macho hockey household. Not just from his dad but from his older brother. No wonder he had issues with his confidence. But I knew what maybe he didn't yet, that he was twice the man his father and brother were.

I followed Lissy's lead and said nothing about Anton, and that seemed fine with Alex. By the time we got to his house I could tell he'd put it behind him and it made me sad to realize that he clearly had a lot of practice doing that.

I sent Dad the promised text when we arrived at Alex's. Their house was in a tract of big comfortable homes. Alex's mom told us Anton was staying there too which Alex wasn't thrilled about, particularly since they'd have to share a room, with Lissy and me taking the guest room. Alex said he'd sleep on the sofa.

I'd never shared a room, and it turned out we'd be sharing a bed too. It didn't seem to faze Lizzy as she'd shared rooms and beds at skating camps and competitions. There was a push-button lock on the bedroom door that I set before I took off my mask and took my turn in the shower. I was kind of surprised when I heard Lissy brushing her teeth at the sink next to me and talking through the shower door, but I guess sharing a bathroom was a girl thing. I was still learning. Maybe one day I'd even be like the other girls, with enough confidence to change clothes in the locker room at competitions.

As normal as Lissy was around me all the time now without my mask, I still couldn't imagine her wanting to sleep with my face inches away from hers, but it was just the opposite. When we were in bed she turned to face me, and with our faces as close as could be, we relived the day and the party, and she shared some of the secrets of the female universe.

She told me her ways of telling nice guys from not, and how to be careful when I was in a big social setting like a party. She actually thought I needed the information, which was so flattering. And for the first time I talked with another girl about sex. I got the courage to ask if she was sleeping with Alex and she said no, but that she was both excited and terrified that it was in her future. She said the main thing was knowing she had the right guy. For her, she thought Alex was for life. Probably everybody feels that way with their first love, but I actually thought it might be true for them.

For those precious moments, having a sleepover and talking with a girlfriend about boys and life and future dreams, I felt like a completely normal sixteen-year-old girl.

# 54

We were ready for Nationals, or at least as ready as we could get. Nationals was the biggest event of the year for U.S. Figure Skating, but this year it was particularly important as the top finishers would represent the United States on the Olympic team, only five weeks away in Beijing, China. Up to now, at least for Alex and Lissy, everything had been a prelude to this. This was when it started counting: Nationals, Olympics, Worlds. Over the last few weeks I could see their sessions intensify and their mental focus sharpen. We still had fun off the ice, but they were locked in the rest of the time. My dad was the same way. I was so relaxed by comparison because winning wasn't in my dreams—I just wanted to give an amazing performance.

The only hiccup of the last month was Alex and Lissy having to pull out of their second planned Grand Prix event, the Trophee de France. Alex had pulled a muscle in his back and had to take it easy for a week. No one would cop to it, but I could tell there was an undercurrent of panic. But in a way, the time off might have been good for them. Within days of getting back to work they were just as sharp as before, and probably benefited from the rest.

We were flying to Nationals, but not far since this year it was in Nashville. Alex and Lissy got recognized several times in the airport. As the Olympics got closer, the commercials for it got more frequent, so especially when they were seen together they were identifiable. Thankfully, I still wasn't recognized outside of the skating world.

But all I was thinking about as we neared security was the fact I'd almost surely have to take off my mask. For me, doing so would be just as embarrassing as if they made me strip naked. Actually, given the choice I'd rather take off my clothes. Both my face and my body were private, but only one of them was disgusting.

But I was wrong. I didn't have to take my mask off once—I had to take it off three times. The first time was as we entered the security line when we showed our tickets and ID. Dad had gotten me a passport since I didn't have a driver's license. When I handed it to the lady with the TSA badge she asked me to remove my mask as she compared it to my picture. I kind of flashed it up and back down, thinking that would be enough—but either because it wasn't, or she liked telling people what to do, she said to fully remove it. So I did and stood before her, then after what felt like an hour later she said, "Thank you," and moved me along.

None of us were willing to let our skates out of our sight so I had my skating bag as my carry-on. After I set it down to go through the luggage scanner and walked through the body scanner, I was told to take off my mask again and walk back and put it in the tray next to my bag.

My dad was right behind me and spoke up, keeping his tone polite, but I could tell he was pissed. "It's just like part of her clothing. Can't she just hand it to you and you can see it's . . . safe?"

The man at the body scanner ignored him and repeated the instruction. I kept my eyes straight ahead, like a laser beam, to block out all the people around us looking at me. But I couldn't ignore the sounds. There were hundreds of people lined up around us, many of them already staring at me due to the mask, so I had everyone's eyes when I took it off. I had not heard the sounds that followed since I was six and my mask skidded away when I fell. It was an audible gasp times a hundred. Some people literally pointed. All movement around us seemed to stop and time stood still. I glanced at my father and I could tell as a father he wanted to shout, *"What the hell are you staring at? Do you have no decency?"* But that wouldn't help, just make it worse. My eyes found those of Alex and Lissy, but they were so filled with rage on my behalf, and shame for those around us, that I found no comfort there. For the first time they had their first real glimpse of what it was like to be me.

When I finally walked through the body scanner it seemed to take forever for my mask to finally come through. When it did, I forced myself not to rush to put it on. Instead I did it casually. Everyone around had gotten their good long look already so I wasn't going to let it show that I was humiliated. The moment was bad enough that I admit I wished I'd never left the Ice Castle, even if it meant no Nationals. At least finally it was over.

But it wasn't. After we collected our bags to enter the terminal there were three TSA officers blocking our lane. One of them requested my passport and asked who my parent was, which was pretty clearly the man right next to me with the veins popping out of his neck and forehead. One of the men said, "We need the two of you to come with us please." He indicated the two other security agents. "They will take your luggage."

Alex and Lissy had been behind us in line and had heard the exchange. Alex said, "We're with them, so we're coming too."

I appreciated the united front, but the security man said, "No, you're not. Proceed into the terminal, please."

When Alex started to say something else, my dad just shook his head at him and said, "We'll see you at the gate."

What did the TSA people think? . . . That I was a known terrorist who'd dunked her face in acid to destroy it and hide my real identity, then sneak on an airplane? I doubted a smart terrorist would do something so horrific to draw the attention of every eye, as my face did, but I guess airport security had to be on the lookout for dumb terrorists too.

Dad and I were shown into a small room with glass walls. I'm sure it was so they could see us, but we could also see them put our bags

293

on a steel table and go through them one more time. I didn't care they went through my clothes, but for some reason I was furious when I saw them handling my skates. It was fifteen minutes before a different TSA agent, this one a burly older woman, came in with our passports. She asked me to take off my mask again and compared me to my picture. Then without another word, said "Thank you for your cooperation. Have a good flight." No explanation, but we were free.

I could feel Dad boiling as we walked toward our gate. To cheer him up I said, "Well, I don't know why I was dreading *that*."

But the smile he gave me was fake. In his eyes, he'd failed me, as had humanity in general—well, TSA anyway. But just as I was going to have to adapt going out in the world and its reaction to me, he would have to as well.

None of this detracted from the thrill of my first time flying. I admit I got scared when we took off, but once we were in the air, it was breathtaking. Everyone else acted like the whole thing was one more mundane moment in their lives, opening magazines or laptops. But my eyes were out the window almost our entire flight.

We rented a car and passed the Bridgestone Arena, the site of Nationals, on the way to our hotel. It was a huge arena and the home of the NHL Nashville Predators. I'd heard it seated over seventeen thousand people and it was already a sellout for the long programs. We checked into the Sheraton, Dad and Alex getting their own rooms, Lissy and me sharing. It was only one o'clock and we had ice time at four o'clock at the Ford Ice Center, a nearby rink.

Both the ladies and pairs short programs were Thursday, the day after tomorrow, pairs at 3:45 and ladies at 8 p.m. We were here early to acclimate to the new surroundings and the arena, but Alex and Lissy also saw it as a chance to connect with their friends that trained around the country, so they'd been doing a lot of texting setting up things. My new friend, Tiffany, would be here with Coach Z, and told me she'd be at the same hotel.

The rest of the day was our practice, dinner, and bed for me. Alex and Lissy stayed up a little later to connect with friends.

The next day we had practice time at the arena so got our check-in out of the way—our U.S. National Championship lanyards were *so* cool—then hit the ice. Afterwards, we took the time to check out the arena more. It was *nothing* like Regionals or Sectionals, starting the minute we walked through the door. This was clearly the big time: there was even a separate skater entrance complete with security guards. Alex and Lissy had attended a junior championship showcase here years ago, and Dad had been a newbie coach when the 1997 Nationals were here. The skater area was immense, with lots of sofas and chairs as well as empty space to stretch out, several rooms for U.S. Figure Skating staff, a dining hall set up with a free buffet, and a specific area for media interviews that Alex said was called the *Mixed Zone*, because it was the one place where the skaters and media were both allowed and could literally mix. There was even a room with masseuses and physical therapists standing right there waiting for any skaters who needed their services.

I turned to Alex, "You mean I can just walk up to one of them and say, "I'd like a massage, please?"

"Yup."

"And it's free?"

"Yup, all paid for by the nice people at U.S. Figure Skating."

*Cool.* Since none of them were Bridget, I was going to get one—my first ever massage. If Lissy didn't want one, I'd ask Tiffany and see if she'd want to get side-by-side massages.

They showed me the elevator which went to the upper part of the arena where there was a reserved nosebleed section for skaters to watch their teammates.

When we were back downstairs it was hard to walk very far without someone asking for a picture with Alex and Lissy, or just wanting to say hi. They were the king and queen of this particular universe. And my dad too. I couldn't believe how many people came up to him, many who had not seen him in years. I was like the foot servant walking behind the royal threesome. And you know what? I loved it. After a life of being the one stared at, it was nice to bask in the relative anonymity cast by the shadow of Alex, Lissy and my dad.

# 55

I'd been expecting SoCal weather in Nashville so was surprised to wake to to a sixteen degree day, which the local morning shows were blaming on a blast of arctic Canadian air. But it seemed somehow appropriate for a city hosting a competition held on ice, even if it was the indoor variety.

The juniors had been competing the last few days but today was the first day of senior-level competition. Last night they'd posted the draw for the short programs. Of fifteen pairs, Alex and Lissy were in the first group, drawing the second spot. The reality was they were the overwhelming favorites. The only two teams close to them had retired at the end of last season.

When it was time for their short skate I was up in the skater nosebleed section. The pair before them was just leaving the ice and the minute they were off, Alex and Lissy were on, doing a quick warm-up around the rink. The moment the audience saw them, they let out an appreciative round of applause. It wasn't a sellout since short programs didn't draw the big audiences the free skates did, but the arena was more than three-quarters full.

After the last pairs' scores were read, over the speakers came: "From the Arrowhead Skating Club, Alex Piezov and Melissa Cake." Thanks to Alex and Lissy, the Arrowhead club was getting lots of free pub, despite surely being the tiniest skating club in the country.

When they came out of their starting positions I said a silent prayer that Lissy would ace the first element, a sign she'd defeated her nerves. And she did, just as she'd done at Skate America. The nerves were a thing of her past, replaced by excitement, and maybe helped by a true relationship with Alex. I'd seen their short program over a hundred times in practice, but it felt totally different in front of a big crowd with a national title on the line. Not only did they skate a super clean program, but even from the furthest point in the arena, I could feel the emotion of their skating. All the top skaters in the world check each other out and I could imagine The Big Three watching and thinking, *Oh oh. The gold will be up for grabs in Beijing.* And FYI skating world, the coach who helped accomplish that is my dad, David Cole Wilder.

While we waited for their scores I tried to spot Lissy's dad and Alex's mom and little brothers. Lissy's dad was going to be tougher to spot after she found the courage to lay down an ultimatum. Usually I could just look for the flower arrangement so big it needed its own seat, but she'd told him: no embarrassingly large bouquet of roses, no personal photographer to take publicity shots of him, no supermodel as a date. I was glad to see her tell him how she felt, and that he listened. It was a start. Not so for Alex. It made me sad his dad wasn't here, and Alex had refused to call him. He wouldn't talk about it, even with Lissy. But his dad had to know when Nationals were—so he'd have been here if he wanted—which I guess was why Alex didn't want to talk about it.

I'd actually changed my mind about his father. He'd never win Father of the Year, but that didn't mean he didn't love Alex. He just didn't know how to show it. It hadn't occurred to me until a few days after he'd visited the Ice Castle, but I believe he stole Bridget away just to get her away from his son. Why would an NHL team just happen to need an extra trainer when the season had already started? I think he'd seen enough to know Bridget wasn't good for Alex, and was an obstacle to his relationship with Lissy. Perhaps I was giving him too much credit, and if so, I'd keep his act of kindness a secret. Besides, maybe he wasn't even admitting it to himself.

When Alex and Lissy's scores came up they were monster: 70.18. Since I'm a skating stat geek, I knew that bettered their championship-winning short program last year by four points. They'd go straight from the Kiss and Cry down the hall to the Mixed Zone. I knew Alex and Lissy would be tied up for a while so I stayed and watched the next few pairs.

When I went back down, Alex and Lissy were done with press and were now surrounded by a bunch of friends. Not just any friends: It looked like a Figure Skater Hall of Fame reunion. There was one of the best ice dancing teams of all time, Meryl Davis and Charlie White, who'd won every single event there was to win. Next to them was Adam Rippon, skater turned icon; and Mirai Nagasu, the first and only American woman to land a triple Axel at the 2018 Olympics. And next to her was Scott Hamilton. Scott Hamilton as in *I loved him so much I named my favorite drill after him*. Some of them had broadcasting gigs and some were just there to support. Alex saw me and called me over to introduce me, and everyone was incredibly nice, even when I just stared and couldn't say a word back.


Tiffany arrived for our ice time together. Later we'd have a light meal, stretch again, do the group warm-up, and finally skate. I could tell Tiffany was wired as soon as I saw her. Unlike me, she was here to win—that and the excitement of her first Nationals was probably a lot to handle. I'm sure Coach Z would calm her down, maybe some of whatever he did for me at Sectionals. While we stretched we watched the monitor in the skater area showing the TV broadcast of the remaining pairs' short programs. It was so cool to hear Tara Lipinski and Johnny Weir, knowing they were sitting a few floors above us, looking down on the ice. Weirder still was knowing they'd be calling my skate too.

For ladies singles, there were fifteen skaters, the top four finishers of the three Sectionals, and last year's Nationals medalists: Ainsley Tucker, Savannah York and Jasmine Tishimi. The woman who'd finished fourth had retired. Although Team USA skaters didn't have to go through qualifying like Tiffany and I did, once at Nationals we were all on equal ground. They didn't get any special treatment with things like the amount of practice ice or preference in the skating order, which I though was very cool of U.S. Figure Skating. There would always be the unspoken bonus points that go with having a big rep—but that was fine. In my group was reigning National champion, Ainsley Tucker, as well as Pinky, not that I was giving her much thought. At least in this environment I didn't think she'd try to cut me off during warm-ups.

The Zamboni had come out to cut the ice, then the announcement: "Will the senior ladies first warm-up group please take the ice."

I was already by the gate to enter and looked over to see Ainsley Tucker was right next to me. Amazing. *I'd be warming up with the national champion!* It was for moments like this that I was here.

I'd be skating third and she'd be fifth. When I was on the ice I could see the huge TV cameras on all four sides of the rink, and others higher up—a big difference from the little camcorders at Regionals and Sectionals. When our time was up and we left the ice, we were escorted back into a holding area, with a black curtain up between us and the rink. Unlike at the qualifying competitions, we weren't allowed to watch our competitors from the arena, only on the monitors, assuming a skater even wanted to.

The other girls in my group all had their backs to the screen, and most put in earbuds to listen to music. I knew they didn't want to get psyched by seeing a great program or a terrible one, but I didn't have either worry. There was a cameraman moving around us and it was surreal to see the TV cut away for quick shots of us staying loose as we waited to go on the ice. I could see the cameraman right next to me, and ahead of me on the monitor was what he was filming. At that moment—me—just as people in their living rooms were seeing.

It was kind of freaky.

I watched the first skater, Regan Bailey from Michigan, give a flawless performance. I'd never even heard of her, but her jumps were stunning and she had a beautiful grace. She was the only black skater I'd seen at Nationals which felt wrong somehow. I was always surprised at how "white" the winter sports were. How often do you see a black hockey player? Or a skier? A figure skater? Maybe Regan could answer that mystery for me, or maybe that was a question you just didn't ask. The only black American figure skater who rose to prominence was Debi Thomas, and she skated more than thirty years ago.

When the second skater took the ice I knew my turn was just minutes away. I took my eyes off the screen and put my head down and closed my eyes. Time for my last preparations. I kept changing my mantra—it was like a living, growing thing. Even though I kept telling myself I wasn't here to win—just have fun and skate beautifully—I could feel my adrenaline hit overdrive, more than ever before. But I told myself that was good. More adrenaline meant more power, more speed. Still, I kept taking deep breaths to calm my heart. *I am the Phoenix, risen from ashes, undefeated by fire—unbreakable.*

When I heard the applause for the first skater, I looked up and saw the official at the curtain wave me forward to take the ice. I only had about two minutes before the judges finished computing the scores, so I didn't just skate around the ice, I raced like a speed skater to burn off that extra buzz of adrenaline—too much of it and I'd over-rotate on my first jumps. Serious skating people would have heard about "the girl in the mask," but some of the people in the arena were probably just casual fans who had no preparation for the girl suddenly on the ice. I could hear a murmur rise up like a buzz.

A masked skater. Never been done before—breaking new ground.

You can only live a moment like this once, hearing your name called to skate at the National Championships, and that moment was now. I heard, "From the Arrowhead Skating Club, Katie Wilder." I skated to the boards for the last few words with Dad. I wondered what wisdom he was going to send me on the ice with for what was so far, the biggest skate of my life.

He looked me intently in the eye. "Katie, what did the fish say when it swam into a wall?"

*What?* A fish . . . ? "Um . . . I don't know, what?

"Dam."

It took me a second, then I couldn't help but let out a tiny laugh. And when I did, I realized that despite my efforts to calm myself down, I'd still been too wired. He'd seen that. Now, one stupid joke later, I was perfect. As I took my position I did the most important thing. I spoke to the ice: *"You are my best friend. Take care of me."* And I added something new, *"Let's do something beautiful together."*

# 56

There were no nerves, only speed and power. With Rihanna's encouragement, singing *This is What You Came For*, I practically exploded out of my starting position. Once around the rink and I floated into my triple Lutz - triple toe, to my layback, then the Arakawa Ina Bauer which, even being in the zone, I could hear the crowd reaction. I moved seamlessly from element to element, then closed with a spin I was really proud of: a layover back camel sit spin into a cannonball, to a forward catch foot layback to a twisted intermediate position. Without even thinking about it, I altered my finishing pose to thrust my arms above my head, because *it felt so good!*

The applause was loud and long. A lot of people were even standing—then everybody. I looked up to the skaters' box and could see Alex and Lissy up there, displaying none of the dignity of U.S. National Champions, more like teenagers at a football game, jumping up and down, their arms in the air as well.

When I made my way off the ice, I saw three gates through the boards instead of one. My eyes were so wet it was making me see in prisms. I blinked them clear so I wouldn't end a perfect short program by skating right into the boards. That would be slightly embarrassing, particularly on national TV. Dad gave me a lift-me-off-the-ground hug. "Oh, honey . . . that was magnificent. You were amazing."

We made our way into the Kiss and Cry, and the moment we entered a man with a TV camera on his shoulder moved to within just a few feet of us, the camera literally right in our faces. There was another man holding a pole with a microphone at the end hovering above us. It never occurred to me when I'd see close-up shots on TV of the Kiss and Cry that the athletes had a camera truly right in their faces. How did they act normal? It was so disconcerting that for a few seconds I just stared at the camera like an idiot.

Dad gently turned my head back to him. "Let's sit down."

This was my first time in a real Kiss and Cry. They didn't have them at Regionals and Sectionals. Here it had glass walls, a padded bench and on the wall behind it the U.S. Figure Skating logo sharing space with an ad for one of the sponsors: a tissue company. Smart branding, for the *cry* part anyway. Dad leaned close and whispered, "Remember, they can hear everything we say. And whatever the scores, smile and wave."

Dad and I had compared my base points to the other girls, and mine was the highest, although the required elements of short programs limited our options. Still, I'd chosen the most difficult option for every required category. In theory that meant that if we all skated equally, I'd have the highest score, but it didn't always work that way. The grade of execution for each element could significantly lower or raise the points for each element, not to mention half the points came from presentation and artistry, the component scores. The two girls in front of me had received a 56.19 and a 54.27. The top finishers would be in the sixty to seventy range.

A moment later my score came up: 45.98. The technical score for my elements was good but not what I'd hoped for, 34.08. It was the presentation numbers that were off-the-charts bad: 11.90. There was a loud chorus of boos. I'm talking *really loud* and *really long*.

"Dad?" I had to almost shout to be heard.

He leaned close. "They aren't booing you, honey. They're booing your scores. They wanted them higher. Now smile and wave."

I got to my feet and waved as instructed, although my dad had said "smile" by instinct, even he forgetting no one could see my face. At least as I waved, the boos turned to cheers again. When we left the Kiss and Cry, Dad walked me down the hallway a little way, stopping before the Mixed Zone where the press would be waiting.

"Why were my scores so low, Dad? I thought I skated about the best I ever have." To me it wasn't the score itself so much as it was an indication the judges didn't like it.

Dad said, "Part of it is because you didn't work your way up through junior competition, and it's your first time to Nationals. I don't care if you're the best skater. To knock a Team USA skater off the podium you can't just win by a little. It's got to be by a lot. But . . ." I watched as he fought an argument with himself about what to say. "But there's just no other way to say it. Those component scores were *wrong*. I know you say you don't really care about winning, you just want to perform . . . that's your right. But *my* right as your coach is to question that score."

He was just venting, being more dad than coach at the moment. There was really nothing he could do. Figure skating had by far the most complicated scoring system of any sport in the world. Even gymnastics didn't come close. But unlike other sports, there was basically no way to challenge a score.

When you watch figure skating on TV you can see all the judges have headphones. The public doesn't know it, but the judges are actually being guided through the skater's program by the Technical Panel, who basically oversee the judges' scores.. The Assistant Technical Specialist has the skater's program in front of him and will announce every element coming up, so the judges will hear "triple Axel - double loop combo." Then right after the element, the Technical Specialist tells them if the element was actually done correctly. If he notices a problem, like the skater under-rotated and her landing skate wasn't fully rotated ("cheating" a landing), he will tell the judges, "Axel under-rotated," so it could only be scored as a double.

The panel also decides if spin and footwork sequences were difficulty level one, two, three or four.

The reason scores take so long to go up is because the panel has to review parts of each program afterward in slow motion to make accurate rulings, and a third person, the Technical Controller, then needs to approve the final score. So there were a lot of scoring safeguards, but the judges alone had sole power in giving a GOE for each element, as well as the presentation scores.

My dad knew even better than me that he wasn't allowed to challenge the scores themselves, just see if my elements were accurately entered. And even that was severely frowned on, at least during the competition.

"Don't make a fuss, Dad. I'm just sad they didn't like it."

He shook his head. "No, it's not right, Katie. This is what coaches do. You skate, and let me coach. I'll get your protocol sheet and see what it says. The technical was fine, but that component score was inexcusable."

"Okay, Dad."

He nodded and I could see him mentally switching gears. "You ready for the press? You remember all the things we talked about?"

"Yeah, Dad. I'm good."

"Okay, I'll be right behind you if you need me."

We moved into the Mixed Zone and I was surprised how many reporters were there, maybe forty, not to mention several camera crews. The two skaters who'd gone before me were still there, with reporters surrounding each of them or their coaches. When I came in many of them pulled away and came over to me, making a half-circle around me, mics or cellphones held out, and two big network cameras held above the throng.

—"Katie, Darci Miller, FanZone. Many thought you skated a perfect program but your scores were too low. The crowd certainly didn't like them. Do you have a comment?"

—*"I'm just so grateful to be here. I just trust the judges to give me what they feel is right."* Dad's lessons in my ear.

—"Jean-Christophe Berlot from Skating magazine. This is your first Nationals. Can you describe what it's been like for you?"

—"*Oh wow . . . skating the warm-up with Ainsley Tucker was unbelievable. And just being here is . . . amazing. I see so many people I've watched on TV. I just hope I get to meet them all.*"

—"Tatjana Flade, Golden Skate. Katie, you were seen watching the other skaters on the monitor. It's rare for a skater to watch her competition before she skates . . . What makes you like to do that?"

—"*I don't know about what other skaters do . . . I just wanted to watch them because I love to watch skating and this is my first time at Nationals. If I could go out into the arena to watch instead of on the monitors, I would. I thought Regan Bailey was especially amazing. I'd never seen her skate before.*" Regan was being interviewed not ten feet away and when I glanced in that direction, I saw she'd heard me and gave me a smile and a nod.

—"Robert Brodie, IFS. Katie, can you talk about what it's been like having Alex and Melissa as your training partners? Before they came, it was just you and your father, correct?"

—"*It's been the best thing in my life.*" I waged a short battle inside myself how honest to be. There had to be people out there, hiding from the world like I had been, who could use some help. "*The truth is I was fifteen years old and never had a friend. It was what I wanted more than anything . . . but I was afraid to try. And when Alex and Lissy came to stay with us, they became my first friends. I had to take a chance because . . . I'd be an easy person to reject. But they didn't do that. I'm really grateful to them.*"

The room got quiet and I was embarrassed that maybe I'd shared too much. Finally more questions:

—"Katie, Christine Brennan from USA Today. You came out of Sectionals with more interest than any skater in a long time. Some people were even saying you had an outside chance of winning here. Are you going to do the quad in your long program?

—"*Um . . . I don't know if I'll do the quad or not. I'd like to. If I'm feeling it, I will.*"

—"It has to be hard to skate with a mask, Katie. Can you talk about that?"

—*"Well, yes, it's harder than skating without it. But it's just what I have to do, so . . ."*

—"Would you ever consider skating without the mask?"

—*"No . . . I don't think people would like that."*

A new reporter walked up.

—"Katie, it's being said the reason for your low presentation scores was due to your mask . . . that without your face being visible you couldn't present the emotion needed. Do you think that's fair?"

Wow. Was he serious? If so, my face . . . the gift that keeps on giving. I didn't know what to say. I just stood there. That's when Dad spoke up from behind me and said, "Thanks everybody, I think that's enough questions."

It was the warm-up between groups two and three, so even though he knew I didn't want him to, Dad rushed off to do the one thing he could do: make sure my elements had been entered correctly for my technical score. But the problem had been the component score, which was was solely the personal discretion of each judge.

I headed over to the skater area where Alex and Lissy were waiting.

Lissy said, "You did awesome!"

"Absolutely nailed it," Alex said. "I loved the way everybody supported you with those boos. I have *never* heard it so loud. They only do that for skaters they really support. Judges hear that."

"Is your dad going to question the scores?" Lissy asked. "Those presentation marks were a joke. They couldn't have been entered right." She seemed really angry about it, like my dad had been.

"Yeah, he's going to ask about it, but . . . I really don't know." And I didn't. I just knew it sounded adversarial and unpleasant and not what I came here for. I was tired of the whole topic. I just wanted to watch the rest of the skaters, especially Tiffany.

They had monitors in the dining room so Alex and Lissy said they'd watch with me while we got something to eat. On the TV I saw the scores of the skaters I'd missed. Ainsley Tucker, the favorite to repeat as champion, had a 66.21, and Regan received a 59.19. Tiffany skated well but had to double two of her triples so lost a lot of points. She was in sixth with a 57.25. Savannah York was going to have a hard time repeating as a medalist. She'd given a pretty sloppy performance and was in eighth. I was in eleventh. The four skaters below me, which included Pinky, had all fallen at least twice and had numerous mistakes.

As they were wrapping up the night's broadcast, Tara Lipinski brought me up!

—TARA: "Johnny, more information is coming in on the scores for Katie Wilder that we both thought were shockingly low for an incredible short program . . ."

As she was speaking they cut to footage of my program. *There I was on national TV!* With Tara Lipinski and Johnny Weir talking about me!

—TARA: "It's being said the reason for her low presentation scores was due to the fact she wears a mask. That without her face being seen she couldn't present the necessary emotion . . . What do you think of that?"

—JOHNNY: "What I think, Tara, is that girl might have been wearing a mask, but the judges were the ones with blinders on. That was a beautiful program, beautifully skated. Frankly I thought it was the program of the night."

More footage of me, this time in the Kiss and Cry as the scores were announced and the boos rained down.

—TARA: "Hey, it wouldn't be figure skating if we didn't have a scoring controversy, right? . . . I don't think we've heard the last of this."

When Dad came back I asked him, "Is that true, Dad? Is my mask why my scores were so low?"

His mouth was set in a grim line. "Yes, it's true . . . that's basically what they said. I'm sorry."

I didn't like it, but I guess it made sense. Everyone shows their emotions mainly through their face: happiness, despair, hope, love. But the skaters I'd always admired the most emoted with their entire bodies. Even without seeing their face, you felt their joy or sadness. Skaters like Evgenia Medvedeva, Carolina Kostner, Jason Brown and Jeremy Abbott.

"It's okay, Dad." I admit I was bummed. I thought I could overcome the mask, but it was still holding me back. "As long as people like to watch me skate, I'm happy." It was the one—the only—way the word *beautiful* would ever be connected with me.

Dad said, "Well, I'm glad you're okay with it, but it's not okay to me. If you didn't interpret your music, if you didn't convey the emotion, with or without a mask, that's one thing . . . but you did. You do. No one can say you don't tell a story."

I knew part of what was bothering him. It was what he was always preaching to Alex and Lissy, that painting smiles or sad looks on your face is the lazy way to connect with your audience. It had to come from your heart and your skating. Dad felt if you really had that feeling inside, that connection to the music, it came through every pore of your body and touched the audience, not just the obvious place—your face.

"You didn't make a big deal about it, did you?"

He sighed. "No, I ah . . . firmly registered my displeasure. But the word is out on why they judged you like that . . . and people don't like it. Anyway, you got your wish. You said you just wanted to skate beautifully and you did that, honey. The audience loved it. Don't let the judges take that away from you."

# 57

The next day was a no-competition day for us. It was when ice dancing and men's singles had their short programs. Alex, Lissy and I did our practice session in the morning at the other rink, and later our one allowed session at the Bridgestone. They were out with some friends and I was about to lay down for a nap when my phone rang.

I recognized Barbara's Felsdorf's number and I cringed. I'd seen her yesterday and she'd been so welcoming and excited that I was competing. I'm sure she could remember not so very long ago when she'd invited me to breakfast and I told her I never left the Ice Castle. I figured she was calling about the scoring issue—but it turned out that wasn't it at all.

"Katie, can I ask you a favor? One of our major sponsors is Cellular Star . . ."

Figure skating, like all sports these days, had sponsors to help bring in needed money—it wasn't cheap running an international sports program. Sponsors' names were plastered all over the arena and on the brochures.

". . . Their CEO is Bill Irwin, a very nice man and very supportive of skating . . . He called me about his son. He's twelve and evidently he's autistic. Bill said his son rarely even communicates . . . but when he was watching you on TV last night, he became very animated. Anyway, Bill asked if there was a way you could find the time to meet his son. His name is Noah. I told him it'd be best to wait until after your free skate tomorrow—"

"No, Barbara, that's okay. I can do it today. Dad and Alex and Lissy are all busy so I'm just in my room. He sounds like a nice boy, so . . . yeah. Do you want to give them my phone number?"

"Katie, I really appreciate it. I've never met the boy, but his dad is very nice and is always talking about his son. I know this will mean a lot to both of them."

I let her know I was going to turn off my phone in about ten minutes to take a nap, and not five minutes after I'd hung up, the call from Mr. Irwin came through. He was, as Barbara had said, very nice. He told me about Noah and his autism. Evidently he could speak but rarely did, and only with his mom and dad. Mr. Irwin said when I was skating he started talking more than he had in years and they didn't want to let the moment pass without trying to build on it.

Since I thought Noah would feel more comfortable in a quiet and private setting, I invited them to my room. We agreed on four o'clock so I could get my nap in first. I texted my dad to make sure he was fine with having them in my room, then I was asleep within seconds.

Luckily I'd set my alarm because I was still groggy when it sounded at three-thirty. They knocked on the door at just a few minutes after four. Noah was small for his size and his eyes stayed on the floor. I had never met rich corporate people—but I just assumed Mr. and Mrs. Irwin wouldn't be like normal people. To the contrary, they were very low key and seemed extremely grateful that I was meeting their son. I knew nothing at all about autism, but I'd spent most of my life a self-made captive of my home, so maybe he and I had a lot in common.

I didn't know if he'd like a hug so I held out my hand to shake, which he just stared at and didn't touch. I invited him to one side of the room where there were two soft chairs by the window, and he slowly followed me over. There was a sofa along the other wall and his parents sat there. I didn't know what to say, and I knew he rarely spoke, so I just started talking about my life. I talked about how long

I'd been skating and why I liked it. About my car accident and the burns and why I wore the mask. About my mom leaving but how great my dad was. I talked about my refusing to leave home, or even go to school. About Ice Cream Cheryl and never having a single friend until just months ago, and how my life had changed. I hadn't planned to say all that—but that's what came out. At some point while I was talking, he silently put his hand on mine, his touch so gentle it felt like a resting bird.

He said, softly. "I like figure skating. You skated so pretty yesterday."

Mr. Irwin had told me Noah never talked to anyone but them, so I figured I was doing something right. I told him my secret mantras to deal with anxiety when I went on the ice. I even told him my ultimate secret that no one knew, not even my dad, that I talked to the ice, after getting his solemn promise not to tell anyone.

"I promise," he said. I knew his parents were hearing everything I said, but somehow I knew they'd keep my secrets. And if they didn't, it was worth it to maybe help this little boy.

A little later he said, "I like your mask."

"Do you want to try it on?" I asked.

His first smile for me. "Yes, please."

"Okay," I said untying it and handing it to him. "I'd give it to you, but it's my only one. I need it for tomorrow."

He didn't even glance at my face but he seemed overjoyed at the mask in his hands, like it had magical powers. He held it in front of his face as we continued to talk.

He asked from behind the safety of my mask, "Are you afraid without it?"

"Um. Sometimes. It depends on who I'm with. I'm not afraid with you right now."

We spent almost an hour talking. I did most of it but he did his share. I knew he didn't want to, but Mr. Irwin finally said, "Noah, Katie has a big day tomorrow. She's got her long program to skate and we want her to do well. I know she has another practice today."

I looked over at the Irwins. It didn't seem to matter that I didn't have the mask. Noah handed it back to me but there seemed no purpose in putting it back on.

Noah said, "I'm going to watch you tomorrow on TV. I hope you win."

Winning was impossible after my score in the short and I didn't want him to feel badly when I didn't. I said, "Actually, I don't care about winning. I just want to do a great program and make everyone happy. So hope for that." And that was the truth anyway.

When we stood up he gave me the gentlest hug I'd ever been given, barely touching me, but so sweet. He then walked to the door, waiting for someone to open it. Mr. and Mrs. Irwin each gave me a hug, making those funny little faces people make when they are keeping tears at bay.

Mrs. Irwin said, "Thank you, sweetheart," then walked with Noah into the hallway. Mr. Irwin lagged behind and quietly said, "You are the first person other than us he's spoken to in . . . as long as I can remember. Thank you so much."

I felt embarrassed they were so grateful. Giving kindness is free and it felt so good. I felt bad for people who didn't know that. I was the one who would be glowing all day. I told Mr. Irwin that Noah could call me anytime, and invited them to visit Lake Arrowhead. I was almost sure they would.

# 58

The long programs for pairs would start at ten that morning, with ladies beginning at six in the evening. Personally, I always thought pairs was the most exciting to watch, with the huge throws and lifts, but the big TV ratings were for mens and ladies singles, and the ladies had the primetime spot tonight.

When we got to the arena I went up to the skaters' seating area. I was surprised to find Regan Bailey sitting there. I hadn't talked to her yet, just had that moment of eye contact in the Mixed Zone with the press. I introduced myself and she did the same, adding, "Thanks for the props yesterday. That was nice of you."

When I took a seat next to her, I said, "I thought I was the only one who watched on my skate day."

She playfully held up a finger to her lips. "Shhh, my coach thinks I'm off meditating or something." Cool, she was funny.

I said, "I really thought you did a beautiful job yesterday. Congrats on third place."

"Thanks. From what I saw you skated just as well. Or better actually. I saw the replay . . . along with all the drama."

Since I didn't want to talk about "the drama," I said nothing and we watched the pair taking the ice do their program. Even this early the arena was packed, and while everyone was waiting for the scores

I noticed that a big chunk of the arena had caught sight of us and were staring at us. I mentioned it to Regan.

"Why are you surprised?" she said. "We stand out like there's a spotlight on us. I'm the only black girl in the whole competition, and you've got that mask. Wouldn't you say we're the two most identifiable girls here?"

I leaned close. "Do you know that I'm actually half black?"

She took in my blonde hair and blue eyes. "No way."

"No, really," I said, as I moved my mask a little to the side so she could see the blackened skin. "See?" I don't know what was getting into me lately.

She started cackling and covered her mouth so people wouldn't stare even more. We watched one more pair until it was time for Alex and Lissy. They'd drawn the next-to-last spot, and so far none of the long programs had been outstanding. When Alex and Lissy circled the ice while the last skaters' scores were being tabulated, I could see them look up to the skater area and each pointed at me, almost a *This one's for you.*

"Well, la di da da," Regan said, giving me a nudge. "Getting a call out from the ice from Piece of Cake. Aren't you the one."

I was thinking, yeah, that was pretty cool, but I was also thinking how relaxed they must be to do that—that was the best news. As Steven Tyler began singing *I Don't Want to Miss a Thing,* Regan whispered, "Love their music. Can you believe *Aerosmith?* That takes guts."

She had a point. Many skaters still went conservative and old school with their music. Alex and Lissy's first element, their triple twist, was flawless. Even from the rafters I could see Lissy's height off the ice. Their side-by-side combo jumps were gorgeous. When they got to their footwork sequence, it was crisp and clean, and blazingly fast, just like in our ladder drills back home.

"That's new . . . *nice,* " said Bailey, and I felt such a tingle of pride knowing I'd been a part of that.

316

They flew through the rest of their program, and I mean flew. Their speed was incredible, their lifts more breathtaking than ever. I could feel their glow even in the upper level seats. No one had wanted to admit it out loud, but it had been a foregone conclusion that Alex and Lissy would win. The question was if they'd play it safe, or go max elements. And whether they did it for the audience, or their confidence was that high, they went max. And the audience loved them for it.

When they finished, Regan and I were on our feet, like the whole arena. When their score came in, it was huge: 151.21. That was eleven points higher than their score that won them the title last year. When the final standings went up, Alex and Lissy had won by almost twenty-five points.

Regan and I found Tiffany in the skater area and we peeked in the Mixed Zone. We could tell that Alex, Lissy and my dad were nowhere close to being done, so I suggested we grab some food. Like for me, this was the first Nationals for Tiffany and Regan, and they were just as blown away by the hugeness of the whole event.

We passed a beaming Barbara Felsdorf, obviously thrilled with Alex and Lissy's performance and what it meant to Team USA's chances in the Olympics. She pulled me aside and said, "Bill Irwin called me yesterday. He said you were wonderful." She paused then said, "You made a very important friend yesterday." It turned out she meant Mr. Irwin—I'd assumed she meant Noah.

When we'd finished eating and I figured Alex and Lissy had to be done with doing press, I asked Tiffany and Regan if they wanted to walk over with me to congratulate them. Tiffany had met them but Regan hadn't. When we found them, they were surrounded with friends, but as we walked up, that group drifted away. I was so excited I had to give them crushing hugs.

"You guys were *amazing*. You had to feel incredible out there."

I introduced Regan, who it turned out trained with some of the same skaters Alex and Lissy knew. As we were talking, the photographer for *Skating* magazine walked by and Regan called to her, "Hey, you better take our picture. We've got the whole freakin' United Nations going on here . . . a black girl, a half-Polynesian, a white guy and a mixed-raced girl in a mask. How often do you get that in figure skating? Hurry up, take our picture."

The *mixed-race* part was just to make me laugh, and it did. Even Alex and Lissy didn't know what she was talking about. The flustered photographer did take our picture, but we'd see if it made the pages of *Skating* Magazine. Regan was right though—it would make a good recruiting poster.

# 59

My long program was four hours away. In the back of my mind, I'd wondered if I'd be too excited to take a nap: national TV, the Olympic team being determined, seventeen thousand-plus people hoping to see some amazing things on the ice. All that should have been on my mind—but it wasn't. My two best friends had given an incredible performance and were going to Beijing, my dad's reputation was golden and I'd been here to see it. With that, and all the incredible things I'd experienced, and the new friends I'd made, I'd already exceeded my dreams. I'd be the only skater out there tonight who had already won.

Dad knocked on my door: time to go to the arena. I had my skating bag all ready, so I was set to head downstairs with him. On the way down I could see his eyes were twinkling.

"What?" I said.

"Have you turned on your TV or been online?"

"No, I took a nap. Why?"

He just smiled. "Nothing. Just . . . a lot of talk about you. How great your program was and why your scores were low. I think you've got more fans now than you would of had if you'd gotten the scores you deserved."

I'd actually been surprised last night to even realize I was included on the prime-time network broadcast. I'd thought a girl skating with a face so disfigured that she had to wear a mask might be off-putting to network TV and they'd edit out my skate. There wasn't enough air time to show every competitor anyway, so they usually just showed the best. So America had seen me, but what they'd make of me I had no idea.

When we got to the arena quite a few skaters and coaches went out of their way to walk over and compliment my short program or wish me good luck tonight. I'd packed my long program with every "trick" I could do: my quad, the triple Axel - triple flip combo, the Pearl variation on the Biellmann, the Arakawa Ina Bauer and my intricate footwork. The level of difficulty was a full six points higher than even Ainsley Tucker. Hers was high at 67.24. Mine was at 74.16.

It was so soothing to have no thoughts about winning, so I didn't have to weigh risks like all the other girls. Someone like Ainsley Tucker could try a quad, but if she fell, that one mistake could cost her the title. So she, like most skaters, passed on the high-risk moves. That, or more likely, they just couldn't do them. None of them had the triple Axel, so opted for the easier toe loop, flip or Sal. I'd skate the performance of the year, or I'd crash and burn but enjoy the challenge.

Since my short program score was low, I'd be skating in one of the early groups of the evening. After the group warm-up I joined the other girls in my group in the holding area waiting my turn. I took my deep breaths and went through my mental steps: feel the adrenaline, welcome it, use it. Power of the Phoenix.

When the skater before me went into the Kiss and Cry, I jumped out onto the ice. Usually crowds give a little round of applause when you entered, but I could literally feel a wall of sound pour over me— a big reaction. But I didn't just take it as a compliment, I took it as an offering—letting me know their energy and goodwill was in the air for me to absorb and use.

I looked up to the skaters' seats and saw Alex and Lissy, and as they had done for me, I gave them a long point. In my gesture was the silent words, *I would not be here if not for you.* I returned my focus to my warm-up laps, but as if someone threw a switch—the huge volume of noise went to complete silence. It was so abrupt and eerie that I stopped skating to look up into the stands . . . and couldn't believe what I was seeing.

Everyone single person was holding a mask in front of them.

A mask just like mine.

Seventeen thousand Katie Wilders.

I could see they were just paper, but they each had the same black accents as mine did, with holes for the eyes and mouth. The change in volume was so sudden and bizarre that even the judges and officials looked up. They saw what I did. At first I thought everyone was making fun of me, then I realized I had it all wrong—they were showing me their support. And making a statement to judges—in fact maybe to all the decision-makers in the world. I felt a tingle run all the way down through my body. I knew they were about to call my name so I skated over to Dad waiting at the boards. He looked stunned.

"Dad, did you know about this? Who . . . who did this?"

It was the first time I'd seen my dad speechless.

"Got any fish jokes?" I asked.

That brought him back. "You don't need a joke today. I know you feed off the audience. Well, this audience has nothing but love for you. So go out there and savor it. Do what you love to do and have fun. One element at a time."

The loudspeaker: "From the Arrowhead Skating Club, Katie Wilder."

The applause went on so long they had to delay my starting music. That was okay, more time for me to talk to the ice: *You are my best friend. Take care of me. Let's do something beautiful together.*

With the first piano notes of *One Call Away,* I was into my triple Lutz - triple toe - double loop combo, then the triple loop. I felt in such control on each of the jumps, like I was weightless in the air and came down only because I wanted to. I had gone on the ice thinking "quad," so there was no decision to be made when I got to it, and it was flawless. It was almost as if the love in the arena kept me suspended in the air with their support.

The hardest part of a program is to relax and not even think about what you're doing. To be unconscious. But it's almost impossible to do when so much is on the line. Not today. My body was on auto-pilot, skating flawlessly, while my mind was filled with images. Dad. Lissy. Alex. The sight of the arena full of masks. I could visualize my mom opening the letter I'd finally mailed and crying welcome tears. She and my sisters sitting in front of their TV at this moment, willing me on.

When I got to the Arakawa Ina Bauer, I savored it, and the crowd applauded so loudly that it brought me back a little bit, aware of them again. Element by element I sailed through my program, finishing big with my spin sequence and the Pearl Biellmann.

I'd put so much into the performance, and the ice had too. If I wasn't in an arena full of people, I would have curled up on the ice to share the moment. It looked like every single person was on their feet and the arena was even louder than it had been for Alex and Lissy. The cheering hadn't even started to diminish after I circled the ice to acknowledge the crowd, so I paused one more time at the gate and waved. Flowers and stuffed animals came flying from the audience and the sweeper girls came out to collect them. I stooped to pick up a rose.

The first time anyone had given me flowers.

I was crying so hard by the time I got off the ice that I could barely see, and had to hold the top of the boards to get to the Kiss and Cry without tripping. Dad could tell so ran the few steps over to me and guided me to the bench.

All I could do was wail and bury my face into his chest. *"Oh, Daddy."* Suddenly it was all too much. I knew the stupid camera was likely right in front of us. No privacy. Dad handed me a handkerchief so I could reach under my mask and absorb the tears that were soaking my face. Finally I could turn around, but I'm glad my dad had his arm around me or I might have fallen right over.

As suddenly as it had been loud, it got completely silent, and I saw that the masks were now held aloft, like flags of one united spirit.

Every single person, a sea of Katie Wilders. They were held so still it was like looking at a photograph. I know I took a picture in my mind to remember forever. Finally, the scoreboard came to life with my scores as the announcer read them, his voice booming overhead. Long program: 155.31; total score 201.29.

That was a *huge* number, bigger than Ainsley Tucker's 148.02 for long in winning Nationals last year. My total score was way behind what won it for her last season though, and I'd likely finish off the podium. But that didn't matter. For four minutes I'd been beautiful the only way I knew how.

Dad and I had the tunnel between the Kiss and Cry and the Mixed Zone to ourselves. I didn't want to talk to my dad through my mask so pulled it up. He put his forehead to mine. "Honey, you were re-markable. I know I've told you for years you could skate like the best in the world, but to do what you just did . . . it was . . . it was breath-taking."

I didn't want to talk. I just wanted him to hold me in his arms. All those years, just the two of us, the world locked outside the Ice Castle, putting in tens of thousands of hours on the ice. But it was never *work*—instead a dad and a daughter spending time doing what they loved together. That made this moment so special for me.

"Thank you, Daddy, for always being there for me. I love you so much."

I put my mask on to get ready for the press, but for the first time in my life, I didn't feel defined or limited by it. And those seventeen thousand mirrors of me in the audience . . . to me the message was not just, *We support you,* but also, *We all wear masks, and we all want to be loved for what is underneath them.*

# 60

The Mixed Zone was packed. Even more reporters and TV crews than before. The previous skater had finished so it was just Dad and me. The questions went on and on. I actually asked *them* a question: Did they know who had distributed all the masks? That took not just desire, but money and organization. But they didn't know either. All they knew was that over a hundred people in the audience handed the masks out in each section shortly before I skated.

One of the reporters had one of the masks and gave it to me. As I'd thought, it was just card-stock paper cut into a mask like mine. When I turned it over I saw the back was filled with words of hope: *kindness, forgiveness, love, charity, tenderness, courtesy, patience .* . . Then words with a line through them: *hatred, prejudice, apathy, cruelty, injustice, spite* . . . Clearly I was only part of the message. I answered questions for a long time until finally my dad said it was time for me to rest. We headed to the media-safe zone of the skater area and found a quiet corner to sit and watch the rest of the skaters.

I was in first place with my 201.29, but that was only because the best skaters were still to come, so I'd be dropping down when they got to the final group. Tiffany was just coming up to skate and I watched her go to the boards to get her final advice from Coach Z. I wondered if she was getting a fish joke. Probably not. She was in sixth, within striking distance of a bronze medal and a trip to Beijing.

Tiffany's program wasn't as demanding as mine, but it was a clean skate: 135.91; total 193.16. In second for the moment. Last year's silver medalist, Susannah York, fell on her triple-combo and was clearly tired by the end of her program: 127.90, total 181.24. Third place. Jasmine Tishimi wasn't right from the start. It can happen to any skater. She fell on her first jump, a triple Sal, then doubled the rest of her planned triples. She was off the platform.

Ainsley Tucker had drawn the first spot in the final group. She showed why she was the defending gold medalist and received a 150.32; total 216.53. I actually had the higher score for the long program but she had the overall lead, giving her first place.

Just as they flashed the standings, Tiffany and Coach Z came out of the media room and joined us. Other than getting up to give Tiffany a hug and exchanging "nice jobs," nobody was talking. National championship medals were hanging in the balance.

With only Regan left to skate, Ainsley was in first, I was in second and Tiffany was in third. It took me a minute to process what that meant: No matter what Regan did, Tiffany and I would be on the podium, the question was just how high. When Regan took the ice, I can honestly say I was rooting for her success. As she skated she made me think of a firecracker. Her jumps were so explosive, big and bold, and her spins were lightning quick. She had a great personality that showed on the ice. She received a 144.52; total 203.71. She'd earned the silver. Nationals had four spots on the podium: gold, silver, bronze and pewter—bronze for me and pewter for Tiffany.

For the next year, we were officially Team USA.

The four of us were celebrating when Tiffany said, "Katie, I'm so happy for you. You deserve it more than me." At first I didn't know what she meant. We'd both be on the podium, the ceremony we'd watched so many times on TV and dreamed being a part of. Then I realized what she meant. There'd be four on the podium, but only the top three would move on to Beijing.

I was going to the Olympics.

# 61

Travel was new to me but I could see one reason people did it—just for the joy of coming home. I missed the solitude of the Ice Castle, and the forest that surrounded it like walls to the world. After Nationals, life changed. As a new skater on the scene taking third place, even at Nationals, it was not a big story except in the skating world. Add being one of the few women in the world to land a quad, and it was a bigger story, but still only among skaters. Add the mask and the hermit aspect, and being the daughter of David Cole Wilder, and it became a big mainstream news item, what evidently the media termed a "feel good" story—of which apparently there were never enough. Then when you have seventeen thousand people hold up a mask in solidarity and support, you had one of the lead stories across the nation.

Within days, agents were calling, endorsements were being offered and interview requests were pouring in. My *KatieWilderSkates* social media accounts suddenly had more followers than Alex and Lissy's combined and was growing at a ridiculous pace, although I still did nothing but share pictures of the Ice Castle and slogans about good character and sportsmanship from people my dad was always quoting, like Michael Josephson and John Wooden.

Alex and Lissy's manager called and made a pitch for his services, telling me my *Q rating*—which he said was the measurement of a person's familiarity and appeal with the public—was off the charts. Being the only person who lived behind a mask did make me pretty identifiable, but the word *appeal* wasn't one I'd ever think to associate with myself. Needless to say, my conversation with The Weasel was short. None of it was of any interest to me.

For the first couple of weeks back, Alex and Lissy and I focused on nothing but skating. Their visibility was rising with the Olympics on the horizon, but Alex liked to kid me that since Nationals, more people were talking about me than them. The sad thing was that it was true—and I was once again hiding from the world. Dad said it would slowly fade away, but not until after the Olympics. I hoped he was right, that a year from now I'd be just a trivia question on a game show: *"What was the name of the Olympic figure skater who competed in a mask?"*

Like most skaters, Alex and Lissy's programs were not changing. But my dad and I decided to up my game. If I was landing the quad so well, why only do it once? And the same with the triple Axel. At the Olympics I'd be facing Tatianna Petrova, Russia's seventeen-year old quad queen. So my long program now had two quad Lutzes, one in combination with a triple toe loop, and two triple Axels. No female skater in history had ever landed two of each. Only three women in the world, not counting me, could consistently land a quad. But for some reason, the few that could couldn't land a triple Axel. Put the two most difficult jumps in the same program, and the points were massive. And the truth was I got quickly bored with the same routine, so I relished both the changes and the challenge. I'd have put the quad in my short program but it still wasn't allowed under ISU rules, although the rule was expected to change next year. Why the men could do a quad in their short but not the women made no sense.

We'd take a break to go into town every few days, and thankfully the locals just smiled and said hello, but the tourists always wanted to talk and take a picture. It was impossible not to be nice—but it was tiring. The irony wasn't lost on me that I'd initially worn my mask so no one could see me. Now the mask made me the most easily spotted person in the country.

Without a doubt the coolest thing to happen since Nationals was Jordan Cowan posting both Alex and Lissy's and my videos on On Ice Perspectives. As Alex predicted, his and Lissy's exploding phones alerted us. Together we watched our videos over and over, marveling at how good he made us look, like we were doing things that should be beyond the human body, which in a way we were. Then I went to my room to watch alone. I didn't want anyone to see me cry. I was so happy. No one had ever made me look beautiful before.

I had a phone number I'd been meaning to call. I guess my name showed up on his phone because when he answered, Mr. Irwin said, "Hi Katie." I asked how Noah was doing and if I could say hello. He put Noah on the phone and we talked for a while—at least I did. I repeated the invitation for his family to come and stay in one of our cabins after the Olympics. When he put his dad back on the phone, I asked him my overdue question.

"Mr. Irwin, was it you who made all those masks?"

He had the money and motivation to put something like that together so quickly. He probably even bought tickets for a hundred of his employees to hand them out.

A pause, then, "Yes. I'm sorry. I . . . I thought it was one of my better ideas when I saw the judges score you so unfairly, but I didn't anticipate it'd be the story it became. I'm guessing you didn't really want even more attention."

"You don't have anything to apologize for. I just wanted to thank you for caring . . . and I'd like to ask your advice if that's okay."

"As far as I'm concerned, Katie, we are friends for life. What would you like to know?"

How to say it? "Well, it seems I'm suddenly famous. For a little while anyway. People are calling and wanting me to do commercials and go on talk shows . . . and I don't want to do any of that. We have enough money and all I want to do is skate, or teach skating. But . . . people like Scott Hamilton, and Miley Cyrus . . . do you know who Miley Cyrus is?"

"I'm fifty, Katie. Not dead."

"Oh, sorry. Anyway, they're two of my favorite performers and they're both really active in helping other people, like Miley Cyrus has her Happy Hippies charity to help kids, and Scott Hamilton has his for fighting cancer. So I was thinking . . . not that I'm a big star like they are . . . but since so many people are, um, *looking* at me . . . is there a way I can use that to help other people like they do?"

I explained to him about the people who messaged me on Instagram and Twitter, or wrote me letters, and how it seemed so many of them were facing some kind of challenge, even if it was self-imposed. Maybe I could do something more than skate for them.

When I finished rambling there was a long silence and I wondered if he was still there. Finally he said, "I understand completely. And Katie, you're already doing more than I think you know. Just being out there, facing the world, I think every time you skate, or even do an interview, people with challenges are inspired. Like Noah. Win or lose, you're out there fighting to be in the world and not be denied your place. So to answer your question, you're already doing something amazing."

I'd hoped for more from him. "Well, thank you. But it still feels like I could be doing something more. Can you please think about it?"

"I'll tell you what, Katie. You've got just a few weeks until the Olympics. Can you put it all out of your mind for now and just enjoy your skating? And after the Olympics we'll sit down together and come up with something for you. Okay?"

Sounded like a plan.

# 62

The sky outside my small window was quickly darkening as our plane seemed to race away from the sun. There had been some highlights and low-lights in our last few weeks before leaving for Beijing. One of the highs had been the Olympic Processing Center in Houston, our first stop on our three-flight journey. The Processing Center was like a store just for Olympians. It was a first-time experience for Alex and Lissy too. We were literally each given a shopping cart to push as we were "processed."

There were about twenty rooms. There was one for our Opening Ceremonies outfits, another for the Closing Ceremony outfits, and even outfits for the Award Ceremony in case we were lucky enough to medal. For each outfit we were measured, and tailors instantly made any needed alterations. America and Ralph Lauren wanted us looking sharp.

Then there were rooms full of t-shirts, tennis shoes, warm-up clothes, hats, sunglasses, underwear, water bottles, Olympic pins, plus a Nike swag bag full of even more. I got at least one of everything. Well, except the condoms. They actually had huge barrels full of them, different colored little foil squares with the Olympic logo. I'd picked up a handful thinking they were wet wipes before Alex whispered what they were. At the very end, there were even sets of designer luggage to pack everything up in. All free, and thankfully shipped to us overseas, as we sure couldn't tote all those extra bags. When we got home I was going to have to reclaim some of my closet from Lissy. A few weeks before we'd left, we'd received by FedEx our official Team USA Olympic jackets, and we were all proudly wearing them on the airplane.

Those had been the highs.

The low was the whispers about a photo of my face being circulated online. At first I tried to ignore what I read, then began to see more and more references about it. At least it was outrage by people and not gossip, although many people did evidently check it out and said it was clearly a fake picture. I knew no one from U.S. Figure Skating would leak my lanyard picture, and I didn't let anyone else take my picture without my mask, so I assumed it was a sick joke. But when I clicked on the link to go to the scuzzy site that posted it, I saw it was indeed me.

It took a minute to realize where it was from, but it was real. It was my profile, sleeping in the guest room at Alex's after the party. The lighting wasn't great, and I could see why people thought it was a joke. The head on the pillow looked like a clump of misshapen clay, with hair. I think people's imagination of what was under the mask was kinder than reality. But that was the real me.

Alex came to see me, shaken. He and Lissy had seen it too, and recognized the background. Evidently Alex didn't even need to think about who had done it: his brother, Anton. Alex said Anton hadn't even denied it when he called. Getting past the simple push-button door lock had been easy for him. Anton had waited until he thought I'd reached maximum "fame" and sold the picture. Evidently he got five thousand dollars for it.

That was the low.


I couldn't believe the immensity of Beijing as we descended into Beijing Capital International Airport. I'd read the city's population was 22 million people, which my dad told me matched the total population of Oregon, Washington, Nevada and Arizona combined. That didn't seem possible, but I guess that explained the smog everyone kept talking about.

U.S. Figure Skating wanted all its skaters to be in China a full week early to acclimate to the time change and the environment. They rented a rink for the team's private use in a city about forty minutes outside of Beijing. Once we were out of the city, it was all very pretty and rural. Everywhere we looked were pictures of the official Olympic mascot for these Olympics, a cuddly panda. He seemed to be on billboards and in shop windows everywhere.

The team rented an entire small hotel near the rink for all the skaters, coaches, trainers and U.S. Figure Skating staff. The size of the whole endeavor was almost unfathomable to me. I'd watched the Olympics on TV but had no idea the depth of preparation involved.

I was glad they had us come early because it did take me several days to feel normal. We had a lot of breaks in training so Dad would drive us around the countryside. The people were incredibly friendly. We ate the local food and ended up having our picture taken with about every person we met. We'd been given the "You are an ambassador for America so be on your best behavior" speech, but it was easy to be nice with everyone we met. They were so happy and excited to host the Olympics and show off their country and culture, and it actually made it more fun that almost none of them spoke English.

Every day when we were out at least one small child ran up to me, pointing at my face and shouting, "Bing! Bing!" I knew they weren't being mean because they were so happy and excited. We finally learned what it meant when someone handed me a little stuffed animal. It was the Olympic panda mascot, and I was told his name was Bing. In mandarin it meant *ice*. And I realized why the kids had been pointing at me. The panda's face was remarkably like my mask, all white with black accents. Making it all the more magical was that the panda was a symbol of trust and friendship in their country. Kids were literally jumping into my arms, to the embarrassment of their parents.

Lissy kidded me, "Man, Katie, you are going to be sooooo popular. You're their freakin' mascot." The funny thing was that adults were blind to the similarity, only small children seemed to see it. For some reason that made it all the more special, like a secret identity only the truly innocent could see.

I felt bad for some of the skaters who basically never left the hotel, either because they, or their coach, felt it unwise to venture out. But all of us had a great time at the hotel every night and I got to know the whole team really well. Ainsley's coach, Rafael Arutyunyan, who I'd never met until we got here, turned out to be a lot of fun. One day he came back to the hotel with China's version of Monopoly. Instead of moving around the board with the tokens we were used to, like a thimble or a race car, they had a roller skate, a laptop and a cell phone. And when we bought properties it was crazy trying to find our deeds because they were all in Chinese. Ainsley told me she'd considered quitting skating last year until she changed coaches to Rafael, and she was now recharged and loving skating again.

Coach Z also knew how to keep us loose. One day he came back with kites, which he said were invented in China 2,300 years ago, originally used by the military to send messages. They were really fancy . . . dragons and birds and fish, so one day the whole team was out in the snow, flying kites. So I'd always think my dad was the best coach in the world, but Coach Z and Rafael came a pretty close second.

We had seventeen skaters on the Olympic team. How many entries a country has for singles, pairs and ice dancing depends on how well the country did at the last World Championships. For ladies we got the maximum of three: Ainsley Tucker, Regan Bailey and me. Ice dancing and pairs had also earned three spots, but just two for men's singles.

A few days before the Olympics would start, we had the option to move to the Olympic Village, or continue to stay in the hotel with the coaches and support staff. Even though it would mean more driving to come back each day for our practice sessions, it was an easy decision for me. I wanted to experience everything, and Alex and Lissy felt the same way, so the day before the Opening Ceremonies we'd be relocating to the Village. All the skaters were, except for the men's singles skaters.

When we moved into the Village, it was cool to see the apartments were brand new. There were two bedrooms in each one and we'd be two to a room. Lissy and I took one and Ainsley and Regan the other. This was Ainsley's second Olympics, finishing seventh four years ago, but she was a leading contender for gold this time. She was twenty-six, which was old by today's standards for female singles skaters, but if she felt overwhelmed by three teens in the apartment she didn't show it. It was great to have her there to walk us through things, kind of like a second coach.

The rest of the Village was amazing. It was *our* space, which was cool and seemed to honor the tradition of the Olympics—young people getting together from around the world to become friends, learn about each other's cultures and compete in sports. I think our governments often forgot about that. The common areas were like a luxury hotel. There was a huge cafeteria with all kinds of different food stations, and hair dressers, nail salons, a movie theater, even a laundry service, dry cleaners and a florist. And of course there was a huge gym with an indoor pool. Security was so tight even coaches needed a special pass to get in.

The Opening Ceremonies were Saturday—tomorrow night—then the figure skating events started the following day. Pairs were scheduled first and Alex and Lissy's short program was Sunday afternoon, followed by the free skate on Monday. Tuesday and Wednesday was men's, Thursday and Friday was ice dancing, then Saturday was the ladies short and Sunday the long program.

In the Sochi Olympics in 2014 a new figure skating event was added—the team competition. It was a smart move, copying the Summer Olympics, where they had not only individual gymnastic events, but a team competition as well. So for the third time there would be a special team event where each of the top countries would have just one entry in each discipline. The team event would be last, so U.S. Figure Skating was not going to announce the team until after the other competitions were done, but we all knew who the teams would be, surely Ainsley for ladies and Alex and Lissy for pairs.

My short moment of fame in the United States had not spread overseas, so I was getting the expected first looks, and a lot of questions in languages I didn't understand. But word seemed to spread pretty quickly what the mask was about and the stares lessened.

One nice thing about the Winter Olympics was that there were fewer events and fewer athletes than at the Summer Games. Everything was more intimate. Except for speed and figure skating, most events were held outdoors on mountainsides. None of our events were held in giant stadiums seating a hundred thousand people.

For the Opening Ceremonies, all the countries were packed together outside the open air stadium waiting for each team to be brought inside. With us were all the other American athletes—skiers, bobsledders, snowboarders and hockey players. Even though we were all bundled up, it was cold and we all huddled together for warmth—all the countries packed together, side by side, distinguished only by the colors of our outfits. It was one of the most communal feelings I'd ever experienced. We edged closer to the tunnel into the stadium as each country was announced, and the closer we got the louder the crowd's roar became.

When it was finally our turn and we moved through the long tunnel, I was overcome with emotion. I was so proud to be there. I was proud to be representing America, although I wasn't sure exactly what that meant. Maybe that's normal for a girl who has never been to a Fourth of July fireworks show or a Memorial Day barbecue, or sung the national anthem at a football game or said the pledge of allegiance in a classroom. I kind of felt like I carried my own flag—a flag representing everyone who had been rejected for who they were, or for simply the way they looked.

Inside the stadium it was a celebration of noise and light. I heard the announcement, "The United States of America!" and the roar got even louder. Eighty thousand people could make a lot of noise. I didn't know how the crowd could keep up the constant volume for each country as it entered. After we came through the tunnel we could spread out and I found myself in a row holding hands: Alex, Lissy, me, Regan. But we kept letting go to wave. It was like being a rock star, coming onto the world's biggest stage, music playing and lights flashing. I'd read that the TV audience would be over a billion people. *A billion!*

There were TV cameras everywhere and whenever Regan saw one she dragged me along and we'd run up to it and give it a close-up wave and thumbs up. I could only imagine what people in China and Russia and Brazil and a hundred other countries were thinking of the girl in the mask as I filled their TV screen. Were the announcers furiously looking through their notes to find out who I was and why I wore a mask? Or did they cut away to another shot and avoid a screen full of mask and scars? I was actually fine either way.

# 63

Since the pairs short programs were the day after the Opening Cere-monies, many of the pairs teams from other countries didn't march. The thinking was it would be tiring and could hurt their performance the following day. My dad had left the decision up to Alex and Lissy. Their thinking . . . how could they *not* go? They were glad they did.

I watched from the skater seats in the top rows of the arena as they took the ice for their short program. With me was Regan and Ainsley, and all three ice dancing teams. Team America, in support. So far, two of The Big Three had skated, Vrenko and Vlatoya, 76.13, and Roma-nov and Ludnova, 72.88. An unexpected great performance from the Japanese team earned them a 73.26.

No one could say Alex and Lissy no longer skated without emo-tion. And it was the best type—transparent—nothing fake. I thought they outshined everyone and they received a 76.35, putting them in first place by less than a quarter point. That left only Peligrino and Maples as the last of the elites to skate.

They were masterful, as always, but still fell short of Alex and Lissy, with a 75.61. Afterwards, if Dad, Alex or Lissy were surprised by being in first, they didn't show it. Celebrate, yes, but they'd con-vinced themselves they'd be at or near the top.

The long programs were scheduled for the following evening, so that made it easier for the entire team to be there to give support, even the men singles skaters who were staying at the hotel. Last night I'd been afraid Lissy would be too excited to sleep, but she laid down for a nap at 7:00 p.m. And never woke up. She slept eleven hours. Had to be a good sign.

The draw had Romanov and Ludnova up first. They shockingly had two falls and likely wouldn't medal at all: 128.69, total 201.57. Even the best have off nights, or maybe they feel the pressure of a gold medal. The Japanese pair was next: 134.99, total 208.25.

Next up were Vrenko and Vlatoya. I knew their program by heart, so I knew they'd altered it when they upped their throw from a triple to a quad. They were going for broke and it backfired. Vrenko under-rotated and fell and was slow to get up, making them skip the planned transition to follow and hurting their presentation scores even more: 133.45, total 209.58.

Lissy and Alex skated like their Piece of Cake nickname. Their program was fluid and effortless while at the same time being big and powerful and fun. Not that that made it easy to watch. Honestly, it was harder to watch than to skate. Watching, you're powerless.

When they opened with their triple twist, I was sure Alex had tossed Lissy too high and she'd over-rotate. But she landed perfectly in his arms. The height had been incredible. High enough to have been a quad-twist. The side by side triple loop - double toe was perfectly timed, each a mirror image of the other. Their faces radiated such a calm and confident joy, I knew they were in the zone and I felt my body relax a tiny bit. Each of their lifts felt massive, even from the rafters, and that power contrasted beautifully with the delicacy of their choreo sequence. As they finished with their combo spins, I thought it had been everything they could hope it would be. And it was. 147.36, total 223.71. First place, with only Peligrino and Maples left to skate.

When they did, they matched the beauty of Alex and Lissy and showed just as much spectacular power. They had been flawless. It would just be a matter who impressed the judges the most. Our eyes were glued to the scoreboard, waiting for it to come to life. When it did, it showed: 143.23, total 223.84. The Canadians had won the gold by thirteen hundredths of a point.

Alex and Lissy took the silver.

For a split second I was disappointed—so close to gold. But then I was high-fiving my teammates. Alex and Lissy had done all they could do—a great performance, defeating both of the supposedly unbeatable Russian teams, and were taking home an Olympic silver medal.

We all stayed in our seats as the platforms were brought out to center ice. They didn't waste any time in awarding the medals. The arena lights dimmed for the announcements and spotlights circled each of the pairs as they were announced and skated out on the ice. I couldn't imagine how Alex and Lissy must have felt at that moment. To have given such an incredible performance for the world, and now to receive an Olympic medal. I'd heard the phrase "happy tears," but had never experienced them as fully as I did at that moment. I literally sobbed. I was getting some looks from my teammates, but that was okay.

It felt so good to love someone that much.


In the men's free skate the next day, we didn't fare very well—no medals for either of our guys. But ice dancing was turning into an American strength the last few Olympics, and we won the bronze, with our other two teams finishing tenth and seventeenth.

My turn.

Every day my dad would pick up Alex, Lissy and me early in the morning to take us to the team rink, then drive us back by mid-afternoon. That left us plenty of time to enjoy the Village and even watch some of the other events. Alex and Lissy's pairs competition was over, but they were still practicing for the team event. We were doing only two light sessions a day because Dad didn't want us overtraining.

There were so many women entered in the ladies' singles competition that after the short program, only the top twenty-four would advance to the free skate on Sunday. Ainsley had been at Sochi and was really helpful in giving Regan and me a better feeling of what to expect. It was the first international competition for both of us.

And now here I was, taking a few laps around the rink, my short program just two minutes away. Although the feeling off the ice in Beijing was so different, with all the different languages being spoken around me and the feeling of tight security all around the rink—once I was on the ice I felt at home. And helping me even more were the masks. I hadn't expected them, but there were a few hundred being held up around the arena. Americans, I guessed. They looked like the ones Mr. Irwin had made for Nationals so they must have made the trip overseas. I wondered what the predominantly Chinese crowd was thinking with a masked girl on the ice, and now a smattering of people holding up matching paper masks. All I knew was the ice suddenly felt even more solid under my feet.

I went through my mantras and took my ready position. *You are my best friend. Take care of me.* I had to hope Chinese ice understood me.

No joke, I actually thought about that as I spoke in my head.

My short program was fast and strong and clean. Unlike all my competitors who never watched the other skaters, both before and after I skated I watched those I knew would be among the best. It sounds conceited, but I felt I'd skated better than anyone else. Unlike at Nationals, though, here all the top skaters maxed out on their short program's level of difficulty, so I had no point advantage there. Still, I thought there had been slight edge errors and even a few uncalled under-rotations—and none had the height or length I did on my jumps. Still, I couldn't complain that I was in third after the short with a 77.48. The favorite to win gold for Russia, Tatianna Petrova, was in first: 80.64. Ainsley was in second, 78.52. In fourth was the winner of the Grand Prix final, Oksana Trankova from Ukraine. Regan was in eleventh.

It turned out I was the only one thrilled with my third place. Alex and Lissy, and the teammates who were there said I'd skated the cleanest program. I asked Dad and he said all bias aside—he thought I'd out-skated the other girls. But he also said that when the margins were that close—especially given the fact the international judges had never seen me skate in person before—that there was nothing even he would complain about. He agreed I should be thrilled with my scores. One thing everyone felt the same about was the appearance of the masks. We were all used to seeing flags waved by each country's fans, but no one had ever seen something for an individual skater like that.

The big blow came just after the short programs had wrapped. Dad informed me that the Ukrainian Skating Federation had filed a complaint and asked that I be disqualified. They claimed I violated the International Skating Union's rules regarding permitted costumes. After Katarina Witt's sexy showgirl costume prompted the "Katarina Rule" in 1986, the rules were changed on what could and couldn't be worn.

But they wanted to apply it to my mask?

"*Dad, are you serious? . . .* Wait *. . . is* there a rule like that? Are they right?"

What worried me was that he didn't immediately rush with the "No!" I expected.

He said, "Ah . . . it's complicated. There's nothing specific in the rules about masks. It's an interpretation thing. Rule 501 forbids anything that is overly theatrical, or anything that could be considered a prop. Something that would be a distraction. But—"

"A distraction for who? I'm the one who has to look through the mask! Do they know how hard that is? Wouldn't the distraction to the judges be if I *didn't* wear my mask? This was just so . . ." I thought the Olympics were all about friendship and sportsmanship. "Oh Dad, I have so many people counting on me."

341

"I know, honey. Listen, we'll argue it and U.S. Figure Skating will be there with us fighting too. And I have the feeling when word gets out . . . I think Ukraine has no idea how this makes them look."

"So we'll win?"

"Honey, I honestly don't know. I've never appeared in front of an Olympic Committee. This is really unprecedented. But . . . yes, I think you'll get to skate. I just can't imagine them taking that chance away from you."

"But why would some country even do this? What did I ever do to them? And I don't even know their skater."

He gave me a no-nonsense look. "What you did was show you're one of the world's best skaters. They want their skater to win gold. They're afraid of you, Katie. Take it as a compliment."

Right. Not a compliment I wanted. "So when do we do this? Now?" It was already late.

"No, they can't get it put together tonight. They've set it for to-morrow at ten."

"But Dad, free skates start at one!"

"I know, honey. I'm sorry. I'm going to see if I can talk to one of the Ukrainian coaches and see if they can convince their federation to withdraw the complaint, but I just needed you to know what was go-ing on. I know it will be hard, but try to put it out of your mind. Worrying about it isn't going to change anything."


When I got back to my room, not only were my roommates there, but some of the others on the team. They'd heard what was happening and were livid. I was exhausted from the excitement of my first Olym-pic skate, then dealing with the attempt to disqualify me. From the highest high to the lowest low. I just wanted to go to bed, but I sat with them and let them vent and come up with sweet but silly ideas, like go to the committee and threaten a boycott. I told them no. My dad and I would go alone and we'd abide by whatever was decided.

As we were talking there was a knock on the door. That was no surprise even this late since the socializing and partying seemed to go on until quite late. Ainsley went to the door and came back with the girl I recognized as Oksana Trankova, the Ukrainian skater. I didn't know how old she was but I guessed about sixteen. She walked in hesitantly, not made any easier with a team of angry Team USA skaters glaring at her. She stopped in front of me. Her eyes were red like she'd been crying. When she spoke, her English was stilted.

"I am coming to here to apologize . . . This thing that my federation do . . . It is not good thing. It make me feel very bad . . . I ask them to stop do it, but they say no. Is embarrass to me. Please to forgive."

Gold was a precious resource, either in the ground or around our necks, and governments would find a way to fight over it. Oksana actually ended up staying a while, and I got to know my first foreign skater. It sounded like both she and her country put tremendous pressure on her to win; she'd been living at training centers since she was recruited at age four. It was sad that I didn't sense much joy for skating from her.

When I went to bed I thought at least being so tired would mean I'd sleep well—but I didn't sleep at all. I had so many emotions . . . anger at people in the world that tried to push people down rather than help them up . . . shame that my mask and I were indirectly hurting other people, like distracting my teammates, and even Oksana, whose performance might be affected by all this . . . and anxiety as I watched the hands on the clock pass four a.m., worried what a night without sleep, and skipping my morning practice, would do to my performance.

I was still awake when the sun came up.

Dad told me that the Ukraine Skating Federation had refused to back down, so at ten o'clock we were waiting outside the locked doors of the meeting room. We weren't alone. Barbara Felsdorf was there, along with the entire Olympic staff of U.S. Figure Skating, and so was every member of the team except Regan and Ainsley, who were getting ready to skate. Alex said, "I know you told us not to come. But we're here. We won't say anything, but if they're going to take away your chance to skate, they'll have to say it in front of all of us."

The American media was there in force as well, even Johnny Weir and Tara Lipinski. I still hadn't met them in person and almost had the desire to walk over and tell them what a big fan I was, but at the moment I couldn't focus on anything but my fate to be decided by the committee.

The locked doors were opened at ten on the dot. The room was large and set up like a courtroom. There were seven men and women already seated at a long table at the far end of the room, each with a microphone in front of them. There were other people off to the side, one of them a stenographer. The man who opened the door said, "Parties only, and federations. The rest of you must wait outside." Some of my teammates started to protest but Barbara held up a hand. She knew arguing wouldn't change the rules.

There were two tables facing the committee. Dad, Barbara and I sat at one and the Ukraine representatives took the other. Oksana wasn't there. A man I'd never seen before was standing next to Barbara. The proceedings finally started when a woman sitting at the center of the panel started speaking.

But when she spoke it was in *French*.

I looked to Barbara. She whispered, "The official language of the Olympics is French, and everything has to go into the record that way." She nodded at the man standing next to her. "He will translate everything for us."

And so it went, French to English, English to French, Ukrainian to French and French to Ukrainian. Tedious. The Ukrainians spoke English so they didn't need translating of what we said, but we didn't speak their language, so that was a third translation. When Ukraine gave its position, it was just as Dad had explained; that my mask was theatrical in nature, a removable prop, so barred. They also argued something we didn't anticipate: that wearing a mask was a competitive advantage because part of presentation scores was judging a skater's facial expression, and that could not be judged if I was masked.

When Barbara spoke she addressed the lack of anything in the rules specifically about masks and pointed out how the Katarina Rule was created in response to costumes that were showgirlish, with decorations like feathers, or overtly sexual in nature. And she pointed out that a mask couldn't be considered a prop when it was serving the same function as clothes, covering what was for me a private part of my body. She closed stating that wearing a mask could only limit, not enhance, my presentation scores as my face could not be viewed, so I had only my body to show my musical interpretation and emotion. When she sat down I thought she'd done a good job, but I thought several of the panel looked supportive of Ukraine.

It wasn't planned, but I stood up. "Excuse me please, but may I say something?"

It was strange to hear my words followed by the French, *"S'il vous plait. Puis je parle?"*

When I got the nod of approval from the panel, I said, "I don't believe my mask gives me any advantage. It actually makes it much harder to skate with it. To see and breathe through it. But if you want me to skate without my mask, I will."

As the French translation was in progress, I took off my mask and stared first directly at the Ukraine delegation, then back to the panel. The translator was mid-sentence when he glanced over at me and his words died in his throat. The faces of the panel were what you'd expect. It was the usual range of reactions. Those with kind hearts showed empathy, those without them showed poorly hidden repugnance. But after the first glance, both groups looked anywhere but at me. I was glad my teammates had not been allowed in or I may not have had the courage.

One of the panel politely said, "You may put your mask back on if you'd like." He didn't bother to say it in French, maybe thinking that would delay by a few seconds my face being covered up. The woman at the center of the panel said, "We will confer and have our decision shortly."

As they started to stand up, Dad said, "Excuse me, but my daughter is set to skate in only ninety minutes. There isn't any time left."

Her cool-as-a-cucumber reply through the translator: "You may wait here."

With that they left the room, but were gone less than five minutes. When the panel marched back in, the same woman spoke, and our translator said, "The complaint of the Ukraine Skating Federation is denied. Katie Wilder may wear her mask to skate."

Just like that it was over. My guess was they got to that back room and imagined all the TV sets turning off—one billion buyers of Pepsi and Tostitos and tampons and tires—when my uncovered face appeared on their screens. That was what I had been counting on. In reality, I couldn't imagine skating without my mask.

We gave the good news to everyone outside. Tara and Johnny were gone as they had broadcasting duties, but the rest of the media was there. Barbara handled talking to them because Dad and I had to rush to the rink. I knew we'd be cutting it close so I was actually wearing my costume under my clothes.

# 64

By the time we drove to the arena and got through security, there would only be time to stretch, then my six-minute group warm-up. Regan had already skated and done well, but didn't have a chance to medal. When Oksana and I saw each other we had a long hug, which I noticed was caught by the TV cameras. Was she thinking like me: *This is how it's done world.* Hopefully that wasn't going to get her in trouble with her federation.

I'd missed her performance but I'd heard she hadn't skated as well as in her short. Only one fall, but no sparkle in the performance. Maybe she didn't get much sleep either.

I was the first up of the final three. As I circled the ice, I waited for the adrenaline—but it wasn't there. There was *nothing.* It felt like my skates were made of cement. And the ice felt like it was melting, my blades in quicksand. There was the smattering of some Americans holding masks in the audience, but unlike for my short program, I was too tired, too drained, to feed off their energy.

I took my starting position and waited for my music to begin, willing my body to finally respond. As the first notes played, I glided into my program. I was positioning for my first jump when I realized I'd forgotten to talk to the ice.

After my skate, the first thing I did when I got back to my room was take a nap. Eleven hours later I woke up and it was dawn. Some nap. I turned on my laptop so I could watch the replay of my first Olympic long program.

—TARA LIPINSKI: "And here comes sixteen-year-old Katie Wilder to take the ice. In two minutes, the moment of her life . . . her first Olympics and the chance to win gold. And she's upped her program. Can you believe it . . . two quad Lutzes and two triple Axels. If she lands them, she'll be the first woman in history to do it. And I've heard she's nailing them in practice. What do you think makes her so good?"

—JOHNNY WEIR: "Well, first off, she's the fastest skater I've ever seen, man or woman. She literally eats up the ice. It's amazing to see. The power and length of her jumps is breathtaking. And when you know her story, what it took to get here . . . it's a real-life Cinderella story."

—TARA: "But can it have a Cinderella ending? A lot of people in the figure skating world are furious over what's being seen as an attempt to sabotage her chances here."

—JOHNNY: "Well, we'll see how she'll do. The Ukrainians' attempt to have her disqualified has to have taken a huge toll. She didn't get in *any* ice time today except six minutes for her group's warm-up."

The screen cut to an image of Oksana and me hugging.

—TARA: "I was so happy to see this. This is Katie and Oksana Trankova, the Ukrainian skater caught at the center of this debacle. These are just two sweet kids who want to skate. None of this was Oksana's doing."

—JOHNNY: "But the damage has been done, Tara. I spoke to Katie's roommate and training partner, Lissy Cake, who said Katie didn't sleep at all last night. Can you imagine . . . to go through the emotions of your first Olympic short program, then learning you may be disqualified, not sleeping all night, then arguing in front of a rules committee to be allowed to skate? Then a couple hours later, you're on the ice?"

—TARA: "Well, one thing we know is, this girl is a fighter."

—JOHNNY: "Well, here we go. She's going to open with a beautiful combo, a triple Lutz - triple toe - double loop, and she always nails it . . . oh . . . It looked like she under-rotated, but she's back up . . . and now here's her triple loop . . . she gets so much height on this . . . oh no . . ."

—TARA: "Oh, that had to hurt. She came down hard."

—JOHNNY: "She went way outside the takeoff . . . but she's right into her footwork sequence . . . I think the most difficult in the field this year . . . that was nicely done . . . now her triple toe . . ."

TARA: "Oh, Johnny."

JOHNNY: "But she's up on her feet again and . . ."

And so it went. Three falls and . . . well, who cares what else went wrong when you fall three times. I didn't do either quad. No point to trying them, and the way I was feeling, I could have hurt myself. I finished last of the twenty-four girls, as my performance deserved.

Ainsley blew the lights out. She was like a mash-up of my two favorite skaters who inspired me growing up: Evgenia Medvedeva and Michelle Kwan. She managed to combine energy and sizzle with grace and elegance. Ainsley didn't have a quad, but she did two exquisite triple Axels. More importantly, she told a story on the ice and everyone felt it. She put up a giant number: 152.60, total 231.12.

The last to skate would be Tatianna Petrova. It seemed every year Russia churned out another teen phenom to dominate ladies skating. It was like they had a factory, which they sort of did. For her long program, Tatianna was copying the strategy of her fellow Russian, Alina Zagitova, who'd won gold in 2018 by putting her highest scoring jumps into the second half of her program. That gave her a ten percent bonus for every element, and with three quads planned, it added a lot of points. One advantage Ainsley had over her was she couldn't land a triple Axel so was only doing a double.

But the potential drawback to backloading your program with your most difficult jumps is fatigue. I could see her tiring in the third minute. A skater can tell. I wondered if she'd even go for the quads. To her credit, she did, and she landed them both cleanly. Good for her. Gutsy. But then she was out of gas. She gave back the points she'd earned with the two quads by popping the third one. Her score: 148.41, total 229.05. As they flashed scores with the "2" next to Tatianna's name, everyone knew Ainsley had won the gold. Rafael lifted her up like she weighed five pounds. So thanks to Ainsley and Rafael, a gold for the U.S., the silver to Russia, and Oksana held on for the bronze.

At first we all thought Ainsley was just feeling under the weather the next morning when she woke up feeling tired and with an upset stomach, but by afternoon it was pretty clear she had the flu. They moved her to the team hotel so they could watch over her, but also so Regan and I wouldn't catch whatever she had in case one of us had to take her place. The team competition would be contested over a three-day period with the men and ice dancing short programs tomorrow, and ladies and pairs the following day. So Ainsley had a day to get better, but Barbara met with Regan and me together to let us know she needed us to practice as if we were going to skate, just in case Ainsley couldn't go. I knew if it came to that, the choice would probably be Regan after my three falls and last place performance.

I didn't know what to feel. My Olympics had been a disaster. Part of me wanted another chance to skate like I knew I could. To skate for the world like I had at Nationals. But I also didn't want to let people down again. It didn't matter to me that everyone was making excuses for me: no sleep, the attempted disqualification, yada yada. I'd had my chance and I'd blown it. I'd thought there couldn't be pressure matching Nationals, but the Olympics were at a level so much higher, there was no comparison. Ainsley had proven she could handle it and she'd give us our best chance of a team gold.

The next day was a Team USA disaster. Figure skating was like that, where one day you skate great and the next time your body just won't cooperate. There were ten countries in the team event, and after the men's and ice dancing shorts, we were in sixth after error-filled performances. Russia, Japan and Germany held the top spots, followed by Canada and Italy.

The good news was Ainsley felt better and had been able to put in a solid day of practice. I was happy for her and the team, but as soon as they told me, I realized how much I'd actually wanted another chance to skate. As part of Team USA I'd be competing in just a few weeks at the World Championships in Italy—and Worlds was a huge event—but there was nothing like the Olympics, and it killed me that my last skate on Chinese ice was going to be that embarrassment.

The next morning I got to sleep in; the only job ahead for me was as a cheerleader. First for Ainsley and Alex and Lissy for their short programs, then the long programs in the evening for men's singles and ice dancing. For Alex and Lissy they'd be battling Vrenko and Vlatoya, the team Russia selected, and the gold medal-winning Peligrino and Maples for Canada. For Ainsley, it would be the same girls with the exception of Oksana, since Ukraine wasn't strong enough in the other disciplines to qualify for the team competition, so that helped her odds.

And then everything changed.

Barbara called as Regan and I were finishing breakfast. "Katie, is Regan there with you?"

"Yes. She's right next to me."

"Good. Can you put me on speaker so I can talk to both of you?"

I did, and Regan said, "Hi Barbara. I'm here."

Barbara got right to it. "Ainsley can't skate. Maybe she overdid it yesterday . . . I don't know, but we just got off the ice and . . . she's not ready. She thinks she can do it, but I'm making the call." The sound of a deep breath, then, "Regan . . . we've decided to have Katie skate for Ainsley. Katie . . . are you ready to take her place?"

For a moment I couldn't even speak. *Was* I ready?

I knew she meant emotionally. And it was a good question. Suddenly I had so many thoughts and emotions racing through my mind. My great short program . . . and my abysmal long one. The chance at Olympic redemption . . . or being the weak link that could cost us a medal. And, oh yeah, I'd literally be on the ice in just three hours. I wasn't even going to think about the fact Regan and I had just celebrated the end of our Olympics with a rare total pig-out breakfast, not the light meal I'd normally do before a big skate.

I said, "Barbara, are you sure? I mean, I finished *last*. Last out of twenty-four skaters. Regan finished eighth. Shouldn't she—"

"Katie—" Barbara cut off me, but before she could say anything, Regan cut *her* off.

That wasn't surprising. Regan could do about anything, except hold her tongue. What Regan thought, Regan said. I figured she'd make her case why she should be skating. And rightfully so. We were friends, but I understood.

"Excuse me, Barbara," Regan said, "but let me take this . . ." She turned to me. "*Stop it.* After the short you were in third, by *a fraction*. And everyone knows you actually should have been in first. Of course you should be skating. Now shut up and listen to Barbara."

And so I did. As soon as I got off the phone Regan and I literally ran to my room so I could grab my skate bag and have enough time to get in a warmup. The ladies' short programs would start in just three hours.


This time, with no sleep deprivation, no fears of being disqualified, and not forgetting to talk to the ice, I could not have skated any better, although the judges still gave the edge to Tatianna Petrova, making it: Russia, U.S., Japan. Alex and Lissy were also in second after their short, finishing between Canada and Russia. Keeping us neck and neck in the competition was the fact that Canada's men's singles skater had finished eighth, and Russia's ice dancing team was ninth. So the gold was still up for grabs.

That afternoon, the men and ice dancing teams did their long programs, wrapping up that side of the competition. In men's singles, thanks to Coach Z's skater, we moved up to fourth. Then a second place finish in ice dancing moved us up to third. The point total with only the pairs and ladies' long programs still to come had it: Russia, Canada, U.S., then Japan, with Germany a distant fifth.

Except for Ainsley, the whole team met for a late dinner in the cafeteria. There were TVs all over the Village, but especially in the social and eating areas, huge screens constantly showing live or replayed events. I almost coughed up my food when my face, six feet high, suddenly appeared on all the giant monitors around the room. Thankfully the extreme close up was short.

Over the last week I'd caught myself being shown briefly on Chinese TV, along with all the other skaters, but this story seemed to be just about me. It was in Mandarin, so none of us understood what was being said, but we all stared at the screen nonetheless, hoping for a clue. I could see a lot of the other athletes in the room turn and look at me. The real me that is, as I watched myself on TV.

It must have been quite a detailed story. There was an exterior shot of the Ice Castle, which made me absurdly proud for some reason, then some highlights from both Sectionals and Nationals, including the arena full of masks. They spent a lot of time on the masks, maybe because masks were a big part of Chinese culture. Finally, there were shots of my dismal long program, followed by footage of the Ukraine skating officials, clearly taking a lot of heat from the media.

A few minutes into the story, a boy tapped me on the shoulder. His warmup jacket had the Chinese colors we'd all come to know, and a logo identifying him as a member of their speed skating team.

He smiled and said, "I sit?"

Regan and I made some space between us on the bench.

He sat down and said, "My name Li Wei." Then another big smile and a little head bow to everyone around the table.

He must have known none of us could understand what was being said. He nodded toward the nearest TV. "They say . . . ah . . . China. Like. You."

He seemed very happy to share this, which was sweet. He started to say more then paused, clearly struggling to translate more of what was being said. Finally, he pointed to the nearest screen and said, "We hope. . . you win."

Wow. I was sure the Chinese newscaster didn't actually say China was rooting for Katie Wilder, but still, it must have been something nice. It made me feel funny that all of China had just learned my life story. I guess the announcement of the Olympics first masked girl taking Ainsley's spot, along with the drama of the Ukraine protest, was putting me front and center.

I thanked Li Wei and he pulled out his phone. He said, "Picture please?" and held it out for a selfie.

"Yes," I said and he moved his head next to mine, a big grin on his face.

As he got up to leave, he said, "You win. Yes?"

What could I say? So I said it. "Yes."

# 65

The next day, pairs were first up for the long programs. Alex and Lissy had already earned their silver medals in the regular pairs competition and that took a lot of pressure off them to perform well in team. As much as I wanted to watch them, I had to get my ice time in to skate my best tonight. I was practicing at our team rink when I got the results by text. Proving how equal the new Big Four was, the results had flipped from just a few days ago. The gold-medaling Canadians finished third. Vrenko and Vlatoya won the event with Alex and Lissy again second.

Before I skated I knew the bottom line—we were in second to Russia by a fraction. If I could take first, we'd win the gold. Canada and Japan were too far back to challenge.

It was old-school: U.S. v. Russia.

The draw for the free skate had Japan, followed by Russia then me. For once I took my dad's advice and didn't watch the other skaters. I found a quiet spot and imagined I was at the Ice Castle. I visualized skating my program on my home ice—ice that had been my best friend and never let me down.

When Tatianna finished her program and left for the Kiss and Cry to await her scores, I took the ice. I knew all my teammates were watching me from high above, but my eyes were locked on the ice as

I circled. Something felt wrong and it took me a moment to realize what it was.

The silence.

Usually there was at least mild applause when a skater gets on the ice for their warmup, then full applause when their name is announced a couple of minutes later. But there was nothing. Not a sound. And when I looked up, I saw why.

The arena was filled with masks.

But they were not the masks like Mr. Irwin had made for Nationals, perfect copies of mine. These were different. They all appeared to be handmade, just simple oval cutouts to represent my mask. Most with no holes for eyes or nose, or drawn lines. Just ovals. And every single person in the arena held one up.

They were all slightly different sizes and were cut from different colored paper. Most were white like my mask, but a lot of them were black, or brown. Some were even rainbow. They had clearly all been made at home, and brought with them for this moment. I imagined families at their kitchen tables, scissors and paper in hand, talking about the message they were sending.

I don't know if they were holding up the masks for me, for themselves, for someone they loved, or for the nameless outcasts of the world. But they were making a statement for the entire world to see. I felt like I was in the middle of something so much bigger than me. Or my skating.

I felt so proud. And ashamed I'd been blind for so long. I'd spent so much of my life cursing the "bad things" I'd had to endure: a never-ending list holding me back. *If only* I'd never had the accident. *If only* I looked like other people. *If only* my mother hadn't left me. *If only* I'd had at least one friend.

But life *was* obstacles. Lissy had them. Alex had them. My dad. My mom. And me, yeah, more than most—a lot more actually—but that just meant the more I overcame, the stronger I became. It had been those challenges that got me here.

Not despite them.

Because of them.

I don't know how long I stood there, just turning in a circle to take it all in. Then the masks came down and rhythmic clapping took its place, sounding like overpowering but friendly thunder in the enclosed arena. It jarred me out of my reverie and I started moving around the ice to finish my warmup.

I heard the click of the microphone indicating Tatianna's scores were going to be announced, but I tuned out the score and kept my eyes off the scoreboard. I didn't want a number in my head that I had to beat. All I knew was I had to skate my best.

When I heard, "And now representing the United States of America, Katie Wilder," I got the full force of adrenaline and commanded it to give me more speed and power. I am the Phoenix, surviving fire, indestructible. I pulled the crowd in and let them strengthen me. There had never been a crowd willing to give me so much. I took my starting position. *You are my best friend. Take care of me. Let's do something beautiful together.*

I'd heard of other athletes who have said their performances were like an out-of-body experience. That's how my free skate was for me. I felt like I was watching myself from above. When I landed my big triple combo, I looked so light that it seemed I might stay in the air forever. I moved through the program with so much speed and elegance that even I was surprised. Mid-air in my Axel I could feel I wasn't precisely over my hips, but as if I was in slow motion, I made the needed correction. When it came time for the quads, one right after the other, I could hear the *crunch* and *hiss* of two perfect landings even from my spot floating high above. My second triple Axel covered more distance than I'd have thought possible. In my closing layback spin, it wasn't humanely possible to spin any faster. As I moved through my variations I somehow seemed to build speed rather than lose it. And when I finished perfectly in time with the last note of my music I watched myself raise my arms up high. I didn't feel I had re-entered my body until that moment, and then the roar of the crowd hit me like a tidal wave.

So many flowers rained down it looked like a nuclear spring blooming through the ice. I knew I was supposed to go to the Kiss and Cry, but I was the last skater to perform, so there was no reason I had to leave the ice. Hands reached out all around the rink, something I'd never seen in any of the competitions I'd watched throughout my entire life. So like I'd done at the impromptu show with Alex and Lissy at the Ice Castle a lifetime ago, I circled the rink touching extended hands and giving high fives. But this time, I did it alone. If anything, the roar in the rink only kept growing.

It was a victory lap—for me and everyone watching—even before the scores were read. They knew what I knew, that the win had been in just getting here. To skate that performance. To have fought for my moment to literally talk to the entire world through my skating. It was an international audience, both in the arena and watching on TV, and although everyone spoke different languages, for four minutes I'd found a way to communicate with each one of them.

I could see the technical panel conferring about something. Clearly there was some dispute going on. Someone was fighting for me. Someone was fighting against me. That would never change. But it didn't matter and I didn't care. Some things couldn't be taken away. I saw them break apart and I knew the score would finally be posted.

With a final wave to the audience I joined my dad in the Kiss and Cry. I wasn't even going to look at the score. There was always that brief moment when the scores appeared just as they announced them. It was always a race between sight and sound to see which would register first in my brain. I looked up to Alex and Lissy and our team but their eyes weren't on me. They were glued to the scoreboard, waiting like me, and the crowd, which had suddenly gone completely silent knowing the moment was finally here.

I was going to look next to my score, for my placement. I was the last skater, so if it flashed "1", that would mean I'd finished first and we'd won the gold. I looked up to my teammates in the skater seats, high above. They were all there. We'd be winning a medal—the only question was what color. I was looking at them when the scores came up behind me. As they jumped up and the crowd roared, I knew we'd won.

I turned around and saw the "1" next to my name.

While the podiums were brought out onto the ice, our team and coaches gathered together and celebrated. The Russians and Canadians waited with us, and although I know they had to be disappointed, they showed nothing but goodwill for our win. The podiums were larger than the usual to accommodate all six skaters from each team. As I looked out into the arena, I could see that not a single person had left. They, and a billion people watching around the world, would watch us receive our gold medals, and see our flag raised above us. But for me, I still felt like I represented a second flag, the one representing people like me.

I was raising their flag tonight.

I wished coaches got to stand on the podium too, but Dad and the other coaches would have to stay off ice. Finally, each team was announced, first in French, then English and finally in Chinese, to skate out on the ice and take their spots on the podium. First the Canadian team for bronze, then the Russians. Finally, over the loudspeakers, "Gold medalists, and Olympic champions, representing the United States of America . . ." My teammates sprinted out onto the ice, but I stayed back and looked to my father.

"Do you think it's time, Dad?

I didn't have to tell him time for what, and he didn't need to answer. The fact that I asked the question told him I'd already decided. I turned around so he could untie my mask. It was only right that he be the one to do it. As he held my past in his hands, without looking back I skated onto the ice to join my friends.

# 66

*Lago de Resia, Italy*

I wanted the perfect place, and when I described what I was looking for, Dad was the one who found it. Lake Resia, nestled in northern Italy, just below the borders of Switzerland and Austria, not too far from where the World Championships were being held in Montpellier next week. I'd never skated on a frozen lake, and as it turned out neither had Alex and Lissy, or Regan and Tiffany. We were all rink rats, never trying the real thing.

The Worlds were only three weeks after the Olympics, so there had been just twelve days at home before Team USA sent us off early for the traditional pre-competition acclimation. Ainsley Tucker had done what everyone expected and retired after her gold medal. I was happy for her to go out on top. I was even happier that the next in line for Team USA was none other than my friend Tiffany who'd been fourth at Nationals. Barbara even let me make the call to give her the news. Helping your country win a gold medal at the Olympics does have its perks.

Returning home to the Ice Castle, away from the world, had felt like old times. Welcome times. But I knew I could never go back to those days. Not in the same way anyway. I had not put my mask back on since the moment I had my dad take it off. It was actually harder than I thought it would be, but I wasn't doing it for myself. That made it easier. How could I encourage people to not hide behind masks if I was wearing one myself? The irony wasn't lost on me that one of the most famous faces in the world at the moment was a girl without one.

I declined every single interview and I wasn't even sure if I'd keep skating after Worlds. Skating I'd do forever, but competitively, that might be it for me. My success, and that of Alex and Lissy, had Dad as the most sought-after coach in the world, and he was going to be able to pick and choose his skaters for next season. He would be hiring another coach at the Ice Castle and when I told him I might want the job, he said it was mine if I wanted it. I'd let him know soon.

I'd never understood why so many of the best women skaters in the world retired so young—Tara Lipinski and Oksana Baiul at only fifteen—but now I was thinking about it too. How could I experience more than I already had at Nationals and the Olympics? And I don't even mean the medals.

Mr. Irwin had waited only a day after the Closing Ceremonies to call me as promised. His idea: a charitable foundation, with a simple white oval as our symbol. He said we'd just got a billion dollars worth of free publicity when the world saw all those masks go up—and everyone knew what they stood for and what needed to be done. All we lacked was a name. Later, when I told him I thought one person couldn't change the world, but one person could change their *corner* of the world, and if everyone did that, we *could* change the world, he said we had one: Foundation One.

One person.

One act.

One commitment toward kindness and non-exclusion.

One pledge to not stand silent in the face of prejudice or cruelty.

One.

So whenever the time came and Foundation One became a reality, *that* I'd do interviews about. I'd laughed when he said I'd soon be seeing people wearing t-shirts and ball caps with the white oval and the word *One* below it, but I wouldn't bet against him.

The lake was about three square miles, surrounded by pine and spruce-covered mountains. There were other skaters, but the lake was so huge it was like having it to ourselves. We'd arrived an hour early and we used it blissfully. The idea that we could just take off in any direction and not have to turn in a circle was exhilarating, like nothing we'd ever experienced. Like caged birds set free. When it was time, Alex, Lissy, Regan and Tiffany stayed in the distance, their balletic movements like a silent orchestra, as I skated closer to the ice's edge. I had finally found the right time. The right place.

And there they were, right on time.

Three blonde heads skating toward me, the tallest one sprinting ahead of the others, her arms outstretched to embrace me even from fifty yards away, tears freezing on her cheeks. Behind her, two twin girls with nervous smiles on their faces.

# About the Authors

Randall Hicks and Hailey Hicks are father and daughter. *The Girl Without a Face* is their first novel together.

Randy became a fan of figure skating at age 19 when he—like all of America—fell in love with Dorothy Hamill as she skated to a gold medal at the 1976 Olympics in Innsbruck.

As a young man, Randy was a television and film actor. Upon realizing he had no acting talent, he moved to Nice, France, where he worked as an English teacher. After he realized he had no French language talent, he returned to the United States. He attended Pepperdine University Law School, and for more than 30 years as an attorney he has specialized in family formation. He has authored several books on adoption and parenting (featured on many news and talk shows, including *The Today Show, CBS This Morning* and *Sally Jessy Raphael*). He has also written two mystery novels. His first, *The Baby Game*, won the Gumshoe Award (Best Debut Mystery), was a finalist for the Anthony, Barry and Macavity Awards, and was selected as the Book of the Month by the Independent Mystery Booksellers Association. He lives in southern California. When not writing books or practicing law, he pretends to be a tennis player.

This is Hailey's first novel. After receiving her bachelor's degree from San Diego State University, she moved to Thailand, teaching English and leading cultural immersion programs. She is now the director of a company which assists foreigners wishing to relocate to Chiang Mai, Thailand. She also helps coordinate international music and arts festivals which support environmental awareness and healthy communities. She enjoys yoga and exploring the world on her motorcycle.

# About the Ice Castle

The Ice Castle is as much a character in this story as Katie, Alex and Lissy. It is a real place and exists almost exactly as described, nestled in the little mountain town of Lake Arrowhead, California.

It was one of the first international training centers for the world's best figure skaters. As described in the book, the championship banners of those skaters hang from the rafters, and it is one of the few skating rinks without hockey boards. Fun little facts contained in story, like Michelle Kwan's escaping hampsters and the international athletes singing their national anthems on a nighttime boat ride on the lake under Fourth of July fireworks, are true.

In its heyday in the 1980s and 90s, the celebrated coaches who trained there included Frank Carroll, Irina Rodrina, Peter Oppegard and Rafael Arutyunan. Skaters making the Ice Castle their home rink included Robin Cousins, Lu Chen, Nicole Bobek, Surya Bonaly, Michelle Kwan, Jeffrey Buttle, Mao Asada, Shen & Zhao, Klimova & Ponomarenko and Bourne & Kraatz, to name but a few.

During its most popular period, there were not just bungalows, but a dormitory, dining hall and a swimming pool, although as the years went by these were slowly sold off.

As new facilities opened around the world, the Ice Castle became outdated and it closed its doors in 2013. It still exists, but is empty and abandoned. We love that Katie's story has brought it back to life.

◆　◆　◆　◆　◆

We hope that you believe in Katie's message and want to share it with your friends, and with others via social media. And big thanks for posting your review on Amazon, Goodreads et cetera.

As Katie Wilder says, "One person can't change the world, but one person *can* change their own corner of the world, and if everyone does that, we *can* change the world." Thank you!

CPSIA information can be obtained
at www.ICGtesting.com
Printed in the USA
LVHW051453121020
668590LV00003B/816